EVIL ROMAN EMPERORS

The Shocking History of Ancient Rome's Most Wicked Rulers from Caligula to Nero and More

Phillip Barlag

Prometheus Books

Guilford, Connecticut

 Prometheus Books

An imprint of The Rowman & Littlefield Publishing Group, Inc.
4501 Forbes Boulevard, Suite 200
Lanham, Maryland 20706
www.rowman.com

Distributed by NATIONAL BOOK NETWORK

British Library Cataloguing in Publication Information Available

Library of Congress Cataloging-in-Publication Data

Name: Barlag, Phillip, author.
Title: Evil Roman emperors : the shocking history of ancient Rome's most wicked rulers from Caligula to Nero and more / Phillip Barlag.
Description: Lanham, MD : Prometheus, [2021] | Includes bibliographical references and index. | Summary: "Evil Roman Emperors puts the worst of Rome's rulers in one place and offers a review of their lives and a historical context for what made them into what they became. It concludes by ranking them, counting down to the worst ruler in Rome's long history"—Provided by publisher.
Identifiers: LCCN 2020043435 (print) | LCCN 2020043436 (ebook) | ISBN 9781633886902 (paperback) | ISBN 9781633886919 (ebook)
Subjects: LCSH: Emperors—Rome—Biography. | Rome—Kings and rulers—Biography. | Rome—History—Empire, 30 B.C.–476 A.D.
Classification: LCC DG274 .B368 2021 (print) | LCC DG274 (ebook) | DDC 937/.060922—dc23
LC record available at https://lccn.loc.gov/2020043435
LC ebook record available at https://lccn.loc.gov/2020043436

CONTENTS

ACKNOWLEDGMENTS

I have to begin with my family. Erin, I love and appreciate you so much. I couldn't do this without your support. Ethan, Everett, and Harper, you each inspire me individually and as a trio. You are terrific human beings.

Mom and Dad, you are always behind me, and I never can adequately express my gratitude for everything.

Pat, you cheer me on like none other. Thank you for your encouragement.

Amy, Charles, and Roxanne, you each, and as a family, enrich my life.

Ryan Masters, I am running out of ways to thank you for all of your help, guidance, encouragement, and mentorship over the years. I am in awe of your brilliance and cherish our friendship.

John Willig, thank you for being in my corner and guiding my way through this strange industry.

Jake Bonar, thank you for getting behind the vision of this book. It certainly wouldn't have happened without you!

Finally, one of the reasons to write another book is to correct mistakes made in the previous one. One of the people to whom I am indebted is my friend Marisa Levi. My book *The History of Rome in 12 Buildings* would not have happened without you.

INTRODUCTION

Absolute power corrupts absolutely. As conclusive evidence of this unfortunate truth, I present to you the Romans who ruled during the height of the Roman Empire. This singular collection of deranged sadists and ignorant egoists terrorized the people of Rome in ways that boggle modern sensibilities.

But this is just the beginning, and the title of the book is only half the story. Rome wasn't built in a day, and neither was its empire. From its very foundation, the history of Rome is replete with people and stories that shock and horrify. The story of Rome begins and ends with wicked rulers. The dark chasm at the heart of Roman history is irresistible, tempting us to peer over the precipice. After all, a careful study of the lives and careers of totalitarians can teach us a lot about the human condition. These monstrous men reflect the darkest parts of our own psyche, and if they invite comparison, I hope you share little with them. This rogue's gallery of rulers consists of contenders for world's worst human being.

So which ruler is truly the worst? An internet search for "worst rulers of Rome" results in an exclusive list of emperors. Makes sense, but Rome's history is long and complicated. Not all who ruled Rome—and certainly not all of its worst rulers—were emperors. Although these rulers make up the list's majority, a complete and accurate view of Roman history and the nature of power in the ancient world requires a more expansive net. Narrowing our consideration to emperors would exclude some delightfully awful people.

Yet before we continue, an editorial note: The history of ancient Rome comes from limited and often biased sources. A lot of this stuff happened a few thousand years ago, and a lot of it likely didn't happen at all. In the absence of a confirmed historical record, Roman historians and scholars codified legends and myths into history. This mythology-turned-history subsumed the Roman psyche. What actually happened mattered less than what people *thought* happened. No matter how outsized, unlikely, or just plain weird some of the founding mythology of Rome came to be, it was the history around which the Roman identity was formed.

Even when contemporary historians were working at or near the time of events, they often skewed their work to align with a personal or political agenda. For example, the Roman historian Tacitus was a senator who lived and worked during the reign of Emperor Domitian. Domitian violently persecuted the senatorial class. Consequently, Tacitus's description of Domitian glosses over the many positive aspects of the man's life and rule, instead emphasizing their substantial shortcomings. We simultaneously must believe historians' accounts and take them with a grain of salt. To qualify every historical detail would make this book long and tedious. As a result, some of the history is downright questionable. It's not just skewed; it's quite possibly fabricated.

Particularly troublesome is the *Historia Augusta*, an anonymous work of uncertain date and dubious reliability. It is likely that much of this work is fabricated. However, for some periods, it is the only ancient Latin history that exists. So reliable or not, it's necessary. Sorry in advance, Elagabalus. The stories about you in the *Historia Augusta* are just too good to pass up. Given the challenges with the bias or reliability of sources, some events will be presented as straightforward historical fact despite the fact that the truth is far thornier or subject to multiple interpretations. Consider it the cost of a conversation about ancient Rome.

Second, many think that the Roman Empire is part and parcel of Rome. In reality, it took centuries to build the Roman Empire. Consequently, historians generally break up Rome's history into four phases:

1. the kingdom, starting with Romulus and the other mythical or semi-mythical kings of Rome;
2. the republic, where the oligarchs in the Senate seized control and ruled;
3. the principate, the age of the emperors and the height of power; and

4. the dominate, when the military ruled the state and appointed the emperors themselves.

In reality, the four phases of Roman history are not so easily delineated. Within this book, we will address each of the four phases, and—despite the title of the book—we will cover periods and people beyond empire and emperors.

To tell the full story of Rome's most wicked rulers requires us to look through a wider lens. However, the majority of our stories will be drawn from the principate (i.e., stories about emperors from the time period considered to be the empire). During this phase of Roman history Rome was at the peak of its power and influence. Thus, during the principate emperors had the most power to use for positive or negative means. Some of the best—and by best we also may mean worst—stories of Roman rulers come from the people whose names have become synonymous with sadistic lunacy, such as Nero and Caligula. Because we will be traveling between different periods in Roman history, we will need to set some context from time to time. Bear with me as I set the stage; the "murder and mayhem" arrive quickly with this lot.

Third, some of the rulers not directly featured in this book did some pretty terrible things. For example, when Julius Caesar slaughtered the Gaulish tribes in his self-serving quest for glory, he ineradicably stained his legacy. Although Caesar did not warrant a chapter in *Evil Roman Rulers*, his omission should not be considered an endorsement. We are after the worst of the worst, where their legacy leaves little doubt and little to admire. Caesar's life and legacy are much more complicated than, say, Nero's. Caesar founded an imperial dynasty. Nero burned it to the ground. Caesar was a brilliant leader, one of the greatest in all of human history. People followed him—quite literally—to the edge of the known world. Nero drove everyone away and died a pathetic disgrace. To distill Roman history to the worst of the worst, we must dispense with nuance and focus on the irredeemable. Caesar will just have to answer more fully for his actions in other works.

That said, it also would be a bit tone deaf if I were to ignore some of the deeds and actions that still shock modern sensibilities. Without distracting from the very worst of the worst, I want to highlight some people who fall outside this bull's-eye. Good and bad are subjective, after all. Some of Rome's "best" rulers did terrible things. These deeds deserve consideration even if their committers did enough to keep themselves off of our list. This book contains a few brief detours—"(dis)Honorable Mentions"—which examine these horrors. Again, failure to include a particular deed or action should not be taken as an endorsement. We have *so many* things to choose from. We simply cannot cover them all.

One challenge anyone who writes about Rome faces is names. Roman names didn't quite work in the same way modern ones do. Everyone knows Julius Caesar. But Julius wasn't his "first name" in the way we think of it today. It was his family name; he hailed from the Julii family. There were a lot of Julii. In fact, at periods in Roman history when one family was ascendant, you often find lots of people with similar names central to the story at the same time. Not enough name variation in a short period of time can lend itself to confusion. In this book, I periodically opt for clarity over historical precision in naming conventions. For example, I refer to the king Servius Tullius as Servius, even as historians may shorten his name to Tullius. Why? Because his daughters were both named Tullia, and having Tullius, Tullia, and Tullia is confusing. Any adjustments to historical naming conventions are done for the benefit of the reader and do not alter the underlying history.

This is a history of certain Romans, but not a history of Rome itself. This book identifies the worst of the worst of its rulers and puts them all in one place. More than 1,350 years passed between the legendary date of Rome's founding and the guy we meet in the epilogue. That's a broad swath of time, the better part of two millennia. To cover this much ground, we have to pick and choose our spots. I'm not trying to cover all of the details. I couldn't if I wished. This book is less about the larger picture and more about the character of Rome's rulers.

For example, when we get to Nero, we will skip the big native revolt in Britain led by the warrior-queen Boudica. Not that this isn't interesting. On the contrary, it's fascinating. It's just that it didn't really contribute to the development of the picture of Nero's character. The lens will focus on the ruler. Things happening on the periphery will be outside the focus. This book is not and cannot be all things Rome during the life spans of its subjects. We have to draw the line somewhere, even if it means leaving out some really interesting stuff. Fortunately, opportunities to explore Roman history in all time periods from almost every lens imaginable are almost limitless. Except this one. So far as I can tell, nothing out there is quite like this book.

Sure, there are rankings, and people have their opinions about who was the worst emperor, but this book breaks with tradition by considering more than just emperors. One of the people on the list was one of the kings of Rome. His life and actions easily warrant inclusion in any such list. This book also takes a unique and provocative stance by specifically considering not only people, but also institutions that had an outsize influence on Roman life, and that, often quite violently, tilted the trajectory of Roman history. The Senate and the Praetorian Guard were not individual people, but they ruled and projected power. They held sway over life and death, with the power of their institutions behind them to enforce their will. All too frequently, members of these groups used that power for nefarious aims and in direct opposition to the interests of the Roman state itself. Neither of these institutions ever is treated as a "ruler" in the traditional sense, and thus their inclusion in this book adds a differentiated way to define and study power.

What is so striking about all these people, both the individual rulers and the institutions we discuss, is that they all found different ways to be awful. In a way, they were all innovative in finding new ways to manifest the darker elements of the human soul. With that said, this book's intention is not to be excessively gruesome or voyeuristic. The book does not seek to wallow in the more disturbing details that could accompany this subject matter. It is impossible to tell the stories of why some of these people's actions are evil without getting into some pretty uncomfortable territory. However, the intention is to be more focused on the nature of the rulers than the gory details of what they did. That said, it's hard to make a case that someone was evil, or just plain incompetent, without describing why from time to time. Some things these people did, and commanded others to do, are genuinely shocking.

During a particular period, Roman emperors rose and fell so quickly they didn't have enough time to earn access to this ignominious club. In the fifty-year span from 235 to 285 CE, at least two dozen people claimed to be emperors. They didn't rule long, but that doesn't mean they should be overlooked. Being evil or awful takes no time at all. It can also get you killed in a hurry. Some rulers from this period would possess far more impressive résumés if they hadn't been assassinated young, though to be fair, a couple of people we will meet, namely Caligula and Elagabalus, managed to pack a whole lot of crazy into about four years each. They

PROLOGUE

A City Founded on Blood

The earliest days of Rome are shrouded in mystery and folklore. To-day's historians struggle to separate fact from fiction. But the Romans themselves didn't suffer from such historical indecisiveness. They knew Rome was founded in blood. It was common knowledge, part of their identity, even sequenced into their DNA. In fact, the city's very name enshrines a homicide.

Once the Roman Empire was secure, its historians looked back upon its founding and development from the vantage point of conquerors. In these shaky early years, the city needed cunning and determination to survive. In their accounts, the means always justified the end because they wrote from a place where ultimate victory has been realized. Not surprising, then, that the Romans believed their city was founded with a purpose, by a serious, charismatic leader, with a clear vision of the city's destined greatness. This idea was central to their founding myth. The Romans believed that their city was founded by an act of murder. The soil of the Palatine Hill, the heart of the city, was fertilized by blood, and in this rich mixture the roots of empire took hold.

Myth notwithstanding, archaeology suggests the site that eventually grew to the imperial capital of the world had very humble agrarian roots, dating back much further than the mythical date: thousands, perhaps as much as ten thousand years earlier. The first settlers almost certainly chose the Palatine Hill as home. Easily defensible, overlooking a narrow ford in the Tiber, the site had inherent commercial and martial advantages.

Roman mythology tells the story of the twin brothers, Romulus and Remus. Born of noble birth, they were the grandsons of the king of a city called Alba Longa. When granddad was usurped by his brother, the newborn twins were famously abandoned in a basket by the Tiber and suckled by a she-wolf before being saved by a kindly shepherd who slowly came to understand the royal blood flowing through their veins. When they came of age, the precocious twins set off to reconnect with their lost family and help their grandfather reclaim his throne. After righting the wrong, the twins decided to establish a kingdom of their own. They found the famous seven hills and knew they were in the right spot. But which hill to make the center of their kingdom? Remus believed the Aventine Hill was best. Romulus made the case for the Palatine. The disagreement morphed into argument. Heated words were exchanged. The tension escalated until the rival camps came to blows. In the end, Remus was cut down, butchered at the hands of his brutish brother and his thugs.[1]

Bloodshed. The destruction of the vanquished. The killing of one's own flesh and blood. These were ideas central to the very foundation of the Roman identity. Might makes right. Few remember the vanquished, but the name of Rome itself enshrines and celebrates power seized through fratricide. Subsequent generations of Rome's rulers took careful note that power was consolidated by the sword. More than twenty-two hundred years would pass between the founding of the city and the collapse of the Eastern Empire. Over these millennia, hundreds of people would come to hold absolute power. Some would use this power with wisdom and benevolence. Some avoided problems and conflict at all cost, kicking the can downhill to leave challenges to their successors. But others used their power to terrible and bloodthirsty ends, liquidating enemies, slaughtering innocents. Some were brilliant but genocidal. Some were just strange, indulging bizarre habits that shocked ancient contemporaries and modern readers alike. When there is little to stop the impulses of mad men, bad things happen.

It is a testament to the Roman system that the empire could survive the likes of a Caligula or Commodus, and, in some cases, even thrive in the long run. More often than not, though, the relentless bloodletting eroded the foundations of Rome, sapping it of its strength, and often destroying

The legendary twins, Romulus and Remus, being suckled by a she-wolf. Romulus murdered Remus, founding the city that bears his name through bloodshed and betrayal. *Wikimedia Commons.*

the empire's most talented leaders, generals, and citizens. It's hard to help further the cause when you're dead.

Case in point: with Remus dead, Romulus was in sole control. He was the king now. In those bloody first days, Romulus looked around and saw one serious drawback to the motley group of people he'd assembled as his cofounders; they were men and mostly fellow miscreants. At first, they had plenty to do. They had to organize a society, develop a military, feed people, all the usual stuff of a people trying to move from the Bronze Age to the Iron Age. To help give advice and counsel to the king, Romulus rewarded the founding families with representation in a prestigious advisory group, the Senate.

No matter what moves they made to stabilize their nascent kingdom, it would be impossible to build on their success without subsequent generations. The men needed wives and families. They weren't exactly the most eligible bachelors. Undeterred, Romulus proved that he could be not only brutal, but also cunning. He called a big festival and invited all the neighboring tribes, especially the Sabines, with all their marriable young women. Once everyone was nicely liquored up, Romulus gave the signal, and the men abducted the Sabine women and drove off their families. Angry, and presumably now sober, the fathers and brothers of the stolen women regrouped and planned their revenge. They armed themselves and marched on the city. Both sides drew swords and planned to cut each other to pieces. But then the ladies intervened. The Sabine women, now married to their Roman captors, sued for peace. A deal would be struck. The Sabines would appoint their leader to be co-king to rule alongside Romulus. The tribes would share power. Their people would be united, and what started with the abduction of the young Sabine women resulted in a stronger, more powerful kingdom, richer in lands and armies.[2]

Romulus and company had done it again. Resorting to fratricide was one thing. This was wholesale kidnapping. And it worked! Not surprising, Titus Tatius, the Sabine coruler, was murdered a few years later. None of the sources point toward Romulus as the instigator, but it sure was convenient for him. He was in charge again. Solo. With no one to question his actions or decisions. For a time. Eventually that body of senators started to get ideas. Romulus had a long run at the top. A few people were getting itchy for their turn.

After a thirty-seven-year reign, Romulus vanishes.[3] He either ascended to heaven in a cloud or was murdered by a jealous Senate. In the latter version of events, he was torn apart by the rampaging oligarchs, and the ascension to heaven was a convenient cover-up for their treachery and regicide. Given Romulus's original seizure of sole power, convenient symmetry of murder marked both the beginning and end of his eventful reign.

Whether he ascended to the heavens after a peaceful end to a divine life or was delivered there via murder, the top job was available. Romulus would be succeeded by a series of kings, who established many of Rome's institutions and began its relentless radiation of power in all directions. The results speak for themselves. Under these kings, Rome went from a tiny little backwater to a burgeoning power, developing rivalries with nearby city-states. As Rome's power grew, so, too, did the power of the kings. Generally, they used this power to benefit their kingdom. For more than two centuries, the kings guided Rome's ascent from its founding to its regional dominance—until one grasping, scheming tyrant seized the throne in a bloody coup and set a new bar for evil leadership for centuries to come. This king was so bad that the monarchy would be officially abolished, and to be accused of aspiring to be king was enough to get someone killed. Clearly, someone this evil is someone we need to get to know.

I

THE PROUD

Legend has it that after Romulus ascended to heaven to become a god, or was torn to pieces by senators, or just sort of vanished, a year passed before a successor king was elected. Wanting to get a taste of kingly authority, the senators each took a turn at the helm, ruling for five days before passing it along to the next guy. This nonsense lasted a year until an election was held and the Senate appointed Romulus's brother-in-law, Numa Pompilius. Where Romulus was hawkish, Numa was peaceful and gods-fearing. It is said that in his reign, many of the Roman religious institutions took shape.

For example, the pious Numa built a temple to the god Janus. When Rome was at war, the temple's doors would be open. When peace reigned, the doors would be closed.[1] Preferring peace to war, Numa promptly closed the doors and kept them shut for the duration of his reign. When he died at a respectable old age, it didn't take long for his bellicose successor to shove open the doors and go out a-conquering. The doors would remain open for *four hundred years*—four centuries of perpetual warfare. When they were finally shut, the peace lasted for all of eight years before being swung wide for another two centuries.[2]

Over the decades, the crown passed from ruler to ruler. Along the way, Rome's farmer-soldiers projected the power of the upstart city farther and farther. The little settlement on the Tiber was evolving into a force with which to be reckoned. The kings of Rome, advised by the Senate, that body of men who traced their days back to the founding of Rome in the glory days of Romulus, oversaw strife, conflict, and near constant warfare. These kings of Rome ruled for an average of thirty-five years, a near-miraculous run of assassination-free longevity and good health. Granted, the stories of these kings went a long way in explaining the origins of Rome's social, religious, and martial institutions. These legends crystallized the Roman identity, grounding the people in a shared past, never mind the fact that this past is wholly or partly myth. Or maybe the Romans just needed to justify its rulers' savagery and bloodthirstiness.

Being king was a good gig, and eventually someone came along who would stop at nothing to seize control for himself. Actually, a few tried, but the first to succeed in a bloody power grab would fate himself to be the last king of Rome, a ruler so reviled that afterward the Romans vowed never to let any ruler hold supreme power alone. You know you're bad when a country reorganizes itself so there can never be anyone like you again. The twists and turns of how things got to this point are a bit confused, but there's plenty of murder, betrayal, and ruthless ambition along the way.

When the aged king Ancus Martius died in 616 BCE, the Roman monarchy was still technically an elected position, not the birthright of the king's kids. On Martius's death, a wise regent who had served as Martius's sons' tutor lobbied for the gig and was duly elected king himself.[3] Thus began the rule of Lucius Tarquinius Priscus: a competent ruler, acknowledged by all as the right man for the job. Except, that is, for Martius's sons. They burned with resentment. They wanted power for themselves. While they schemed, Priscus ruled well, managed Rome's ongoing wars to good ends, and married his daughter to a talented and promising man, Servius Tullius.

The years rolled by. Eventually, the scheming Martius sons made their move. They hired a couple of brutish thugs to murder King Priscus in order to clear their path to rule.[4] The assassins enacted their scheme by pretending to get into a violent shouting match, each accusing the other of horrible things. Whipped up into a frenzy and with shouted abuse raining down on one another, the two put on quite a show. People got worried. They turned to their wise king to adjudicate the impassioned argument. Whatever it was about, it was big, and the king dutifully agreed to intervene.

Eventually, the two combatants were brought before the king to settle their disagreement. Having gained the royal audience, they dropped the pretense of antagonism and worked together for their true aim: to kill the king. One brandished an ax and buried it in the head of the unsuspecting king.[5] The assassins fled; the mortally wounded king was taken to private quarters. The sons of Martius who had hatched the scheme never came close to seizing power. Instead, they fled Rome in disgrace, only to be tracked down and executed.[6] The first murder of a Roman king had failed to secure the throne for the assailants. The second would be more successful.

Priscus died from his head wound, but before word could spread, his quick-thinking wife, Tanaquil, had him brought upstairs to his private rooms in the royal palace. She knew she had to act decisively. Appearing from a second-story window, she spoke to the gathered citizens holding vigil and declared the king's injury just a flesh wound. She promised everyone he'd be back at work in no time. Meanwhile, knowing that the wound was mortal, she played the role of kingmaker behind the scenes.[7] But who to rule in Priscus's place? One on side, her son-in-law, the just, wise, and talented Servius Tullius. On the other, her own sons with the stricken king Tarquinius Priscus. She looked at her boys and knew they were lacking.

Tanaquil chose well. Skipping over her sons, she made her move. While keeping up the charade that King Tarquin would be better any day now, she asked the people to trust Servius Tullius as a stand-in while the king convalesced. It would help the king heal faster, she suggested, if he could recover at his own pace and without the stress of his kingly duties. By trusting Servius's leadership, Priscus would be back on his feet in no time. At Tanaquil's urging, Servius began to appear wearing the royal robes and standing in as a proxy for the stricken king. By the time it was apparent that King Tarquin was actually dead, everyone had already come to accept Servius as king.[8] It just sort of happened. Everyone shrugged and got on with their lives.

The wisdom of Tanaquil's choice would bear out over the long, successful reign of Servius. But just as Martius's kids seethed at being passed over, so, too, did the younger Tarquins. Well, at least one of them did. Servius Tullius had two daughters, both, confusingly, named Tullia. In order to create some semblance of family order, Servius had married his two daughters—again—both named Tullia (confusing, right?) to the sons of the good and now dead King Tarquin, Lucius and Arruns, the same two boys who had been passed over by their own mother.[9]

As it turns out, Lucius was violent, brooding, and power hungry. Arruns, it would seem, was of milder disposition. One of the Tullias was like Lucius; the other, like Arruns. The vicious Tarquin prince Lucius married the sweet Tullia. The sweet Tarquin prince Arruns married the vicious Tullia. Confused yet? Don't worry. The picture will get a lot clearer in a moment as people once against start murdering one another in the craven quest for power.

Vicious Tullia and vicious Tarquin saw in one another a vehicle for their ambition, a partner in crime in the very literal sense. The Roman historian Livy summed it up perfectly: "Evil attracts evil."[10] Being married wouldn't be a deterrent for either of these two. Lucius and Tullia schemed in a way that would feel very comfortable to Alfred Hitchcock. They plotted together to arrange the deaths of their respective spouses/ siblings. The gentle prince and princess, Arruns and the other Tullia, were duly dispatched through well-placed poison. With them dead and gone, Lucius and Tullia (there's only one left now, so she gets sole possession of the name without qualifier) dropped the pretense of mourning and promptly married one another. From two royal couples to one, there was now a concentration of ambition, ruthlessness, and a crazed desire for power.[11]

Just to reset: Servius Tullius is king. His surviving daughter, Tullia, is married to Lucius Tarquinius, the son of the dead Tarquin king. Servius is father-in-law to the son of the previous king. Tullia and Lucius are cold, calculating murderers, having dispatched their respective spouses/sib-lings so they could plot and scheme together. The only thing standing between them and the power they crave is Tullia's dear old dad and Lucius's father-in-law, the noble and aged King Servius. They'd killed their own siblings and spouses. They had one more family member to betray, and power was theirs. It didn't matter to them that Servius was a good, just, and wise king, that he guided the state with a benevolent hand and was universally admired by subjects and senators alike. He stood in the way. Family be damned. The old man had to go.

It didn't take the brute Tarquin long to make his move. At first, he worked in the background, whispering in people's ears about how much the old king stunk, and how much better things would be for everyone once Tarquin was calling the shots. He bribed, pleaded, and cajoled people to give him their support when the time came, making outlandish promises about all the wonderful things he would do for them once he was in charge.[12] Then one day, while Servius was off doing whatever kings did, Tarquin assembled a posse of armed thugs, marched through the Forum, and stomped up the steps to the Senate House. He went straight for the king's chair and demanded that all of the senators assemble and acknowledge *him* as the king.[13] When the aged Servius arrived to register his protest, Tarquin grabbed the old man by the waist and tossed him down the steps of the Senate House. Dazed and bloodied, poor Servius stumbled away, seeking the protection of the palace. Tarquin promptly sent his armed goons after the poor old man, and they hacked him to death for all to see.

Tarquin wasn't the only one whipped into a frenzy of bloodlust. The lovely Mrs. Tarquin, you will recall, was the daughter of the deposed and now dead King Servius. If she mourned the loss of her father, she sure had a strange way of showing it. Having gotten word that the coup had succeeded, she drove her wagon into the Forum and hailed her husband as king. Then, as she left in her wagon, she saw the corpse of her father lying in the street where he had been butchered on her husband's order. Rather than collect the body to ensure a dignified burial, she whipped the horses to go faster, promptly picked up speed, and crashed right over the body of dear old dad, desecrating his corpse and adding one last indignity to a man whose only crime was to have really awful kids.[14]

Let's take a quick look at how Tarquin was doing on his to-do list as he trod his path to the throne:

1. Murder spouse? Check.
2. Help plot and pull off the murder of your brother? Check.
3. Marry your brother's widow to form a power couple of doom? Check.
4. Threaten the Senate and people into recognizing you as king, despite a perfectly good one already on the throne? Check.
5. Murder father-in-law? Check.
6. Seize power in a bloody coup and displace a good and wise ruler in the process? Check.

Not bad. Not bad at all. Job well done, Tarquin and Tullia. What a swell couple you two are! Things looked bleak for Rome. The nature of their new king wasn't lost on anyone. However, although Tarquin may have gotten to the throne by horrible means, once he was in control, he surprised everyone by being a humble, visionary ruler. Oh, no, wait . . . That's not it at all. Grasping and vicious, Tarquin was about to take things from bad to worse for his subjects.

King Tarquin's first order of business was to figure out which senators had objected to his heavy-handed seizure of power. He made his list, then murdered the whole lot of them. Aware that he had now set a precedent that all one needs to do to be king is to murder the previous one, he armed his retainers to the teeth and had them surround him wherever he went. Thoroughly unpopular for having displaced and murdered a popular ruler, Tarquin trumped up charges on leading citizens, personally overseeing sham trials. He served as both judge and jury and gave over to his thugs the role of executioner. Liquidating political enemies, both real and imagined, was also good business, as Tarquin seized the estates of the vanquished men, disinheriting their families and gobbling up all the cash for himself. One gets the sense that as bad as all this was, what really bugged the historians writing about the events down the historical road was that he turned his back on the Senate. No longer bothering even to pretend to care about them, he carried on as he pleased, striking deals with foreign powers at a whim, making all policy decisions, and generally acting as though his opinions were the only ones that mattered.[15]

Tarquin killed some nobles and relegated others to irrelevance. He was accompanied by an armed horde and threatened people with violence everywhere he went. And this was just in the first few months. The people could do little but mutter laments to themselves and hang the moniker "Superbus" on Tarquin. Far from meaning "superb," this meant "proud," but not in a cool way. Superbus was meant in an arrogant, obnoxious, and thoroughly unlikable way. He didn't care. And besides, no one called him that to his face.[16]

As his reign progressed, he ruthlessly guarded his power and generally was a jerk to everyone. He embroiled Rome in countless wars and diplomatic tussles, wasting lives and resources. He ignored and undermined the Senate, and generally proved the accuracy of his nickname. No matter how horrified and frustrated the Romans were, there seemed little they could do about it, as Tarquin was always surrounded by his retinue of vicious, armed brutes.

Where the long-dead Servius had been done in by his progeny, Tarquin was the beneficiary of the machinations of his son, Sextus, who took after dear old dad in the worst ways possible. Once, while embroiled in a conflict with a neighboring city-state, Tarquin had Sextus flee to the enemy camp, pretending to be a persecuted refugee. The cover story of Tarquin being a jerk was believable, and the gullible rulers took him in, offering shelter and comfort. They felt bad for the kid. Everyone knew what an ass Tarquin was, and no one suspected anything when his own son showed up with a woe-is-me story.

At first, Sextus made a grand show of fighting against his dad and the Roman armies, winning the confidence of his hosts and earning a senior position in their leadership. Sextus waited until they let down their guard to spring his trap. Once thoroughly entrenched and with full access to his father's enemies, Sextus rounded up the city elders. He did more than betray their confidence. Sextus slaughtered some, imprisoned others, and drove everyone else into exile. He then promptly surrendered the city and all its possessions to dad. The apple really didn't fall far from the tree.[17] But not all his kids' scheming would reap profitable ends. They would, in fact, lead to his downfall.

Tarquin was determined to build lavish monuments to himself. Money was always short, and he frequently declared war on generally peaceful neighbors, with a mind toward sacking and looting to bolster his coffers. When that still wasn't enough to pay all his expenses, he conscripted the commoners into forced labor.[18] While Tarquin sought to build monuments to himself, resentment for him and his whole family grew and spread. Speaking out against the family was a death sentence. Conspiracies had to be kept secret in order to work.

One person who detested the Tarquins was Marcus Junius Brutus. His family was full of smart, capable people, and, as such, had drawn the ire of the Tarquins. Brutus had seen many of his relations slaughtered to prevent them becoming threats to the murderous tyrant king and his family. To keep himself safe, Brutus pretended to be a simpleton. Although it exposed him to countless cruel jokes from the Tarquin family, he stayed alive, biding his time and waiting for his moment.

Fortunately for Brutus, the Tarquins were the Tarquins, and his moment wouldn't be long in coming. One night, Sextus Tarquin—he of the pretend to be an exile and ruthlessly seize control of a rival city variety—was drinking with his pals. This, apparently, was not an infrequent occurrence. In fact, Sextus and his entourage were often out partying, causing trouble, and generally being assholes. The prince and his retainers hit it hard late into the evening, getting plenty drunk and arguing over who had the best wife. One came up with the questionably wise idea that they should all go see what their wives were doing at that very moment. Nothing would help determine the virtue of these ladies like showing up unannounced and seeing what they did to occupy their time when their husbands weren't around to keep an eye on them.

They hopped on their horses, one of the earliest recorded instances of drunk driving, and galloped off into the night. At their first stop, they found most of the royal princesses having their own party, feasting and dancing deep into the night. But from there they went to the home of Sextus's cousin, Lucius Tarquinius Collatinus. This whole crazy thing had been Collatinus's idea in the first place, and he was proud that when they arrived at his home, the entourage found his wife, Lucretia, at home, tending to her weaving.[19] No party for her. The work of a virtuous Roman matron was never done. He was declared the winner, and the whole party was invited into the home of Collatinus and Lucretia to continue their festivities. A little drunken boorishness: not great, but definitely not the worst the Tarquins had ever done.

But Sextus Tarquin had one look at the lovely Lucretia and was overcome with lust. He didn't care that she was married to his drinking buddy/cousin. In fact, that probably increased the appeal. He waited. Just a couple of days passed before Collatinus was called away for one reason or another. Sextus rode to their home, knocked on the door, and accepted the invitation inside. Lucretia was a gracious hostess, and she fed the prince and then showed him to a guest bedroom for the evening. Sextus duly retired for the evening, waiting for the household to be quiet.

When everyone was sound asleep, he grabbed his dagger and broke into Lucretia's bedroom. She resisted his overtures as best she could. He made serious threats to kill her, yet she resisted. Turning her virtue against her, Sextus threatened to kill both her and a slave, placing them in bed in such a way as to implicate her as having died in the throes of impassioned adultery. Her resolve weakened, Sextus duly raped the poor woman.[20] Satisfied with his latest conquest, Sextus rode away from the scene of his crime, content that his royal status gave him immunity from, well, the need for even the most basic decency.

Understandably, Lucretia was devastated. She sent a messenger to summon her father and husband, and told them to bring a witness. Collatinus brought Brutus. When they arrived in her presence, she told them what had happened. She demanded revenge, making those present vow to

The tragic nobility of Lucretia led to the downfall of the vicious Tarquins and inspired the Renaissance master Titian more than two millennia after the events. *Wikimedia Commons.*

avenge her mistreatment. She made them make a solemn vow. To a Roman, a vow was sacred. Defying such a vow would be unthinkable. They were committed. When they affirmed their vow, the chaste and heartbroken Lucretia drew out a dagger and said that she could not live with what had happened. She plunged the dagger into her chest, killing herself. Her grief-stricken husband and father were shocked. Their beloved and virtuous Lucretia was dead. Tarquin Sextus had driven her to suicide, and they had just sworn revenge on the son of the king. They weren't exactly sure where to start. But one man had been present for the whole thing, and he'd been waiting for this moment for a while. Brutus's moment had arrived.

He pulled the dagger from the corpse of poor Lucretia and, with it dripping her blood, vowed that with that very knife, he would drive away all the Tarquins, not just Sextus but the whole rotten family.[21] He passed the knife to Lucretia's heartbroken husband, then father, and made them do the same.

Together they rode off into the night. News traveled fast, and the locals in the closest village were furious. Enough was enough. The Tarquins had to go. Brutus managed to make way to the army and convinced them to join the revolt. Seemingly unassailable just a day before, the Tarquins suddenly were overrun by angry mobs. The people gave vent to their pent-up anger, and King Tarquin, his horrid wife, and the whole rotten family were driven from Rome in disgrace. They were lucky to escape with their lives. The doors at the city gates were shut behind them as they fled into the night. In a fitting twist, Sextus Tarquin sought refuge in the very city he had betrayed to his dad, and the locals, still seething, cut him to pieces.

King Tarquin, meanwhile, fled to one of the countless cities that viewed Rome with jealousy and suspicion. Desperate to get his throne back, he formed an alliance with a rival king, and together they declared war on Rome. From king to would-be conqueror in just a few days. It was an epic fall from grace. Tarquin died in exile, having spent the rest of his life trying—and failing—to seize by force the throne he had seized twenty-five years earlier with the murder of his father-in-law.

In a way, he got off easy. He lived. He caused so much death, pain, and suffering in his two-and-a-half-decade reign of tyranny. Whereas so many others died a violent death at his instigation, Tarquin was spared what might seem a more just retribution. But consider that, for the rest of his days, Tarquin seethed at the loss of his kingship. For a decade and a half, he plotted and schemed, his mind twisted with angst over his lost throne. He woke up every day trying to regain Rome and went to bed every night a failure. It's not exactly justice, but at least we know he didn't ease into a comfortable retirement. It consumed him, tormented him. And not that he would know it at the time, but he would go down in history as the worst and last king of Rome.

In the immediate aftermath of the overthrow of the Tarquins, the monarchy was abolished, the control of state given over to the Senate. Only from their ranks could senior administrators be drawn, and never fewer than two people would share the highest job, the consulship, and even then, for a term of only one year. The first two consuls to share the job in the newly formed Republic? Collatinus and Brutus, of course.[22] Together they had mobilized the people, won over the army, driven out the Tarquins, and established a new system of government. They saved Rome from its first truly evil ruler. They honored the vow of revenge they'd made to the martyred Lucretia . . . and then some.

You have to be pretty bad at ruling if an entire system is created just to prevent anyone else from ever having the same job again. And if the name Brutus sounds familiar, then it should. Marcus Brutus, some five hundred years or so later, would etch his own name in the history books as one of the assassins of his famous cousin, Julius Caesar. One reason this Brutus pulled out a dagger and joined the conspiracy against Caesar? They thought he wanted to be king. Five centuries later, and fear of another Tarquin was enough to seize otherwise rational people with a bloodthirsty frenzy.

2

THE OLIGARCHS

In 123 BCE, violent rioting erupted across Rome. Vicious mobs, frenzied by bloodlust and armed to the teeth, roved across the city, hunting down their enemies. Unlike most urban riots from the span of history, this was not a case of the urban poor revolting against their oppressors. No, the malevolent actors were the rich, elite rulers of the upper classes, seeking to wreak vengeance on those who would dare speak up and demand a more equitable share for the rest of the citizens. Rather than consider long-overdue reforms, the rich armed themselves, fanned out across the city, and cut down thousands, murdering them where they stood. Then, their fury not yet slaked, they dragged the butchered corpses through the city and dumped them in the Tiber River. All told, nearly three thousand Romans lost their lives that day. The leader of the reform movement being so violently repressed was not just any citizen. He was of the upper levels of the nobility. A man of impeccable credentials. His attempts to reform did not just bring about violent reprisals; they put a target on his back. His social station couldn't save him. The murderous mob hunted him down so they could visit upon him the same fate as thousands of his followers: savage death.

Seen by his contemporaries as a traitor to his class, the patrician Gaius Gracchus was a reluctant entrant into public life. His older brother, Tiberius, had likewise been a reformer, fighting for balance and fairness across Roman society. It hadn't ended well. Most attempts at social reform during the republic—the historical period when the Senate called all the shots—ended badly. At least, for the reformers and their followers.

The republic was far from a representative form of government, and certainly not the proto-democracy that America's founders looked to as an example of how to achieve life, liberty, and the pursuit of happiness. At this point, Rome was firmly an oligarchy, with wealth, power, and prestige consolidated in the hands of a small handful of the upper crust of society. These people saw their dominance of Rome as their birthright, and they clung to it with an iron grip. They dominated the official apparatus of government, the Senate, the body of rich men who got to decide everything.

When Tiberius Gracchus, older brother of Gaius, began to agitate for a reform agenda, Senators worked themselves to a boiling fury. In 133 BCE, they armed themselves with crude clubs, marched to the Forum—the heart of civic life in ancient Rome—and bludgeoned Tiberius and many of his followers to death.[1] Their actions cost Rome one of its farsighted leaders, depriving the city of one of the few people who could organize the reforms so desperately needed to keep the rickety republic from crashing and burning. Seeking to avoid the fate of his older brother, Gaius Gracchus went into self-imposed exile and fled not just the city, but the whole Italian peninsula.

Camping out on Corsica, Gaius Gracchus kept his head down and tried to leave Rome to its own devices. But the call to public service was strong, as was his sense of justice. Ending his exile, Gracchus encamped to Rome and went to work picking up where his brother had left off. At first, he met with a bit more success. But the senatorial distrust of populist reform, not to mention that group's ardent desire not to share a shred of their wealth, could only withstand so much.[2] As Gracchus pushed harder to shake things up, the patricians began shaking their heads and fists with righteous indignation. The harder Gracchus pushed, the angrier the patricians became. Their anger turned to hatred, their hatred to violence.

On that fateful day in 123 BCE, as the senatorial death squads fanned out across the city, Gracchus fled for his life. He found sanctuary at the foot of a statue of the goddess Diana, protector of childbirth and hunters. Unfortunately for Gracchus, the ones *doing* the hunting found him. Rather than respect the sanctity of this holy place, the thugs tore Gracchus from the statue and hacked him to death. He was rejoined to his followers as his lifeless body was tossed into the Tiber.[3] As the slow-moving river wended its way through the city and toward the sea, its waters turned red with blood. Rather than stabilize the system by ridding itself of unwanted troublemakers, the violence of 123 BCE accelerated the end of the republic. There would be more cataclysms of violence before the foundation collapsed, and the republic would limp along for almost another century, but it was in its death spiral. How had it become so bad?

* * *

After Tarquin was driven off in 509 CE, he didn't give up his ambition to rule. For the rest of his life he formed alliances with other cities and rulers, trying to coax them into war with Rome, to humble his former kingdom, teach them some manners, and place himself back in charge. But Tarquin was a spent force, and so was the monarchy. In its place, the senators puffed up their collective chest and proclaimed a new era of prosperity, slapping each other on the backs and lauding themselves for their commitment to freedom, equality, liberty, and blah blah blah. They would have a pretty good run, in terms of holding on to power. As a governing body, the Senate got to call the shots for about five hundred years. The only hiccup? Senators had to disenfranchise, exploit, and murder *a lot* of people along the way in order to do so.

But still, the Senate did debate, make decisions by consensus, and had a membership that, in theory, one could work his way into. As such, it's easy to romanticize the Senate, with its faint whisper of democracy. The concept of sharing power is indeed noble. This was a class of several hundred, sharing power and working together to set policy and guide the ship of state. But too often the romance of this idea was held in stark contrast to reality. Sometimes a particularly ambitious or bloodthirsty senator would get his hands on too much power. Other times the whole group perpetrated atrocities. Either way, in its long and complicated history, the Senate as a whole, and individuals working on its behalf, had enough examples of brutality to warrant mention in our review of the worst rulers of Rome.

Let's take a half step back and take a quick look at class divisions in the ancient Roman world. In its simplest terms, we can look at this divide two ways: socially and politically. Socially, there were patricians—the families that claimed their descent from those present with Romulus at the founding of Rome—and everyone else. Non-patricians were called plebeians. Patricians versus Plebeians would be an epic battle line tearing at the fabric of Roman society.

Politically, the top of the oligarchy was the Senate. Initially organized—or so the legend says—as an advisory body to Romulus, with

Tarquin gone, the Senate assumed responsibility for making all policy decisions for the state. As Rome's power grew, so, too, did the power of the Senate. At the time Brutus and company drove off Tarquin, the Senate had existed for several hundred years. Aside from the Senate, several more classifications existed, all, in theory, ranked according to wealth and property ownership. Membership in the Senate was not exclusively patrician. But it was overwhelmingly so, and it also *was* exclusively rich. If there was one thing the average stinking rich Roman really didn't like doing, it was sharing those riches with lots of poor people. This was an age when people assumed that social and financial status was a sign of divine favor. If the gods favored you, then they must not favor the poor people. To be a member of the senatorial order was to be a member of the most exclusive club in ancient Rome. They learned pretty quickly to take care of their own.

They were paranoid that too much power in the hands of one person (remember how much Tarquin sucked?) was dangerous. The Romans solved this problem by having not one, but two senior-most magistrates, called consuls. Their terms were for one year. In theory, they could not serve another consulship for a decade. Consuls were drawn exclusively from the senatorial order, as were the other senior administrative and military positions in the republic. To hold any of the prestigious posts, to have any real power, one had to be a senator. Lots of people wanted in, or at least, a fairer slice of the pie.

It's important to remember the social and political divides: patricians and plebeians, Senate and non-Senate. Because the trouble really started when the have-nots started to look around and realized they were getting a raw deal at the expense of a few rich snobs.

The Senate really came into its own with the overthrow of Tarquin and the abolishment of the monarchy in 509 BCE. For the next five centuries or so, all the important administrators were drawn from its ranks. To be a senator was a pretty good gig. You owned lands and estates, you collected revenues, mobs of the great unwashed stepped aside to let you pass on the street. Slaves toiled on your farms, growing crops, making oil and wine, and breaking their backs during long, grueling days as you strolled through the Forum, content to be the social better of all you passed. The size of the Senate varied over the years, but so far as can be told, always measured in the hundreds. Most sources seem to point to three hundred as the magic number at this point. But as Rome's influence and population expanded, the Senate came to be an increasingly tiny fraction of the population, with enormous amounts of wealth, power, and prestige concentrated in the hands of a fractionally small group of people who were often out of touch. The number of poor and dispossessed grew.

The Senate's membership was dominated by patricians. Plebs were to be exploited, not have a voice in governance. Despite the successful rhetoric of their coup, in which they decried tyranny and oppression, the senators rigged the system for themselves. To the rank and file of the Roman world, this was exploitation by another name. As the senators controlled the strings of government and policy, the plebs toiled in a state of near servitude. Days were long and brutal. Food was always short. Life for the plebs was nothing like the comparative opulence of their senatorial overlords. In short, little changed for them. Tarquin might have been a tyrant, but at least he didn't cloak himself in the veil of liberty. The Senate's sugary words held no sweetness for the plebs.

Maybe the system of government had changed, but to most, things remained more or less the same. The change affected the top of the social order. When a coup succeeds on the rhetoric of "liberty" and "ending tyranny," but nothing changes for everyone but the upper crust, then it's understandable when the rank and file become disaffected.

It only took a few years before the Senate as a whole became insufferable. Collectively, the senatorial caste owned just about everything. They also controlled all the political offices. They preferred to keep things as they were. Everybody else had to fight for their daily bread. The rich senators could talk all day about liberty, but they enjoyed their exalted position on the backs of exploited labor and ceaseless toil from the everyday folk. As the first few years of senatorial rule progressed, the working classes worked harder and harder for less and less. Debts mounted, conditions worsened, and a disinterested Senate couldn't be bothered to consider the welfare of fellow Romans who had the unspeakably bad taste not to be born to the upper class.

So, after just a few years with the Senate as the apex of Roman governance, the majority of citizens were understandably not too thrilled that *they* were still oppressed. Wages were paltry, food scarce, days long and brutal. After just a few years, the plebeians looked around and realized their one advantage: numbers. Many more were outside the loftiest social order than inside it. While the fat-cat senators luxuriated, the plebeians existed in a state of near slavery, accumulating massive debt with no hope of financial independence.

Enough was enough. In 494 BCE, tired of being exploited, the plebeians walked out. They got up and left, en masse, decamping to a mountain outside the city.[4] They quit. In what is likely the first organized labor strike in human history, the plebeians fled the city and wouldn't return until their grievances were addressed. How bad must things have been for an entire social order to leave a city? Less than two decades in power, and the senatorial order had effectively forced creation of the first labor movement, denying their fellow citizens basic human rights and governmental representation. Fueled by a sense of natural-born superiority, their condescension toward the majority of plebeians showed their true colors. The senators and their caste cared only about themselves and looked upon everyone else with scorn and contempt.

But faced with a labor shortage, the economic life of the city screeched to a halt. Negotiations took place. Some concessions were granted, grudgingly. The wary plebeians came back to work. Life went on, but the plebeians took a first step in understanding their power when organized. This movement gained a few considerations from the stingy Senate, most important being the creation of a new political office, the Tribune of the Plebs.[5] This office held a few powers, but most important, it held veto power over certain acts of the Senate and was considered sacrosanct, meaning that while in office, the Tribune could not be harmed in any way. It was a mild check on senatorial arrogance, but in the creation of this office, the Senate sowed the seeds of its own destruction. Our friends Gaius and Tiberius Gracchus were two of the Tribunes of the Plebs who would use the office to crack away at the foundations of the republic.

This labor strike, known as the first Secession of the Plebs, marked an inauspicious start to senatorial rule and proved to be a predictor of how the Senate would run things for the next four centuries. It also kicked off a period in Roman history known by a somewhat sterile and clinical name: The Conflict of the Orders.[6]

In many ways, this conflict defined the evolution of Roman society for centuries. One on hand, plebeians were fighting for basic rights such as representation in government and protection under the law; and on the other, patricians were using their domination of the Senate to deny these things to others and keep everything for themselves. The Secession of the

Plebs wouldn't be the last such labor strike; the plebs would reach a breaking point and quit several more times. This also wouldn't be the last time the senators' grasping for power and refusing to care for the rest of their fellow Romans would tear at the fabric of Roman society. For the first Secession of the Plebs, a peaceful labor strike with a negotiated settlement would turn out to be a high-water mark for Senate–plebeian relations. Down the road, the senators would skip the particularities and just start killing populist upstarts. As history took its course, bloodshed became alarmingly frequent.

As senatorial rule progressed, their behavior didn't improve. Roman society, plebeians especially, needed a formal legal code. Just a few decades after the first Secession of the Plebs, a formal committee of twelve magistrates set to work to draft a formal legal code. When their work was incomplete after their first year in office, a second group of twelve took over. This group of senatorial elites decided that instead of creating a more egalitarian society, they should consolidate power further.[7] They surrounded themselves with bodyguards, seized the government, and proclaimed themselves in charge. When they were finally run off, and the legal code was completed, Rome was left with a system that protected the rights and lives of the plebeians. So, of course, the senators refused to implement it. They were just words with no force of law. Rather than respect their fellow citizens, the Senate left the law code in permanent draft status, fighting off with all its might even the slightest shred of reform. It took another Secession of the Plebs for the Senate grudgingly to put the law code into effect.

While the plebeians gained a foothold in terms of legal protection, the Senate looked for other ways to exploit the masses. Over time, the senators would deploy such tricks as denial of the highest elected offices to anyone other than patricians and keeping their chosen people in office by extending the terms of office of patricians long past their expiration date—anything to hold on to power.

Later in the republic, as Rome expanded its territory, its battles were increasingly farther afield. Soldiers were rounded up and sent to faraway battles. When they returned, they found that their lands had been seized, their crops stolen, their families and laborers evicted. As the soldiers couldn't both fight and farm at the same time, they couldn't keep up with the rent, and as such, their lands became property of the "people," which meant the "Senate." Thank you for your service.

In other places on the Roman peninsula, the Senate laid claims to large swaths of fertile lands, even as citizens starved in the streets. The Senate steadfastly refused to give these lands to the citizens for farming and thus to alleviate the starvation. The Senate would rather people starve to death than allow those same people to grow crops. It was agrarian reform that pulled the Gracchi into public life. Making this the cornerstone of their reform agendas, the brothers turned away from patrician precedent and fought for a more equal society. Empathetic to the plight of the common people, they fought for land distribution, enfranchisement, and basic human dignity.

When Tiberius pushed the senators to the breaking point, they armed themselves with clubs and beat him and his retainers to death in the Forum. When Gaius caused such a stir, they not only murdered him, but also three thousand of his followers. The Senate seemed willing to hold on to power and maintain the patrician social standing by any means necessary.

In 100 BCE, another populist sought to push for needed reform. Rather than play by the rules, he sought to cut corners, make deals, and use bribery and intimidation. Essentially, he tried to reform the system by the same playbook the senators had used to fight reform. Outraged, the senators attacked the reformer, named Saturninus. A full-scale battle broke out in the Roman Forum, with armed mobs fighting a pitched battle to the death. When the senators and their thugs prevailed, Saturninus and his followers were arrested and thrown into temporary prison in, ironically, the Senate House. Despite the promise of safety from the leading citizen, the senators wanted to skip the whole "trial by a jury of peers" thing and pursued their own form of justice. Climbing onto the roof of the Senate House, the senators tore up the terra-cotta roof tiles and threw them down at the cowering men below.[8] In what must have been a terrifying and gruesome way to die, the shower of tiles crushed the prisoners below. Those who didn't die fled through the front doors, where a waiting mob of senators beat them to death.

The "leading man" mentioned above was Gaius Marius. In time, his ambition to win respect and his great rival's refusal to grant it would lead to armed conflict that mortally wounded the republic and created the conditions that the most famous of Romans—Julius Caesar—would use to destroy it.

Marius's most notable accomplishment had been the complete reorganization of the army. He not only modernized its tactics, but also recruited soldiers from the poorest ranks of society and trained them relentlessly, drilling into them a sense of professional discipline that previously had been lacking. Under Marius's vision, Rome's military was less a citizen militia, hastily organized in times of war or crisis, and more a standing army ready to fight and crush anyone who dared stand against Rome.[9] Marius's reforms also marked a dark shift in the trajectory of Roman history. By recruiting from the poor of the Roman world, Marius had given access to opportunity to a group of people who had enjoyed little such favor. So far, so good. But from here on out, the standing armies developed loyalty to their commanders, not necessarily the state, and certainly not to the Senate. This creation of a cult of personality could spell doom, depending on who was there to exploit it and who was presumed to oppress it.

Marius had not been born into the upper echelon of Roman society. He slowly and methodically built a career of odds-defying social mobility. Some of his subordinates chafed at taking orders from a commoner. One of these, Lucius Cornelius Sulla, hailed from a family that held rank and prestige even over other patricians. Like many good patricians, he served in the upper ranks of the army's officer corps.[10] He was present at and an active commander in some of the late republic's great victories. He was lauded and awarded some of Rome's highest honors. He also came to be the torchbearer for the senatorial party, the Optimates, or "the best men." This political group fought to maintain senatorial and societal power and prestige in the hands of the oligarchs at the very top of the social order, and not share much of either with anyone else. Their adversaries were the Populares, those who sought a more equitable distribution of wealth and access to social advancement.[11] The Populares, not surprisingly, were populist. Sulla hated them.

Marius had been born of low rank. Nevertheless, he clawed his way into the Senate and attained the consulship—the highest office in the land—an astonishing seven times by the time of his death. As a non-patrician, Marius had a hard time winning the respect of his social betters. But he saved the day on the battlefield, and that was enough to keep him moving up the ladder. Beneath Marius in the military chain of command, Sulla seethed at being subordinate to a plebeian.

When Sulla finally got his independent command, he took his army and marched east. Popular agitation got the army reassigned to Marius. Rather than respect the rule of law and hand over command to Marius, Sulla turned his army around and marched on the city. Armed soldiers were forbidden in Rome, but Sulla was not to be deterred. Driven by the frenzied combination of self-righteousness and social snobbery, Sulla marched his troops right into Rome, driving off Marius and his populist agitators. After securing his command, he went back east and resumed his mission.

In his absence, populist agitation again sought to undermine his authority. Sulla completed his mission and again brought his army back to Rome.[12] Rather than sit down and talk with the populists, he sought to rid Rome of them once and for all. He didn't just run off his opponents this time; he condemned them to die. He had himself appointed dictator for life, wholly unprecedented in Roman history. With unlimited power and no accountability to anyone, he could indulge his sociopathy to its fullest extent.

In the name of the Senate, Sulla gathered up a list of his political opponents and declared them enemies of the state, their lives forfeit. The head of the Optimates was about to assert control and wipe out populist agitation once and for all. Senatorial prestige had suffered. Time to settle some scores. A list of the condemned was nailed up in the Forum. Prices were placed on heads. The murders of these unfortunate souls were now legally sanctioned and to be rewarded. Senatorial vengeance against populist reform had devolved into state-sponsored slaughter. Heads were lopped off and nailed up in the Forum.[13] Anyone who spoke against Sulla was inviting his own murder. Those who did so were hunted down and butchered. Sulla's bloodlust was cloaked in the language of patrician prerogative and senatorial domination. His political genocide, officially, was about restoring stability and reasserting senatorial control. The reign of terror went on for months. Giving shelter to someone on the proscription list was itself cause for proscription. Friends, family, and neighbors all turned on one another. The streets ran red with blood, not in the hyperbolic sense, but in the literal one. The stench of death was everywhere. Terror knew no boundaries. As the numbers of dead piled up, new names were added to the list. Old rivals used the opportunity to settle scores, denouncing enemies to Sulla and his thugs in order to prevail in petty feuds. Thousands were killed, their property seized and auctioned off. Sulla and his cronies grew unfathomably wealthy. Many victims had not been politically active but were victims of their wealth, condemned just to be killed for their property. No one was safe.

One victim of the proscription was already dead by the time Sulla reentered the city. Gaius Marius died just a couple of weeks into his seventh consulship, which denied Sulla the pleasure of murdering his old foe. In an act of spiteful and impotent rage, Sulla had Marius's tomb broken open and smashed to pieces, his ashes scattered to the wind. Even in death Marius couldn't escape Sulla's fury. Most wouldn't be so relatively lucky. As many as nine thousand Romans lost their lives at the hands of Sulla and his killing squads. Sulla even banned the male descendants of those proscribed from holding office, thus extinguishing the lives, legacies, and careers of his opponent. [14]

Eventually, a smug Sulla deemed his work complete. Populists had been slaughtered; their descendants could never hold office. The fields were sowed with salt so nothing could grow again. Satisfied, Sulla unexpectedly resigned his post as dictator and handed back the government to his Optimate allies in the Senate. He retired to a life of opulent debauchery, overindulging in all sorts of vices and dying a few months later bloated and diseased. Sulla died knowing that the world was safe for rich senators again, now and forever. Or was it?

One person who escaped the proscription was a young patrician nobleman. His name was added to the list because he was Marius's nephew. Fleeing to evade the death squads, he moved about in the dark and sought refuge with family and friends. Eventually, influential relatives convinced Sulla to remove his name from the proscription list. If the goal of Sulla's purge was to restore senatorial control, then this was a grave miscalculation. As it turns out, this young nobleman would eventually put the final nail in the coffin of the Senate as the ruling body of Rome, giving rise to the emperors and restoration of the monarchy in everything but name. Gaius Julius Caesar would succeed where previous populists had failed. Through his historically unparalleled combination of charisma, ambition, and brilliance, he would break nearly half a millennium of senatorial domination and give rise to the emperors. And with some of these people, the story gets really strange, violent, and twisted. Without Caesar, we wouldn't have had Caligula, Nero, Commodus, Caracalla, and so many others. So, thank you, Caesar?

The dictator Sulla lopped off thousands of Roman heads in the name of senatorial prestige, then retired to a life of drunken debauchery. *Wikimedia Commons.*

To be fair to the Senate, there were good times, too. Senators were in command when Rome fought and won some of its most legendary battles. Their bellicose expansionism gave rise to Rome's dominance, first locally, then regionally, then to peoples and places far and wide. Rome as we know it wouldn't be what we think of, and the foundations of empire were laid in each successive generation trying to outdo the one before it. The senators didn't just see themselves as better than the common folk; they saw themselves as better than everyone else in the world. From a foreign policy standpoint, this led to war and conflict, and, more often than not, victory. From a conquer-the-world standpoint, it has its advantages. Just as no ruler ever failed to do at least one useful thing, so, too, the Senate didn't fail to score its measure of victories. But at the end of the day, the conflict sowed into the daily life in Rome, and the constant tension between the capital city and everyone else, find their root causes directly at the toga-clad fee of the senators. As such, they are responsible for a lot of repression, exploitation, violence, and bloodshed. And if that isn't consideration enough to be included among the worst rulers of Rome, then nothing is.

Eventually, the republic would give way to the empire, where sole power was consolidated into one set of hands. At first, the emperors would at least pretend that the Senate was relevant, its counsel valued. But that didn't last long; emperors dropped the pretense pretty quickly. Many of the historians of this time were of the senatorial variety. They, understandably, longed for the good old days when they and their buddies held power and enjoyed all the respect and prestige it conveyed. So a lot of this history tends to play up the Senate's virtues and downplay its vices, such as, say, slaughtering three thousand people whose sole crime was wanting a fairer piece of the pie, then dumping their corpses in the closest river. But no matter how much they wanted to be nostalgic about the good old days, historians couldn't get around the stark truth: there were plenty of times when individual senators, and plenty more when a whole big group of them, perpetrated atrocities and savagery that shock sensibilities, modern and ancient alike.

Just as present now as it was in Rome's heyday, SPQR meant Senatus Populusque Romanus. Translated as The Senate and People of Rome, it hides one of the basic truths of Roman history—that the oligarchical Senate had very little concern for the everyday citizen. *Wikimedia Commons.*

(DIS)HONORABLE MENTION #1: THE INNOVATOR

It is surprisingly difficult to count the number of Roman emperors. When trying to make a tally, there's usually little doubt whether someone should be counted. It didn't matter that Caligula was nuts; he was clearly in charge, until all of a sudden, he was dead. But, sometimes, it's not so clear. As an example, let's say one guy seizes power in a bloody coup, declares himself emperor, elevates his teenage son to co-emperor, then gets offed by the next claimant to the throne in almost no time at all. Some people recognized him. Some didn't. Does he count? Does his son?

The list of people who actually were emperor and the list of people who claimed to be emperor do not always reconcile. It gets confusing quickly. It is hard to rank the emperors, both worst and best, when a definitive list of all the contenders is elusive. But no matter how you

count them, one person always sits at the top, nearly universally acknowledged as the best Roman emperor.

In the rankings of the best emperors and rulers, Augustus comes out
on top. Number 1. The first emperor gets the tip of the cap as the best. No
matter how many people fall below him on the list, no one is above. The
guy was so good, in fact, that all of his successors, legitimate and acknowledged or otherwise, took his name as part of their title. To become
emperor was to be hailed as Augustus. The name, incidentally, means
revered one. He was viewed as wise, moderate, and judicious.

Maybe these things were true once he matured into his rule and grew
comfortable with his grasp on power. But he did not just start out as
Augustus. His rise to power was complicated, twisty, and frequently
bloody. Rather than wise, moderate, and judicious, as a younger man he
would be better described as ruthless, grasping, and tyrannical.

Before Augustus was Augustus, he was Octavian, the maternal grand-
nephew of Julius Caesar. Octavian had been shoved into the spotlight
when Caesar was murdered. When the dictator's will was read aloud,
people were shocked to find that Octavian had been posthumously named
as Caesar's heir and successor. The young man was a nobody. A distant
relative from a far-off branch of the family. He was nineteen and had no
political following.

But he was smart. Cunning. Calculating. Ambitious. And he now had
Caesar's name. It gave him a good start. But he needed more. He needed
allies. In short order, he formed an alliance with two older, more accomplished men: Marc Antony and Marcus Lepidus. The three, known as the
Second Triumvirate, vowed revenge on Caesar's assassins, who had fled
to Greece to prepare for the war that was sure to follow. But before the
Triumvirs could mobilize armies, they needed cash. They got together
and settled on the most infamous, bloody, and vicious way to raise money: state-sponsored mass murder.

The first proscription happened back in 81 BCE, when Sulla deployed
it to liquidate his enemies and exact revenge on anyone who had dared
oppose his grasp of power. It was a dark period in Roman history. But
from an autocrat's point of view, a proscription was a powerful tool. Kill
or drive off all your enemies. Seize their property. Line your pockets with
cash. What's the downside? None, as long as you don't mind the streets
running red with blood, people fleeing in terror, and having friends,
neighbors, and family members turning on one another.

Joined up in their alliance, the Second Triumvirate met to decide who would live and who would die. Octavian pulled up a chair and the three made their list, deciding who would live and who would be liquidated. They showed no scruples or sentimentality. Antony proscribed a cousin; Lepidus, his own brother. The trio began their shared rule in a sea of blood. Their death squads began the slaughter. Octavian lined his pockets with cash as the corpses piled up in the street. It wasn't exactly the best way to begin a public career. The first time that many Romans dealt with Octavian was while they were fleeing for their lives in utter panic or begging for their lives as the cold steel of an executioner swung down on their necks.

The killing was extensive and horrifying. As Roman historian Max Cary said, "The first practical demonstration of the new dictatorship was a wholesale political massacre. Three hundred senators and two thousand equites (knights) were placed on a list of suspects and delivered to the head hunters . . . the slaughter was on a scale recalling that of Sulla's proscriptions."[15]

Among those who would meet their end in the Triumvir's proscription was the great orator and statesman Cicero. His crime, aside from being rich and thus having assets worth coveting, was that he had spoken out loudly against Marc Antony. When the death squads caught up with Cicero in the countryside, the wise orator stoically confronted his impending death. His courage gave his murders pause, but orders were orders, and they carried out their mission. They cut off his head and hands and sent them back to Rome. The Triumvirs had them nailed up for public display, a grisly trophy of the mounting tyranny of this unholy alliance.

When the first wave of proscription fell a bit short of their revenue projections, the Triumvirs coolly chose a next wave of victims. Taking their chances with divine wrath, they had the Temple of the Vestal Virgins ransacked to appropriate the savings of Romans who had entrusted their savings to the goddess.[16] Afraid that to speak up would bring a death sentence, no one protested. That is, until Octavian and his buddies tried to tax and seize the assets of women, which no one had previously dared to do. One prominent woman, Hortensia, daughter of one of the most famous orators in Roman history, marched to a speaker's platform and denounced the actions of the Triumvirate. They backed down, somewhat, and bypassed their plans to tax so many women.[17] But the corpses just kept piling up.

Once their bloodlust was slaked and their coffers stuffed with appropriated coin, the Triumvirs embarked on war with Caesar's assassins. The most famous, Marcus Brutus, was killed and decapitated. Venting his rage on the dead man, Octavian had Brutus's head packed up, shipped to Rome, and thrown at the foot of a statue of Caesar.[18]

Once that was taken care of, the Triumvirs met again, this time to divvy up the empire. Octavian took Italy. He had a serious problem to confront. He had tens of thousands of troops to demobilize. They had been promised land at the end of their enlistments, but there wasn't enough to go around. Rather than risk angering the armies that had just proved their field effectiveness, Octavian gave his troops land, even whole towns, that already belonged to others. Using their swords as incentive, and with Octavian's blessing, the troops drove off rightful landowners so they could settle down to lives of domestic tranquility. Octavian might have been shrewd, but between murdering some people and stealing the land of others, he was off to a rough start. Said historian Tom Holland, "The same spectres of larceny and violence that had brought terror to the nobility during the proscriptions were now general across Italy."[19]

Octavian didn't just covet land and cash. He also fell in love and, in the process, proved that scruples would not stand in the way of getting what he wanted. By late 39 BCE, Octavian had been married to his wife, Scribonia, for about a year. The object of his affection, Livia, was married, too, to a Roman noble named Tiberius Claudius Nero. Scribonia was pregnant, and so was Livia. Once he fell head over heels for the beautiful Livia, he waited impatiently for Scribonia to give birth to their daughter, Julia. He divorced his wife the same day. He then waited for Livia to give birth, which she did on January 14. He compelled a divorce between Livia and her husband and three days later, on January 17, he married her. In one of the greatest acts of emasculation in recorded history, Livia's now ex-husband, gave away the bride at the wedding.[20]

At this point, it would be fair to ask how this guy could end up shooting to the top of the leaderboard as the best Roman emperor ever. As it turns out, he used one of the simplest techniques. He rebranded himself.

Even into his seventies, the first Roman emperor, Augustus, portrayed himself as young and at the height of his martial vigor. He lived a long life full of brilliant propaganda, carefully distancing himself from his own bad actions. *Wikimedia Commons.*

It was only a matter of time before Lepidus, easily the weakest of the three Triumvirs, was shoved aside. Octavian and Antony fell into a civil war. Antony allied himself with Cleopatra. Octavian won, dispatching his rival and seizing the unfathomable wealth of his lover. Octavian had sole control of the Roman Empire and nearly limitless wealth to finance his administration. He spent lavishly on the city and its people. Rather than a cold, calculating tyrant, he was now a generous benefactor. In a master-stroke of political calculation, he declared all the actions of the Second Triumvirate illegal, almost as though he hadn't been part of it. When he shifted to the name Augustus, the transformation was complete. He was a different guy. All that bad stuff? Some other guy did that.

It was an amazing feat of reputational transformation. Augustus would go on to rule for decades, setting the gold standard by which all emperors would be judged. All would fall short. But when showering him with praise and affection, it's important to remember, Augustus had more than his fair share of cruelty on his résumé and blood on his hands.

Would a tyrant by any other name still be as cruel? History, it seems, says no. In the Roman world, even the very best had elements of the very worst. The line between benevolent and tyrant wasn't always so clear.

3

THE LITTLE BOOTS

Tiberius was utterly detested by the people. At the end of his time, the depraved old man ruled from the island of Capri, some 250 kilometers away. During those years, tales of unspeakable acts and demented sin drifted from his pleasure palaces, and Rome was abuzz with strange and terrible rumors.

Far worse, an air of fear and suspicion gripped Rome during the time of Tiberius. Anyone who spoke out against the emperor was swept up by authorities and swiftly tried for treason. Countless people were exiled, had their property seized, or were simply executed. In the purges and counter-purges, people lost fortunes, or lives. Meanwhile, tucked away on Capri, Tiberius just kept living and living.[1]

In 37 CE, as the old tyrant approached eighty, it seemed he might live forever. But, as death is undefeated, his time came, too, and Tiberius finally slinked off into the afterlife. Elated, the citizens of Rome poured into the streets, chanting "To the Tiber with Tiberius" and calling for the tyrant's corpse to be hurled into the river.[2]

When one emperor dies, another must take his place. Just twenty-four years of age, the new emperor, Gaius, had been in the public eye his whole life. He was the son of one of Rome's true celebrity couples: Germanicus, handsome, fearless, conquering general, multicultural polymath; and Agrippina, beautiful, granddaughter of none other than the divine Augustus himself. Germanicus, Agrippina, and their children were beloved, held in devotional reverence. Unlike most generals, who sent their families away from the front in times of war, this family stayed together, winning hearts and minds with their courage. To boost the morale of the troops, the couple dressed up their youngest boy in full military attire. The adorable little soldier was held by the legions to be a good luck charm. In honor of his soldier's footwear, they gave him a nickname that translated as Little Boots.[3]

It had not been an easy path to power for Gaius. He endured much in his young life. His father died in mysterious circumstances at only thirty-four. Foul play was assumed, as was the involvement of Tiberius, who was said to be jealous of his popular nephew. His mother and two older brothers had been caught up in Tiberius's purges and had been slowly starved to death in exile.

Gaius himself had been summoned to live by Tiberius's side on Capri and had to endure the assassination of his family in stoic silence, one by one, lest he, too, be eliminated. While on Capri, Little Boots was forced to witness the sick depredations of Tiberius, a man with unlimited power and no checks on his sadistic whims. Tortures, rapes, executions. All manner of ungodly acts were said to have happened in that awful place. That he was allowed to live at all was a testament to Tiberius's low opinion of the boy's prospects. In fact, one of his seers is said to have told him, "Gaius has no more chance of becoming emperor than of riding a horse dry-shod over the Gulf of Baiae."[4] In this way Little Boots grew to manhood, a hostage on the vile man's island.

Yet Gaius did not suffer in vain. He outlasted his tormentor. And in the end, his presence at Tiberius's deathbed strengthened his claim to the emperor's throne, a height to which the young man ascended the very same year.[5]

With Tiberius finally dead and Little Boots ascendant, a true wave of joy swept over the city. The future appeared bright.[6] The Roman people rejoiced and thanked the gods for their remarkable reversal of fortune. Gaius was so young. He hailed from impeccable bloodlines. A long era of peace, stability, and prosperity seemed to be on the horizon for Rome and its people.

The first months of Gaius's reign were marked by a whirlwind of accomplishment. To great acclaim from the people, the newly minted emperor recalled those in exile, dismissed charges against countless people, freed prisoners, and publicly burned incriminating documents. Gaius declared an end to the era of suspicion, fear, and recrimination. He vowed never to listen to informants and put an end to the treason trials. Gone were the days of paranoid suspicion, where neighbor would denounce neighbor and families turned against one another.

But he went further. Respectful of the law, and intellectual debate, Gaius restored the courts and invested in them the authority to adjudicate. No more of "the emperor is the final say on everything." Gaius also dispensed with banning books and restored works that had previously been blacklisted, even ones critical of emperors. He called for an era of debate and discourse, where ideas could flourish and create a better society as a result.[7]

Despite the depredations of his childhood, he even remained dutiful to the memory of Tiberius by adopting his grandson, Gemellus, as his own son, making the young man his presumed heir.[8]

He also took care of the people. He worked to reenfranchise disaffected citizens, restoring the rights and privileges of the commoner. He reduced taxes, put on games and shows, and even gave cash to the people to alleviate their financial struggles.

And then, just six months into his illustrious reign, he fell ill and teetered on the brink of death. Wails of lament went up across the city as Gaius lay stricken, unconscious, fighting for his life against a mysterious ailment. For the Roman people, this was almost too much to bear. Gaius had been a godsend, an answer to their prayers. So much waiting, suffering, terror endured under Tiberius, and now, this wonderful son of Germanicus finally in charge, was deathly ill just a few months into the brilliant dawn of his reign.[9] As the citizens lamented their fortune, one uttered an oath that he would gladly give his life to save Gaius's.

Who was this Emperor Gaius? Why has history forgotten such a young, compassionate, strong leader? It hasn't. History simply doesn't remember Gaius by that name. It remembers him by the nickname his father's soldiers gave him as a boy: Little Boots. Or to be more precise, the Latin translation: Caligula.

Slowly, after two weeks of life-and-death struggle, Caligula recovered from his illness. The people rejoiced. But as he rose from his sickbed, it became apparent that he had fundamentally changed. The young, progressive, benevolent Gaius had slipped into unconsciousness. What awoke was not the same man. The historian Suetonius says he could only be described as a "monster."[10] In place of Gaius was a lunatic whose very name evokes images of deranged tyranny. The young man who fell ill and the one who arose from the sickbed were very different people. Two names, Gaius and Caligula, almost two completely different people.

Hearing that a nobleman, in a fit of devoted piety, had offered his life in exchange for his own, Caligula compelled the unfortunate who offered the prayer to commit suicide. Not content with commoners dying by their own hand in his name, out of thin air he pulled trumped-up charges against his father-in-law, Marcus Silanus, and compelled him to slit his own throat.[11] Silanus was a former consul, the highest magistracy in Rome. He'd enjoyed a long and distinguished career and was among Rome's most well-respected citizens. His track record and reputation not only failed to save him, but they were likely the true cause of his downfall. Caligula was an intensely jealous man. Those he envied did not live long. Mrs. Caligula's thoughts on her dad's suicide are lost to history. It's unclear whether she was still alive at this point as she died in childbirth delivering Caligula's first child, which also died. Considering the fate that awaited many of his closest "friends" and family, his widow might have gotten off easy. Regardless, her father's death was a bloody beginning to Caligula's post-illness reign. Far more was to come. In the short and bloody rule of Caligula, no one was safe.

Well, one person. The only one safe from Caligula's megalomania was his sister Julia Drusilla. They were close—rampant rumors of incest close. Although that seems unlikely, it was apparent that she had served as a check on her brother's wilder impulses. As so often happened in the ancient world, an illness befell the imperial princess, and she died at the tender age of twenty-one.

Needless to say, Caligula did not take Drusilla's death well. As she lay dying, a distraught Caligula was by her side constantly. When she succumbed to her illness, he was devastated by grief.[12] With her last breath, the last moorings of his decency were severed, and an impossibly dark era of violent sex and hideous murder was ushered in. In the face of his sister's death, Caligula wanted the Romans to suffer as he suffered. He decreed that anyone who laughed during the prescribed period of grief would be executed. Other capital offenses in this period included bathing or having dinner with one's parents.[13]

Wife and beloved sister were now dead. Before long, he banished his two remaining sisters (one of whom will enter our story much more fully in a later chapter when we meet her and her bratty kid, Nero). Next, Caligula focused on Gemellus, his adopted son and the grandson of Tiberius. Someone with such pedigree could surely make a legitimate claim to the throne. Gemellus knew that he would have a target on his back and sought to take precautions, including taking medicines to counteract common poisons of the day. Smelling the prophylactic on the young man's breath, Caligula uttered, "Can there really be an antidote against Caesar?"[14] Needless to say, in short order the young man was duly dispatched, adding to the rapidly growing body count.

At this point, Caligula began to develop a sense of his own divinity. Rather than wait for posthumous deification like his predecessors, such as Julius Caesar and Augustus, Caligula declared himself a god and demanded that he be worshipped as such. Statues of the god-emperor were erected around the city, worshipped and sacrificed to. He also wanted a

A widespread outpouring of joy and hope met Caligula's ascension to emperor. After a promising start, things descended into legendary levels of chaos and bloodshed. *Wikimedia Commons, by Louis le Grand, CC BY-SA 3.0.*

royal residence more befitting a god. He had the imperial palace extended from the Palatine Hill all the way down to the Forum. He even incorporated the ancient temple of Castor and Pollux as the vestibule to his new palace. He joked that these gods were now simply his doorkeepers.[15]

Of course, a god needed a royal consort, and Caligula didn't wait long to remarry. The fact that he stole his bride from another man only added to the fun. He had been invited to the wedding of two nobles. As the happy couple lounged on couches, the groom took his bride's hand in his. Seeing this, Caligula screamed, "Hands off my bride!" and ordered the poor girl taken away for his pleasure. After a couple days of one can only imagine what, he grew bored and sent her away, but not before ordering her to have no contact with her former fiancé. A couple years later, he heard rumors that she had returned to him anyway, and an enraged Caligula exiled her.[16]

He didn't even have to see the bride to break up a marriage. Once, when told a newlywed descended from a renowned beauty, he decreed her marriage annulled and took her as his own bride, sight unseen. It probably didn't hurt that he was constantly teetering on insolvency and her family was loaded. Break up a noble marriage, claim a beauty as his own, *and* replenish depleted coffers all at once? Triple win! This time, it took him six months before his boredom crept in, and he unceremoniously divorced her but forbade her ever to sleep with or have any association with another man.[17] The poor girl would go on to lead a tragic life, being caught up in a dynastic succession struggle a decade later and being forced to commit suicide by none other than Caligula's sister, Agrippina the Younger. Nice family you have there, folks.

Eventually, he did settle down somewhat and surprised everyone by taking for his fourth and final wife an older woman, mother to three kids.[18] Caesonia was not renowned for her beauty. In fact, oddly, the histories all seem to go out of their way to remind people that she was somewhat plain, as though, given his unlimited power to command any beauty to do as he wished, his choice of a woman of negligible beauty was further evidence of his craziness. Maybe. Or maybe she encouraged the worst elements of his behavior. She certainly didn't try to moderate his excesses. It seems that Caligula liked having her around to challenge him to do even worse, not to restrain himself.

Once Caesonia entered the picture, the trend line to ever more creepy and vile behavior continued unabashed. They even produced a child, a daughter, who seemed to inherit daddy's sadism. Once, when the daughter tried to scratch a playmate's eyes in the nursery, Caligula beamed with pride and pointed out that that was the type of behavior he wanted from his offspring.

Not satisfied to content himself with such pleasant domestic tranquility, Caligula set about to systematically undermine the Senate and all of its old patrician pretensions. As he rode in a chariot, he made senators run beside him, for mile after mile. On occasion, he would invite notable families to dinner, then pick out one of the wives, take her away from the table, rape her, then bring her back, criticizing her sexual performance or commenting on things he liked or didn't like about her body. He is even reported to have made a brothel in the imperial palace, forcing noble women into service as whores, and forcing men to come to the palace and use this new "service." This had the dual purpose of degraded the nobility and raising money to replenish his empty coffers. Because the one thing Caligula liked above all others was spending money. He was obscenely profligate. As soon as he got his hands on a dime, he spent it. He took particular delight in killing two birds with one stone, such as spending money *and* humiliating the Senate.

One way he did so was by lavishing favor on his favorite horse, Incitatus, even as the rapes, tortures, and executions of Rome's elite continued unabated. Caligula ordered troops to walk before Incitatus in order to enforce quiet so that the horse would not be disturbed. Caligula ordered a marble stable constructed, and had Incitatus's stall made of ivory.[19] He was given purple blankets—a color reserved exclusively for use by the imperial family—and a collar laden with priceless gems. His food contained gold flakes. He drank the best wine from golden cups.[20] Caligula even appointed Incitatus to a priesthood.[21] Later, he threatened to make the horse consul.[22] We can only imagine how much resentment he garnered. What Incitatus thought of all this is not recorded.

A couple of years into his reign, horses entered into Caligula's erratic behavior in another way. With a lingering memory and the ability like no other to hold a grudge, Caligula had an old score to settle. Now safely emperor, Caligula sought to mock the seer who said he was more likely to ride a horse across the sea than to succeed Tiberius. He commandeered hundreds of boats and thousands of laborers. He had the boats lashed together, side by side, the entire length of the Bay of Baiae, and used them as a foundation for his bridge. He then had a platform of wood and dirt constructed across the boats. Once complete, and to prove the point, he rode his chariot back and forth across the bay.[23] The seer was wrong. Caligula was in charge, and no one could do anything about it.

He proved this time and again. He left such a bad impression with the ancient historians that they render him capable of anything. Some things of which he is accused have some semblance of logic. Others show a perverse sadism, so it's easy to draw the impression that he liked to cause suffering just for the fun of it. He closed the public granaries to cause starvation. He made parents watch their children's execution. He had a client king executed because the king's clothes were nicer than his own. One time, when a man was about to be executed on Caligula's orders, the man loudly and desperately proclaimed his innocence. Caligula halted the proceedings. But rather than hear the man out, he commanded that his tongue be cut out, then ordered the execution to commence. Another time, while Caligula was out in the provinces, he was gambling with his cronies. When he ran out of cash, he left the table and demanded the census rolls of the wealthy local citizens. He leveled charges against the richest, then had them rounded up, convicted, and either executed or compelled to commit suicide. He then appropriated their property and calmly returned to the table, flush with blood money.[24]

Remember those incriminating documents that Caligula had made a big show of burning at the start of his reign? Just kidding. They were only copies. The originals were produced, he brought a whole new wave of charges, and a whole new wave of people were killed.[25] In fact, you could find yourself dead in Caligula's Rome for a lot of reasons. Didn't fight hard enough in a gladiatorial show? Dead. Failed to recognize the genius of the emperor in a sufficiently awed manner? Dead. Looked at the emperor's bald head? Dead. Sometimes Caligula had people killed one at a time, sometimes by the score. When you read the histories of this period, it's only natural to wonder how any people were left by the time someone finally put a knife into the sociopath.

But by 40 CE, Caligula had a glaring gap on his résumé that even he had to recognize. To be truly great, a Roman ruler needed to claim outstanding martial accomplishment. Orders were given, and the wheels of the Roman war machine came to life. The Roman Empire was built by its legions and their discipline, efficiency, and cold-blooded focus. The soldiery was drilled and drilled, over and over, until they were the most lethal fighting force the ancient world had ever known. It was said of the

Roman legions that their training was bloodless battle, and their battles were bloody training. These guys were *serious*, and very good. Organizing and moving the Roman army took a lot of work and planning. After nearly a year of planning, Caligula was ready to lead the mighty Roman army, some two hundred thousand strong, into the field.[26]

First in the crosshairs was Rome's archenemy, the Germans. Heading to the frontier, he encamped on the Rhine border. He then sent some friendly Germans, who had been traveling in the army's company, across the river. He sent troops after them shortly, "captured" them, had them thrown into chains, and claimed them as prisoners of war and trophies of conquest. He then set his sights on Britannia, the mysterious island at the edge of the known world, and pivoted his army from Germany to the coast of Gaul. But rather than board ships and cross the channel, Caligula ordered his troops to line up on the beach and collect seashells. These he claimed as trophies in his victory over the sea. Satisfied that he had cloaked himself in glory, Caligula turned his army around and marched for home.

He made plans to celebrate a Triumph, the traditional Roman military parade. Not confident that he had enough German prisoners, he ordered the tallest Gallic allies to present themselves as German. In order to do so, they had to grow their hair long, dye it red, dress in German clothes, and learn to speak German.[27] Caligula also ordered his warships to return to Rome to be part of the festivities. But rather than have them sail home, he had them hauled overland. What a sight that must have been. One can only imagine the thoughts of a proud legionnaire, with his kit full of seashells, pulling on ropes to drag a warship across the middle of what's now France, as he watched his Gallic allies dyeing their hair and trying to learn German.

No matter that these escapades were farcical. Caligula declared a great victory and expected everyone to acknowledge it with awed reverence. Upon entering Rome, Caligula felt that he was at the height of his power. Although the plans for his victory parade fizzled, the bloodletting recommenced with a frenzy. What's incredible is not that an assassination plot was hatched, but that it took this long. Enough was enough. Though he clearly didn't know it, once back in Rome the young psychopath had just a few months to live.

In the end, the capricious nature of Caligula's life-and-death judgments were a big part of what did him in. Many around him knew that if they hadn't been condemned yet, it was likely only a matter of time. Better to get Caligula before Caligula got them. A group of conspirators hatched a plan, and their ringleader was an officer of the Praetorian Guard, the elite imperial troops tasked with guarding the emperor. Caligula had taken the extra step of hiring and lavishing rich donatives on a separate set of German bodyguards. They were ferocious warriors and wholly devoted not so much to Caligula as to his pocketbook. It took the conspirators a degree of patience and luck to separate Caligula from these guards.

The fateful day came as Caligula was attending some games and theatrical performances. When he rose to head for the palace to bathe and eat, he passed through a doorway and into a tunnel passageway. Before his German guards could follow, the conspirators barred the door as Caligula walked, oblivious, down the passageway. In short order, the conspirators fell on Caligula and hacked him to death. [28] As panicked observers fled in terror, Caligula lay lifeless on the floor as his blood seeped out all around him. It happened in just seconds. When you consider the horrors that he brought to so many, it's easy to wonder whether he got off easy.

The day's actions were far from over. The conspirators would go on to slit the throat of Caligula's wife, Caesonia, and to kill his infant daughter by bashing her brains out against the wall. [29] They would then go to the imperial palace, find Caligula's uncle hiding behind a curtain, bring him to their camp for safekeeping, and declare him emperor. More on these events in a later chapter. Meanwhile, Caligula's German bodyguards, enraged over the loss of their patron, went on a murderous killing spree. In a last orgy of death to mark the end of Caligula's reign, the German bodyguards cut down and decapitated anyone they thought might even be connected slightly to the loss of their patron. They carried the heads of their victims and threw them into an ever-growing pile in the middle of the theater where Caligula had been taking in the performances. Even in death Caligula wrought death and terror.

Thus, the short life of one of history's great villains ended. But his reputation has endured for two millennia. So, what is the true legacy of Rome's third emperor?

On one hand, you have unhinged Caligula. Violent, capricious, sociopathic. On the other, you have a coldly rational, calculating, and evil young man. In this version, his atrocities fit a pattern. Since the days of Augustus and the beginning of the age of emperors, those who held supreme power in their hands made a great pretense of deference to traditional institutions. The emperors wielded supreme power, and the Senate and the upper classes pretended that they were still relevant and thus maintained their dignity.

Caligula had no time for this charade, and his actions show a pattern of deliberately laying bare the farce. If a senator would offer his life for that of the emperor, why not accept and thus prove the hollow nature of the initial offer? If the senators suck up to the emperor at every turn, why not turn the lot of them into literal whores in a brothel? If the Senate won't really think or act without the emperor's approval, then why not elevate a horse to their level and invest it with high office? If the senators backstabbed an emperor, then tripped over themselves to deify him post-humously, why not skip to the end and declare yourself a god right away? When viewed through the lens of an intelligent and cynical young man, exposing the ritualistic charade at the top of Roman society, a lot of actions seem, if not acceptable, then at least to have a certain chilling logic.

If that is the case, though, then how do you explain the great start to his reign before he fell ill? All his actions at the start of his reign were somewhat obvious, populist steps taken to distance himself from Tiber-ius. Nothing was terribly enlightened. He just did the opposite. Tiberius: treason trials, hoarding cash, fear and suspicion. Gaius: freedom, liberal-ity, build and spend like there's no tomorrow.

It's also quite possible that he was suffering from some form of mental illness that his sickness accentuated. Historians debate his condition and offer clinical diagnoses from the vast distance of time. This seems a pointless exercise because, obviously, Caligula's true nature is unknow-able.

Regardless of the reality of Caligula, whether he was cynical and rational, or truly deranged, some things are true. For one, the net effect was the same. No matter what his motives or mental state, his brief reign was full of horror, death, and dishonor for scores of people. For another, he started "good," then devolved into "evil." At some point, and for whatever reason, he chose to become the cruel monster that led to so many deaths, and eventually his own. One wonders how things would have turned out if he had acted the same way after his illness as before it. What if he'd lived up to his promises to ban treason trials, to enfranchise people, to allow the courts to rule with fairness? What if he'd allowed dissent and debate to enter the public discourse? Would a new era of brilliance in rhetoric and literature have been ushered forth?

Even in the brief, happy time at the beginning of his reign, some disturbing trends point to what was to come. Hiding among his supposed benevolence was a very disturbing profligacy. He spent and spent and spent. Whereas Tiberius had been stingy and left the treasury bursting at the seams, Caligula brought the empire to bankruptcy within a few months. He spent on horses, on actors, on gladiators, on shows and games. He poured countless cash into all these things, and although they were popular with the people, the real reason seems to be that these things gave *him* great pleasure. That the people enjoyed them, too, was an added bonus. Early in his reign, he seemed to take pleasure in being loved. But soon he discovered he enjoyed even more being feared. It would seem that even before he fell ill, a disturbing trend of indulgence and narcissism was emerging in Caligula. Besides, he had kept those incriminating documents from the very beginning, offering evidence that his "benevolence" was just a show after all.

Whether his illness changed him, or the full realization of his power and the accompanying realization that there were no checks whatsoever on his behavior, Caligula's sadism was reaching new horrible depths even as he was murdered. In other words, it's likely that things only would have gotten worse.

Lost in the debates about whether Caligula was crazy is a simple fact: he held absolute power, and he abused it absolutely. Rather than do good for the tens of millions of people under his rule, he did the opposite. Coldly calculating or tormented by madness, Caligula destroyed lives, bankrupted the empire, eroded the social structure of Roman society, and generally earned his historical reputation. In all the debate and analysis about the true nature of his reign, one thing is certain: in the pantheon of all-time murderers, tyrants, and lunatics, Caligula ranks high in all three categories. He might, in fact, have been the very worst ruler Rome ever had.

4

THE LADY KILLER

Mother and son were to be reconciled. They were the two most powerful people in the Roman world. It's easy to understand why they'd become estranged. There was a lot of pressure to rule the known world. It put stress on their relationship. Each had a different agenda, and increasingly, they had been working against one another, not aligned to a common purpose. When the young man had become emperor at the tender age of sixteen, he had needed his mom to help guide the way. He'd had no practical experience governing, and she had been through hell and back in her still-young life. She had helped carve the path to power for her son and was ruthless and single-minded in doing whatever it took to get there. She had bested rivals, survived banishment and exile on a remote island, and even committed incest, all to get the two of them to the imperial palace. She had honed her survivalist mind-set to a razor's edge. Being Caligula's little sister specifically, and a member of the imperial family in general, was always a dicey proposition.

He, for his part, had needed her help. She was all he knew. He had been a tool of dynastic succession, and being a young male in the Julio-Claudian world came with a very short life expectancy. When he came to power, he was overwhelmed with the scope of responsibility. He was the central figure in the largest, most powerful empire of the ancient world, and only sixteen years old. But as he settled into his rule and developed a growing sense of his unlimited power, he'd become more interested in doing what he wanted, regardless of what his overbearing mom told him he should do. He was less and less malleable. As he pursued his own interests, she tried harder and harder to bring him to heel. He pushed back as any good strong-willed teenager would. The friction grew and, eventually, they had a falling out.

He, Nero, had thrown her out of the imperial palace. He had stripped her of her titles, honors, and bodyguards. She plotted and schemed, trying to find a way back to control of her son and, thus, the empire. As he grew in confidence, he felt strong enough to stand up for himself and sent word that he wanted to reconcile. They were to meet south of Rome, at Baiae, to celebrate a religious festival together. His boat accidentally crashed into hers, and Nero made a great show of offering her a replacement. She accepted gladly, rejoicing in her reversal of fortunes and indulging in visions of what she would do back at the capital.

But this was all farce. The gifted boat was purpose-built to be a death trap. Nero had decided to rid himself once and for all of his nagging, overbearing mother. The boat was part of an elaborate ploy. Although he was willing to order his mother killed, he didn't want to witness the killing personally. The boat was designed to self-destruct, sinking in deep water to drown everyone aboard.[1] At the appointed time, while out in the bay, the signal was given, and a confederate triggered the mechanism. It only half worked, and Agrippina managed to make it overboard and into the water before being dragged down to the depths. Languishing in the water, she was picked up by friendly and unwitting locals, who delivered her safely ashore. She made her way back to her villa.

Down the road, Nero was pacing in his own villa, anxious to be told that the deed was done. When word reached him that Agrippina was alive, he panicked. He'd wanted her death to be seen as an accident; he certainly preferred Agrippina not know that her son was behind her planned demise. A boat sinking at night is a tragedy, not matricide. But now she was alive and understood what had happened. Nero made up his mind: he ordered a detachment of troops to her villa with orders to kill. He could always claim that she had been plotting to kill him and that he was only defending himself.

As the soldiers burst in with swords drawn, a furious Agrippina pointed to her midsection and yelled, "Smite my womb." If she was going to die, she at least symbolically could strike at the part of her that had created and nurtured the monster who now commanded her death.[2] They obliged, and Agrippina the Younger was cut down where she stood. When shown the corpse of his mother, Nero could only remark at how beautiful she'd been. He claimed that he'd foiled an assassination plot, and congratulations poured in. But the people weren't fooled. They knew what really happened. So did he. And it haunted him. He was not to be rid of Agrippina just yet; her ghost, and the knowledge of what he did, would continue to torment him for years to come. Even in death, Agrippina hovered over her son.

The man whom we know as Nero wasn't born with that name. Only through adoption and elevation did he accumulate the long list of names under which he would rule. As emperor, he was Nero Claudius Caesar Augustus Germanicus. As a baby, he was Lucius Domitius Ahenobarbus.[3] The Ahenobarbi were an ancient family, and little Lucius hailed from a long line of nasty, violent, and devious men. He might have changed his name, but he couldn't change his nature. Time would show that the apple didn't fall far from the family tree.

Nero's mother herself was a member of the royal family. Because his dad had died when he was just three, Agrippina was a dominating presence in her son's life. She craved power and, through her son, schemed for ways to gain control. She managed to survive banishment to a remote island at the hands of her brother, Caligula. When her first husband died, Caligula appropriated Nero's inheritance. After Caligula's death, his successor, Claudius, recalled Agrippina from exile and restored little Lucius's inheritance. Claudius then arranged for Agrippina to marry a wealthy and prominent member of the upper crust. After convincing the poor guy to name her as his heir, Agrippina poisoned him and claimed the inheritance, at a stroke making her both fabulously wealthy and single.

Claudius, for his part, was anxious to restore the prestige of the imperial family, and he had much damage control to do following the lunacy of his nephew Caligula. He might have carried this a little too far. After the downfall and execution of his third wife, Messalina, Claudius was in the market for a new one. His advisers each proposed a different candidate to become empress. Agrippina had been having an affair with one of Claudius's trusted inner circle, Pallas, and he prevailed. Claudius married Agrippina. Now consider that she was his niece, the daughter of his brother, Germanicus. Even to the Romans, whose ideas on family occasionally differ from our modern sensibilities, this was full-on incest. But he was the emperor, and he got his way. In short order, he adopted her son, Lucius, and the road to ruling the empire was now clear. Nero's public life could begin.[4]

Members of the imperial family were carefully prepared for their public lives. It was understood that a positive relationship with the masses was useful for building a base of support. Populist support helped cement the legitimacy of the imperial family. Even as a young man growing up in his adopted father's court, Nero was in the public spotlight. Before turning sixteen, he had considerable experience being in the public eye. He sponsored games, gave cash to troops and citizens alike, made public speeches, tried legal cases, and even marched in military formation with the Praetorian Guard. The imperial family found ways to give Nero exposure to the public, and he played his part well. Still just a young teenager, he was the adopted son and heir of the emperor. He was known to all the stakeholders who mattered. He was familiar to the people, to the troops, and to the Senate. By all accounts, he performed these acts well and was well liked. In terms of brand building, Nero was off to a good start.[5]

Or was he? Nero's start in public life lacked the practical element of governing. He was certainly too young for political office, but this was a young man destined to rule the world's mightiest empire, and his principal lesson about his role in public life seems to be that it was a performance. Claudius was getting up there in years, already at the life expectancy for the time. This kid would be in charge sooner or later. He had the public performance part down, but was he prepared to shoulder the burden of rule?

Claudius seems to have second-guessed his course of action. Since his marriage to his niece Agrippina (ew), he had shunned his own son, Britannicus, at the expense of her son, Nero. Now, her charm and manipulation were starting to wear off. In his early sixties, Claudius began to think that maybe he needed to elevate Britannicus as well.[6] After all, he intended them to be coheirs. Legally, they were both his sons. Why should he favor his adopted son over his biological son?

Agrippina saw that her son had a head start on a public life and didn't want to lose that advantage. She duly dispatched poor Claudius by sprinkling some poison over a plate of poisoned mushrooms, his favorite food. He had been in poor health for much of his life, and people shrugged off his sickness to natural causes. As he lay stricken, his dying wish was for harmony between Nero and Britannicus, asking senators to be wise advisers to the young men. Agrippina managed to evade suspicion for her actions, and upon Nero's accession, the two covered up their crime by declaring Claudius a god, erecting a massive temple to him, and creating a new priesthood to organize all the proper worship and sacrifices. Of course, it is also possible that he did die of natural causes—he was sixty-three—and that all of the rumors about poisoned mushrooms came out later to besmirch Agrippina and Nero once they had fallen.[7] But given their actions in the coming years, it is easy for them to seem capable of such deviousness. With Claudius, they were united in having a shared motive for his elimination. As time would tell, eventually their interests would come into conflict, and bad, bad things would happen.

But for now, Nero ascended the throne with great pomp. At just sixteen, he was the youngest emperor to rule and would prove to be one of the youngest in the empire's long history. So young, with so much power, and so little practical experience. This could be a recipe for disaster. The only check on catastrophe would be if he were surrounded by smart, capable people whose motives were less about exploiting positions of influence and more about doing right by the empire. At first, that's what he had. His Praetorian prefect, Burrus; his tutor, Seneca; and even his nagging mother, Agrippina, brought immense experience and pragmatism to the imperial palace.[8]

Agrippina herself used every advantage to consolidate power. When Claudius had been debating who to take for his wife, various counselors had backed different candidates. Agrippina had seen to it that those in favor of other brides were eliminated, as were the candidates themselves. Early in her son's reign, she saw to it that coins were issued that included her likeness, and she even pushed her way into the Senate during their meetings, a wholly unprecedented action for any woman. She yielded somewhat to convention and pretended to be modest by sitting behind a curtain. But no doubt anything said in the Senate was said to the listening ear of the empress. A city had even been named in her honor. The capital of the German provinces was named Colonia Agrippinensis, which survives to this day in the place-name Cologne.[9] However, in terms of policy, she had good instincts and was a formidable presence as her son got his feet underneath him. Under Agrippina, paired with other key advisers, the empire could have done worse.[10]

As such, Nero's reign seemed to be off to a moderate, even-keeled start. He took great care to remember the names and faces of everyone he could and was careful always to greet great people as friends and by their names. He lowered taxes where he could and showered gifts of cash, food, jewels, and more on the people. He emphasized arts and literature,

Nero's ascension was engineered by his overbearing mother, Agrippina. As he settled into his role, he tired of her nagging and plotted her death. *Wikimedia Commons, by Carlos Delgado, CC BY-SA 3.0.*

threw games and theatrical performances, and generally made himself well-liked by the masses.

Wait.

Does this sound familiar?

It should. It was pretty similar to Caligula's playbook: A young, charismatic prince, ascending to the throne following an elderly, secluded emperor. But Nero was not Caligula. Not yet, anyway. Early in his rule, when having to sign warrants of execution, he would express regret. Rather than revel in the bloodshed, he lamented that he had learned to read and write and thus had to carry out such unsavory functions of rule. So far, he was off to a fairly good beginning, as senior advisers around him kept him more or less on track.

He was said to hide his growing erratic behavior from his moralizing seniors. Sneaking out of the imperial palace late at night, he and his best friend, Otho, went slumming. They visited brothels, got into barroom brawls, groped women, and attacked men, stabbing some and beating others. Through his late-night escapades, Nero was beginning to get in touch with his baser tastes and appetites.[11]

As strange as this was, it must be said that Nero wasn't devoid of talent. On the contrary, he was applauded for his oratory; his funeral oration for Claudius was well-received, especially for a young man. He could deliver speeches in both Latin and Greek. He wrote poetry of merit and had one of the more well-developed aesthetic senses of those who would sit upon the imperial throne.

But more than anything he loved to perform. Nero took every opportunity to take the stage. The guy just loved to sing, act, play the lyre, and generally perform. He seemed to be genuinely nervous about what people thought of his performances but let himself believe that their constant roaring applause was genuine. Of course, the crowds tripped over themselves to lavish praise on Nero. He was the emperor. His displeasure could mean death. The crowds weren't so much sycophantic as interested in not dying. The people were smart, and they'd gotten used to how the Julio-Claudians tended to treat people who spoke against them.

That said, he wasn't completely hopeless. He seems to have been OK at singing and acting, not particularly distinguished but not necessarily embarrassing himself, either. Well, except for the part where the ruler of the known world was engaging in acting and performing, activities that although valued for their entertainment, were reserved for the lowest

classes of society. But he took his craft seriously. He had coaches and
showed great discipline for voice rest before big performances, even issu-
ing orders in writing to save himself from having to speak. He is even
said to have lain flat on his back with lead placed on his chest in order to
strengthen his chest and lungs.[12] He was completely enraptured of every
kind of performance and contest, to the point that he forced senators and
the Equites—the merchant class—to perform. Unlike Caligula, for whom
such an action would have been purposefully to degrade the senators and
Equites, this was more about Nero just demanding everyone to be a part
of the fun.

One thing he definitely had in common with the dearly departed Caligula was an otherworldly talent for squandering money. He spent on
games, on bonuses for soldiers and commoners, on gifts for friends, on
horses, on foreign rulers, actors, and gladiators. He spent and spent and
spent. But by far the biggest beneficiary of his largesse was . . . himself.
He forced people to throw him elaborate and expensive feasts. Anything
he wanted, he contrived to get. Money was no obstacle. And if he didn't
have money, no problem. Throughout his reign he came up with all kinds
of schemes for raising money. He appropriated people's inheritances. He
invented all sorts of taxes. He took back gifts he'd given to others. He
seized property. He even stole from the gods themselves, robbing temples
of their treasures. His fund-raising could never quite keep up, and Nero's
Rome teetered on insolvency.

Agrippina tried to rein in her son. She was losing control and could
feel him slipping through her grasp. Once, when she was appalled by a
huge cash bonus Nero had granted a retainer, Agrippina heaped that
amount in coin in a huge pile before him, just to show him how much
money it really was. Nero glibly remarked that he had no idea he was
being so stingy, and he ordered the bonus doubled.[13]

Some of his antics were just . . . weird. One day, he and a confederate
resolved to observe the Roman festival of Lupercalia, which honored
both fertility and the she-wolf that suckled the twins Romulus and Remus. Nero and his friend covered themselves in wild animal skins and hid
in a cave while unfortunates were tied naked to stakes. They then burst
out of the cave, ran around like wild animals, and whipped the private
parts of the people tied to the stakes with strips of goat hide. Whipped up
into a state of arousal by these antics, Nero retired to the imperial palace
for a night of orgiastic sex.

To be fair, and believe it or not, these actions were loosely based on established religious rituals. Augustus and Marc Antony had observed a slightly more sedate version of the ritual back in the day.[14] But Nero, being Nero, took things to their weird and lustful extreme. And lustful he was. Nero would sleep with anyone, from older, married women, to young, single boys. He's alleged to have raped a vestal virgin, one of the sacred virgin priestesses. You name it, he'd nail it. But for all of his increasingly weird and sociopathic behaviors, the thing that mattered most to Nero was his musical pursuits.

So caught up was Nero in cultivating what he was convinced was a once-in-a-generation talent, he either missed or ignored the fact that such behavior was seen as way below his office. To many, Nero certainly was degrading the dignity of his position, but everybody kept their mouths shut and got used to it. He certainly was more interested in performing than in ruling. His mother was horrified, and she tried to put a stop to his performances. In fact, as he became comfortable in the big chair, and settled into his role as ruler of the known world, his confidence grew alongside his desire for independence.

On the first day of his reign, he had set the watchword for the imperial bodyguard as "best of mothers." He even was said to keep as a mistress one who looked just like his mother, often joking about how he was sleeping with his mom.[15] But her overbearing, imperious nature began to wear on him. He felt out of control, not his own man. At first, he vented his fury on his younger stepbrother, Britannicus, repeatedly raping the poor young man. But as he grew in confidence, and righteous indignation at her pretensions, he began to assert himself more and more. Furious, Agrippina made noises that she would displace Nero and put Britannicus on the throne. After all, he was the biological son of Claudius; he had as strong a claim as anyone. Undeterred, Nero simply had the boy poisoned at a dinner party. As his mouth frothed, his eyes bulged, and he gasped his frantic last breaths, Nero sat unmoved, simply muttering what a shame it was that Britannicus had epilepsy.[16] Now, just a short time after the death of Britannicus, he was anxious for the same fate for the meddlesome Agrippina. He wanted freedom to do what he pleased without her interference. And he had fallen in love. Sure, he was married. To Claudius's much-beloved daughter Octavia no less. The object of his ardor was married to his best friend, Otho. But still. He was in love. Agrippina didn't approve of this woman, Poppea Sabina. He was ready to be done with his mother's meddling once and for all, and the horrifying matricidal drama at the start of this chapter began to unfold. In her relatively short life, Agrippina had seen and been part of enormous drama. In the end, she survived her brother, Caligula, but was done in by her own son, Nero. [17]

With Agrippina out of the picture, the restraints began to fall away, and the checks against even worse behavior became ever more tenuous.

First things first: he got busy with his love life. With Agrippina out of the way, he could pursue his infatuation with Poppea. Of course, he was married, and so was she. He had plans on both accounts. With his eyes cast directly on the man's wife, he "promoted" Poppea's husband, his best friend, Otho, out to what's now Portugal, congratulating Otho on becoming governor. [18] Their affair began in earnest. Eventually, Nero took care of the other great inconvenience: his own marriage to Claudius's daughter Octavia. To start, he tried to strangle her, but she managed to escape. Changing tack, and despite the almost laughable hypocrisy of it, he charged her with infidelity. The Roman people were shocked. Octavia was beloved, and people remembered her father with great affection. Nero persisted. He had Octavia's maidens rounded up and compelled them to offer testimony to her infidelity. They refused. He had them tortured. Still, the brave maidens swore to their mistress's chastity. Eventually, one gave in to the understandable desire to be released from the unrelenting pain and said whatever they wanted her to say. Either that, or Nero just skipped the formalities and said that she had. Either way, he moved to divorce Octavia and send her into exile. [19]

The people protested loudly. They weren't buying his made-up nonsense. Nero briefly equivocated and considered remarrying Octavia. But he regained his resolve, one can only suppose with the encouragement of his beloved mistress, and sent her into exile to the barren island Pandeteria, where many unfortunate ladies from the Julio-Claudians met their demise, including Augustus's daughter, Julia, and Caligula's mom, Agrippina the Elder. Once the public furor died down, Nero coldly dispatched his killing squads to the island. They lopped off poor Octavia's head, and it ended up in the palace, where Poppea kept it as a trophy. Didn't they just make a lovely couple? Poppea was now empress in everything but name. After Agrippina's death and Otho's banishment, um, promotion, to the edge of the empire, the charming couple would make it official. Poppea snagged herself an emperor. That would prove to be a mixed blessing, to put it mildly.

The two were officially married in 62 CE. That fateful year saw the death of Nero's Praetorian prefect, Burrus.[20] He had been a moderating influence on Nero, toning down the crazy and trying his best to keep the train on the tracks. Around this time, too, his longtime tutor, Seneca, sought retirement from public life. In short order, two of the reasonable, level-headed advisers who had fought against Nero's nature to keep him in line, as much as possible, were now gone. The people who would take their places, instead of helping moderate, were bringing out the worst in Nero, appealing to his wicked instincts as a way of currying favor with the self-absorbed hedonist on the imperial throne. For now, he didn't really notice or care. Poppea had all his attention.

Well, until events demanded his attention, events so traumatic that they echo to this day. In 64 CE, the Great Fire of Rome ravaged the city. Fire was a constant threat in the ancient world. This was neither the first nor last great fire to devastate Rome. What made it so famous, of course, was the rumor that Nero himself had started the fire, or, as legend has it, that he fiddled while Rome burned. In truth, he did neither. Nero wasn't even in Rome during the fire. He was south of the city, gearing up for another smashing lyre performance. When word reached him, he rushed back to the capital. He organized relief efforts. He tried to find shelter for the countless Romans left homeless. He opened up imperial property to the masses and desperately sought food for the victims. In general, he showed empathy for the people and took great pains to provide care for all that he could.[21] So why the rumors?

Nero was, after all, Nero. Once the immediacy of the crisis subsided, Nero looked around and saw a city not in ruins but of opportunity. Much of Rome's infrastructure was obsolete. Roads were twisting and narrow, public hygiene was always questionable, and tenements besmirched the city. Now, with so much of the city reduced to rubble, Nero had a chance to update the imperial capital. Contracts were awarded, rubble was cleared, and work began in earnest. If he had contented himself with improving the city, then he probably would have been fine. But if we've learned anything about this guy by now, it's that his first and primary concern was himself. *So much* prime real estate was now available. Nero designed grand plans for a new palace of mind-bending scale. No expense was spared. The finest materials were brought in. The top artisans from across the empire were called to the capital. Walls were to be inlaid with gold; ceilings made of ivory. The main dining room rotated. At the center of this Domus Aurea—Golden House—was a massive artificial lake. Next to the lake stood a huge, 120-foot colossus of none other than Nero himself. This house was staggering in size and cost. By some accounts, the Domus Aurea took up as much as 25 percent of the entire city of Rome. That's some house for just one guy.[22]

The enormous scale of this project brought Rome to financial ruin. Nero simply ratcheted up all of his avaricious fund-raising schemes and kept building. As his Golden House was nearing completion, Nero said, "At last, I can begin to live like a human being."[23] No wonder the rumors began to swirl that Nero had set that fire deliberately. Nero tried to deflect the growing whispers and flailed about for someone else to blame. He rounded up a bunch of people and claimed that they were responsible. Among these were weirdos from a new cult growing in the shadows of the capital. These unfortunates were, of course, destined to be among the first Christian martyrs. Some were torn to pieces by wild dogs, others crucified. Still others were slathered in pitch and set alight as human torches in the night, a cruel and deliberately symbolic end for those who stood accused of starting a fire.[24]

Historical consensus has settled on the cause: an accidental fire that started in the shops beneath the Circus Maximus. Rather than proclaim the truth, that it was an accident, Nero tortured and executed hundreds of people. Neither satisfied that it was an accident, nor that Nero pegged the blame on the true culprits, the people still suspected him anyway.

As his popularity plummeted, conspiracies began to spring up. One was fairly far along before it was betrayed by one of the plotters. The conspirators were rounded up, tortured, and executed. But shaken by his near-death experience, Nero thought long and hard about what he had done to bring this on himself and vowed to reform his ways. Just kidding. Imperial death squads fanned out across the empire and visited anyone who had even the slightest claim to the throne, in other words, anyone even slightly related to him. Letters bearing his signature also went to top generals and other key members of society ordering them to kill themselves. One person who obeyed the imperial command to commit suicide was his old tutor and mentor, Seneca, thus ending the life of one of Rome's great intellects.[25]

The pen was certainly not mightier than the sword. Anyone who resisted, or even died too slowly, was sped along to the afterlife by Nero's thugs. This killing spree wasn't limited to Rome; it touched every corner

With no checks on his impulses, the once handsome Nero degenerated into a life of pleasure and indulgence. *Wikimedia Commons, by cjh1452000, CC BY-SA 3.0.*

of the empire. Distance from Nero didn't keep anyone safe. Nor, for that matter, did innocence. Blood flowed in torrents across the empire. If the horror of this wave of death wasn't bad enough, the extraordinary cost of Nero's building schemes—especially his Domus Aurea—was stretching things to the breaking point. He was bleeding the empire dry to fund his vainglorious architectural schemes. The taxes levied kept going up and up, and the provinces strained to meet the increasing demands from the capital. This fleecing was a major contributor when the province of Judea erupted in revolt. The first Roman-Jewish War would bring calamity on the Holy Land and lead to the destruction of the Second Temple. Things were starting to unravel for Nero.

But at least he had Poppea. He adored her and doted on her. He seems genuinely to have loved the beautiful Poppea. Except, he didn't love her nagging. On one fateful day, the honeymoon clearly being over, Nero came home super-late after a day at the chariot races. An annoyed, very pregnant Poppea got on his case. In a violent outburst, he viciously kicked her in the belly. She died, as did their child.[26] Nero's outburst that wrought their deaths sent him into a deep, profound mourning. Wracked with grief, and, let's hope, regret, Nero posthumously deified Poppea and ordered others to share in his period of mourning.

After Poppea's death, Nero somewhat pragmatically recognized that he had no heir. Thanks to the murderous intrigues of his antecedents, and his paranoid purges of anyone with even the feeblest claims to the throne, there weren't Julians or Claudians who could rule one day. He needed an heir, and he needed to marry. He turned to the other surviving daughter of Claudius, Antonia. With the fate of Octavia fresh in her memory, she understandably declined his proposal. Rather than save her life, she ended up hastening her own demise. Nero ordered her executed. Clearly, even being associated with this guy romantically, wanted or not, was a death sentence. It was all the same to Nero. Antonia wasn't Poppea.

He was still pining for his true love. Accordingly, he put out word that a search should be undertaken to find the closest look-alike in the empire. People searched far and wide. Eventually, an almost perfect match was found. Everything was similar: height, build, hair color, skin tone. All of it. Well, except for one thing. Poppea's look-alike was a boy. Nero was undeterred. He ordered the boy castrated. As if to add insult to horrible injury, Nero named him Sporos, the translation of which was a euphemism for semen. He adorned Sporos with the empress's clothes, had him wear similar perfume and adopt similar manners. Content that he'd done his best to replicate his dead wife, Nero married the boy and forced Sporos to accompany him everywhere until the day he died, which was, incidentally, not long in coming.[27]

In the province of Gaul, a Roman general named Vindex had had enough. He rose in revolt and despite the real threat he posed, Nero seemed unphased. Luxuriating in his pleasure palace, he initially failed to see the trouble he was in. Vindex's revolt was suppressed by a loyal general, but it made others start to think. In Spain, the governor and general Galba declared rebellion and prepared his army for a methodical march on Rome. This time, no one opposed him, and to rhythmic marching, Galba's legions began to move inexorably toward Rome. Emboldened, Nero's detractors began to deface his statues and openly mock him in the streets.

As Galba's legions moved closer, Nero woke up to the real threat that he faced. With each mile on the long march from Spain, Nero flailed, looking for a solution. He was tormented by nightmares of Agrippina and Octavia, where Octavia dragged him down into the darkness, to be engulfed in a swarm of winged ants.[28] He tried to raise a citizen militia, but no one heeded the call. He went to the Praetorian camp and asked them to defend their emperor. They refused and one mocked him, "Is it so terrible a thing to die?"[29]

On the fateful day, Nero awoke in the middle of the night. He called to his friends, to his guards, to his servants. His voice echoed in the cavernous Domus Aurea. Everyone who could have had slipped away, abandoning him to his fate. He is said to have lamented, "Have I neither friends nor enemies left?"[30] He found a freedman named Phaon willing to help, and along with poor Sporos, they decamped to Phaon's villa, four miles outside of Rome. While there, word reached the party that the Senate, showing some backbone for once, had met and declared Nero a public enemy and his life forfeit. Nero knew his situation was hopeless. The imperial cavalry was closing in; the end was at hand. Still seeing himself as the greatest performer in the empire and proving that he was out of touch until the very end, he lamented, "What an artist dies in me." Nero commanded Sporos to mourn Nero's death like any good wife would and then resolved to commit suicide. But with the dagger held to his throat, Nero couldn't bring himself to meet his end. As the cavalry closed in on the villa, Nero's secretary Epaphroditus put his hand over Nero's and "helped" him bury the knife in his throat. Eyes bulging, Nero gasped until the life finally ebbed away.[31] He was thirty-two years old. He died on the anniversary of his murder of Octavia.

The tyrant was dead! And yet, despite his insanity, a large part of the Roman populace lamented his death. Despite the suspicions that he had started the fire, this was by no means universal. Nero's love of games and theater meant that he had sponsored a lot of entertainment for the people. His inability to hold on to money meant that he had showered a lot of cash on the people. Quite a few people managed to love Nero for all he did for them. Sheltered from the depravity inside the imperial palace, many saw Nero as a beneficent and generous ruler whose actions showed great care for the people. Indeed, Nero did have a side to him that was softer, gentler than Caligula.

Some claimed that Nero had escaped to the east to plot his triumphant return. A series of pretenders even rose, claiming to be the emperor and rallying people to their banner. The ruling emperors had no interest in indulging such lunacy, and each of the false Neros met an end not unlike that of the real one. But still, it says something about the Roman psyche that people let themselves believe. For decades after his death, people placed flowers on his grave. Over time, this place was lost to history, but in a way, Nero is still with us for all to see. While his successors filled in and then used the Domus Aurea as a foundation for later public works, engineers drained the artificial lake and used the reclaimed land to build the Flavian Amphitheatre. It's OK if you're not familiar with that building. It is much more commonly known as the Colosseum, which takes its name from the colossus of Nero, the great statue of himself that Nero had erected inside his pleasure palace. Successive emperors would recast their own head and place it atop the statue, but it stood next to Rome's most famous building for a long time to come. Even as the statue eventually vanished into the mist of history, the name remained, as it does to this day. In this way, Nero is still with us, resting his voice and waiting for his next show to begin.

(DIS)HONORABLE MENTION #2: THE SIDEKICK

Otho sat far off in his province and thought. He had time. He had all the time in the world. To this point in his life, Otho hadn't had to do much thinking. He'd just had to ride the coattails of his best friend. That friend was an important and powerful man—quite possibly the most important and powerful man on earth. Otho and his pal loved to live the decadent lifestyle. They went drinking together, played wingman to one another in their sexual conquests, and generally caroused around town in a way that made elders shake their fists and lament about "kids these days." Yes, for Otho, things were pretty good as long as he remained attached to his best friend. That man, the emperor, tended to get whatever he wanted, whenever he wanted it. Unfortunately for Otho, what Nero really wanted was Otho's wife.[32]

On paper, Otho's career had elevated him to one of the highest posts in the empire. He was a governor of the Roman province of Lusitania. This sounds great, but Lusitania was as far west in the Roman Empire as it was possible to go, well, without going for a long swim in the Atlantic Ocean. Lusitania roughly corresponds to modern-day Portugal. Nero sent his old friend as far away as possible to make his lusty play for his friend's wife that much easier.

Still, to be a Roman governor brought prestige. For a governor willing to overlook scruples and line his own pockets with the riches of his province, it could be quite lucrative. Roman history is littered with unscrupulous governors exploiting the people they were sent to govern, bleeding them dry for personal enrichment. Upon taking up his post, Otho didn't seem like the kind of guy to let scruples get in the way of, well, anything. In around 58 CE, Otho reluctantly took his post in Lusitania while Nero excitedly set his sights on Otho's wife, Poppea Sabina.[33]

Otho came from a family that had greatly elevated its fortunes in the past couple of generations. His grandfather and father had been hailed for their distinguished service to the empire, earning them senatorial and patrician status and declamations of gratitude from the emperors. But Otho had been a disappointment. The family's status got him into the inner circles of Roman society, but he traded his family's prestige for wine, women, and song. He was indulgent and luxury loving, hardly the kind of guy you'd want to entrust a governorship to. But then again, Nero's criteria for the promotion were a little unorthodox.

Much to everyone's surprise, quite possibly even Otho's, he turned out to be a conscientious and competent administrator. Perhaps the apple didn't fall too far from the tree. In his tenure as governor, Otho showed that he really did have the family genes in him after all. He ruled his territory with a firm yet fair hand and won praise for his judicious administration. A little over fifteen hundred Roman miles away, Nero was back in the capital, partying, murdering, and generally earning his way into this book.

Most Roman governorships were temporary postings lasting a year. Otho's term of office went on indefinitely. Year after year, he meekly went about his duties while his resentment of Nero built. He wasn't alone. Nero's antics pushed things too far. In 68 CE, Otho's neighbor Galba, governor of the province of Hispania (modern-day Spain), rose up in revolt. He organized his troops and marched on Rome. Otho saw a chance for a measure of retribution. He declared for Galba and began to make his way to the capital to support the overthrow of the tyrannical Nero. Nero's regime collapsed before Galba even made it to the capital. By the time the stern, curmudgeonly old Galba entered the capital, Nero was dead. He set about to bring some good old-fashioned values back to Rome. He eschewed the big donatives to the Praetorian Guards and generally acted in a high-handed, moralizing, and condescending manner annoying to everyone around him.

Amid all of this, Otho had a plan. Adoption was a great way to gain imperial legitimacy. Otho had thrown his support to Galba from the very beginning. Galba was just shy of seventy years old when he grabbed the throne. Otho calculated that he could be Galba's successor and lobbied the older man to adopt him, thus clearing the way for Otho's eventual—and peaceful—succession to emperor. But Galba doesn't seem to have even considered Otho as an heir; instead, he adopted a member of the nobility whose family prestige went back centuries.

Otho, poor, mistreated, and meek Otho, flew into a rage. Pent-up frustration boiled over. He was tired of being the imperial stepping stool, a tool for other's ambition. His time was now. He made his move. Otho plotted and pulled off Galba's execution, winning the title of emperor for himself. For good measure, Otho had Galba's chosen successor beheaded as well. Both corpses were desecrated before Otho's better nature took over, and he allowed them to be reclaimed by their families for proper burial.

Finally, after all the highs and lows, Otho was emperor of the mighty Roman Empire. If his governorship of Lusitania was any indication, then he might actually be a good man for the job. Early returns were positive, and he appears to have been a decent administrator.[34] Unfortunately for

Otho, and possibly for Roman history, he didn't have long to enjoy his time in the big job. Another general out in the provinces, Vitellius, made his own bid and marched his armies south. Otho didn't have much fire-power, but he scraped together what he could, including enlisting two thousand gladiators, and marched his troops to meet the forces of Vitel-lius.[35] Otho had a reputation for being soft and decadent. Determined to prove himself as a field commander and a worthy emperor, Otho walked on foot to his coming showdown with Vitellius, unshaven and out in front.[36]

But his ragtag forces were no match for the disciplined efficiency of veteran legions. In the first day of battle, Vitellius's forces got the better end of things. But all was not lost. Otho had options and retired to his command tent to think things over. As he reflected, he understood that the longer things went, the more this petty squabble could boil over into a destructive civil war. Maybe he would prevail and maybe he wouldn't, but why put Rome through such bloodshed and disorder for his own personal glory? At what cost would the throne really come? Was it worth it? Otho pondered things and made up his mind. He opened up his veins, taking his life in order to save Rome a potentially costly civil war.[37] Vitellius could have the throne. Otho's final act had been to put the state before himself.

Otho wasn't really a good or a bad emperor. For that matter, he was barely even emperor at all, ruling for three hectic months. But his unoffi-cial career spanned most of his life. Through his friendship with Nero, he was at the center of palace intrigue from a young age. His official public career was more limited, principally his decade-long governorship in Lu-sitania and then his front-row seat in the chaotic sequence of events that surrounded the overthrow of Nero, the final collapse of the house of Caesar, and the rise and fall of Galba. Otho is mostly a sympathetic figure. His best friend stole his wife and banished him, leaving him on the fringes of the empire for a decade. The worst of Otho was mostly harm-less. Well, unless you were Galba, that is. Even his suicide was affable. He was a sidekick who sort of stumbled into becoming emperor.

He was lauded by contemporaries for taking his life and, with it, the possibility of a protracted civil war between his forces and those of Vitel-lius. Not that it mattered much for Vitellius, who would be likewise brushed aside after a few months by a more powerful rival. That rival, Vespasian, would establish an imperial dynasty that would stretch three

Best known as Nero's drinking buddy, Otho became emperor and set a dangerous new precedent for the seizure of power. *Wikimedia Commons, by euthman.*

emperors and bring much-needed stability to an empire struggling to get out of adolescence. But few could have known that at the time.

Otho's enduring contribution to the empire goes way beyond the scope of his three months as emperor, way beyond even his time as governor. For Otho was the first emperor in Roman history who had planned the murder of his predecessor.[38] And this was a bad precedent to set indeed. From here on, the number of emperors who would die a natural, peaceful death is by far exceeded by those who met their end through violent means. Perhaps, with so much power on the line, this was inevitable. But all trends have an origin, and for Rome, the trend of violent assassination in order to claim the throne finds its origin in poor old Otho.

5

THE GLADIATOR

Blade in sweaty hand, the assassin skulked in the shadows of a narrow alleyway. He knew the emperor would have to pass by this darkened spot on his way back from the amphitheater, and he waited nervously for his prey. The emperor had been in charge for three years, and his would-be murderer resolved to make today the last. Despite the dire predictions many declaimed about what would happen when the emperor took command, not much had happened yet. Maybe a new Renaissance hadn't flowered, no new era of culture, arts, and learning, but for many people, the status quo was plenty good and as much as could be hoped for, given the nature of the man who held sway of life and death over so many millions of people. Clearly, though, the new emperor had his enemies, one of whom wanted him dead.

Commodus inherited sole power of the empire when his father, the famous philosopher-king Marcus Aurelius, yielded to the ultimate meditation, and slipped off to the afterlife. Despite being dead three years, Marcus was still providing a steadying hand for Commodus, and by extension, the entire Roman world.

Great lamentations had risen to the heavens when Marcus died. Though only fifty-eight at the time of his death, Marcus Aurelius had shouldered the burden of rule for nearly twenty years and had led Rome through the turbulence of terrible plague and near-constant warfare. Though the Romans might not have been ready for him to die, true to form, Marcus had made preparations. A few years back, he had named

Commodus as co-emperor and had methodically begun to train the youth to take over.[1]

Known for his wisdom, judiciousness, and foresight, Marcus was deeply mourned by the Romans at his passing. They had lost a great leader, a man of remarkable self-discipline and commitment to fairness, a moderate and steady hand guiding the ship of state with firm clarity and righteousness.

Marcus had placed wise counselors and administrators in key positions of power and influence and asked that they guide Commodus as they had guided him. Marcus had always been willing to listen to the people around him, using their input to help him make better and measured decisions.[2] As long as they were around, Commodus would probably be OK. Commodus was reasonably content to let them take care of the boring administrative stuff. As long as he could continue to sleep with every living person with a pulse, then it was all good. It worked more or less that way for the first three years of Commodus's sole rule, until the fateful night when the emperor's entourage approached the would-be murderer lurking in the alleyways near the palace.

The assassin leapt from the shadows, brandishing his sword as he lunged at the emperor. Screwing up his courage, he yelled, "The Senate sends you this!" as he rushed onward. Had he kept his mouth shut, he might have made it to Commodus, and his sword might have found its mark. But the impetuous shout, although it sounded really cool, alerted the imperial bodyguard with just enough time to spring into action. They seized the assassin, and with a little torture, he spilled the whole plot. The designs on regicide had not begun in the halls of the Senate, but in those of the imperial palace itself. The assassin had been sent by none other than the emperor's own sister, who wanted to off her obnoxious brother and clear the path for her own husband. For his part, this husband, a senator of great distinction and unquestioned loyalty to the emperor, was completely oblivious to this scheme.[3]

In this assassination attempt and its immediate aftermath, Commodus quickly learned this wasn't a senatorial conspiracy after all. Why the assassin said so is uncertain. Apparently, he was as inept at wordplay as he was swordplay. But in a way, the words did have a terrible effect. They took root in Commodus's mind, ringing in his head, over and over. Maybe this one wasn't from the Senate, but perhaps the next one would be. Paranoia began to creep into the shadows of Commodus's brain. He began to suspect everyone of treachery. Matched with a dark and brooding personality, this was bad news for everyone, senators and non-senators alike. Things were about to take a dark, bloody, and weird turn in the rule of Commodus.

* * *

Commodus had been the first natural-born son of a sitting emperor in the more than two centuries of imperial rule. That's amazing when you think about it. All of the Julio-Claudians came to power through adoption. Well, that and a penchant for murdering potential rivals in their youth in order to clear that path along the way. Titus and Domitian were the biological sons of Vespasian, but they were adults by the time dear old dad seized power back in 69 CE. Marcus was himself adopted by Antoninus Pius, Pius by Hadrian, and so on, dating back nearly a century.

It was whispered that in this case, biological or adopted, Commodus might not live up to the shining example of dear old dad. One story has a twelve-year-old Prince Commodus dipping his toe in his bath, and, finding it a tad too cool, flying off into a rage. He ordered the attendant responsible seized and thrown into the furnace, to be burned alive. That'll teach him to put cold water in the bath! Horrified, and not about to send one of their own to the afterlife for such nonsense, the quick-thinking imperial retainers scrounged up a sheep's skin and tossed it into the furnace. Commodus, in a presumably warmer bath, could soak and enjoy the smell of roasting flesh.[4] It's quite possible that this story is apocryphal. Some historians see in young Commodus a psychopath hiding in plain sight. Others suggest he wasn't such an awful guy at first, just easy to manipulate and surrounded by people who would exploit the weakness of his character. No one seems to disagree with one thing: he was *not* his dad. The contrast between father and son could not have been starker.

A lot of historians give Marcus grief for breaking with precedent and choosing the most capable man to rule, adopting him as part of a carefully planned imperial succession. But in his defense, not one of them had natural sons. It's not like any made the deliberate choice to skip their son at the expense of a more talented and capable alternative. And besides, it's hard to blame Marcus for wanting to see the best in his son. Parents indulge kids and overstate their talents all the time. It doesn't seem like Marcus ever considered doing anything other than handing over the empire to Commodus.

As such, Marcus had done everything he could think of to prepare his son to shoulder the burden of rule. Marcus himself had experience sharing power with a less competent coruler. Years earlier, he and another Roman noble, Lucius Verus, were adopted at the same time as part of planned imperial succession. Whereas Marcus was studious and responsible, a great prodigy, his new brother, Lucius, was more smitten with mistresses and gambling. Although Marcus insisted that they were true equals, everyone knew who was really in charge, and eventually Verus exited the scene, dying of the plague eight years into their shared rule. Perhaps this all just desensitized Marcus to the consequences of sharing power with an incompetent, because eight years later, he invested his then fifteen-year-old son, Commodus, with imperial authority and began his on-the-job training in earnest, trying to get important lessons into Commodus's thick skull. It was a task that tried the patience of even the renowned stoic, Marcus.

A lot was at stake. To be Roman emperor in the late second century was to be steward of a people that had known great security and prosperity. The famous historian Edward Gibbon, who penned the classic *The Decline and Fall of the Roman Empire*, declared, "If a man were called to fix the period in the history of the world during which the condition of the human race was most happy and prosperous, he would, without hesitation, name that which elapsed from the death of Domitian to the accession of Commodus."[5]

The happiest and most prosperous time in the history of all of mankind? No pressure, kid!

Gibbon's statement reveals that not only was the empire in good standing at the time of Commodus's accession to sole rule, but also that the good times might not last. His rule was proceeded by what history has come to call The Five Good Emperors. In order: Nerva, Trajan, Hadrian, Antoninus Pius, Marcus Aurelius. Their combined rules stretched for nearly a hundred years.

When dad finally kicked the bucket in 180 CE, Commodus ruled alone. Marcus had been away on the frontier, battling this or that Germanic tribe. Hoping to instill some toughness and martial fortitude into the heir apparent, Marcus had dragged his reluctant son away from Rome and to the front lines. Life on the frontier could be brutal, certainly devoid of all the luxurious trappings back in the capital. True to his stoic nature, Marcus admonished himself to stop worrying about his own comfort and commit to the mission. Commodus had been present in camp with his dad, dodging all efforts from the emperor to "grow up," and "take your responsibilities seriously," and so forth. Marcus wasn't asking anything of Commodus that he didn't ask of himself. Commodus didn't listen. He just waited for dad to die. In this way, he was finally more patient than dad himself. Before becoming one of the gods, Marcus seems to have begun to have his doubts that Commodus was up to the task.

It is hard to know exactly what Marcus was thinking when he weighed his son's character. For such a gifted thinker and philosopher, he definitely had a mixed track record as a talent evaluator. His own wife, Faustina, was reputed to have slept her way through the nobility in Rome, with her behavior common knowledge to everyone but the oblivious Marcus. As she hopped from bed to bed, he sweetly, if naively, declared her a goddess and declaimed her virtues to the reaches of the empire. It would seem that son got more of mom than dad.

When Marcus died, Commodus inherited an ongoing war of great complexity. As the veteran legionnaires waited for their orders, Commodus looked around at the hard life of the military camp at the edge of the frontier. His father's military goals were not yet achieved. There was instability on the frontier. Roman allies and citizens were endangered by barbarian incursions, as raiding parties came screaming out of the dark, misty forests, bent on murder and plunder. There was work to be done and, not to mention, a legacy to be honored. The son of Marcus Aurelius had big shoes to fill.

Commodus took a deep breath, looked around, and, considering all the opulent luxury that awaited back in Rome, said, and this isn't an exact quote, "Screw this. I'm outta here." He hastily arranged a peace treaty with the belligerents and beat a path back to the capital. Commodus's sole motivation for leaving the frontier and heading back to Rome was for his own personal indulgence, security of the borders and the safety of the people be damned. He left the frontier in pursuit of pleasure, not love of peace. He was in charge now, and he wasn't about to let the responsibilities of empire get in the way of a good time.

Once back in Rome, Commodus slid into a life of debauchery. No one could say no. No one would dare say no. As long as his antics and depravities were somewhat confined to the imperial palace, things were more or less OK. Marcus's counselors and retainers did their best to keep the ship of state running smoothly. Whether or not they tried to groom the lustful young emperor, Commodus didn't want to learn how to rule. He was learning how to party. He had a few years of fun, but once the assassination attempt was foiled, paranoia spread to every dark recess of his brain, and he began to shoot up the leaderboard in terms of the worst rulers of Rome. He quickly shifted from trusting senators and magistrates to suspecting them of plotting against him. Death squads were duly dispatched. Commodus began a period of bloodletting that hadn't been seen in Rome since the days of proscriptions and civil war.

Informers and denouncers found a ready mark in the paranoid Commodus. Gibbon says, "When Commodus had once tasted human blood, he became incapable of pity or remorse."[6] No one was safe. The closer you were to the emperor, the greater the peril to your life. Two of Rome's greatest generals and statesmen were brothers, Maximus and Condianus Quintilian. These two had done everything together. They rose through the ranks, sharing in great glory and imperial favor. They were loved and trusted by Marcus. Maximus and Condianus loved, respected, and honored one another. They had even shared the consulship, serving together as the two highest magistrates in the land. They were cultured, learned, the finest example of enlightened nobility.

And thanks to Commodus, they shared a horrible death by imperial execution squads. Their true crime was to be competent and prominent at the same time. But Commodus didn't limit his reign of terror to the victims themselves. He sought to wipe their families off the map. The son of one of the brothers joined in death got wind that he was next on the to-do list for Commodus's assassins. Knowing what fate awaited him, he decided to take action. He killed a hare and took a big gulp of its blood. He then mounted his horse and staged a dramatic fall. Making a great show of vomiting blood, he duped everyone into thinking his condition grave. He then continued the charade, faking his death, adding the corpse of a ram to his coffin to give it some heft, and vanished into the shadows of history.[7] Word crept back to Rome, too late for Commodus's thugs to kill the clever fellow.

In prior imperial purges, such as those under Caligula, the selection of victims had a certain chilling logic. Commodus just seemed to like killing people. It was almost an involuntary reflex. The ability to hold someone's life in his hand was too much for him to handle. Person after person. Dead, dead, dead. Commodus even invented a fake assassination plot just to denounce and kill the alleged plotters.[8] The consequence was more than the spread of terror across the empire. By systematically removing everyone in sight, Commodus was erasing the lives and thus contributions of the empire's most talented and devoted officials. Into this power vacuum stepped people who exploited the emperor's sickness for their own ill motives.

Even the very worst of Commodus's predecessors had paid homage to the Roman traditions of intellectual and artistic pursuits. Caligula was a gifted orator. Nero wrote poetry of decent quality. A good Roman aristocrat was taught these higher-order functions as part of the standard education. Commodus had ignored his lessons as a kid. Now, as emperor, he turned up his nose at all such things. In fact, he went out of his way to target and kill Rome's intellectuals. There was to be no Commodian Renaissance. But for the emperor, a return to the heroic age of Hercules was the true goal. Commodus, it seems, began to suspect that he might, after all, be the living reincarnation of the great Hercules himself.

It was a long-standing Roman tradition for members of the upper classes to write checks and commission great works, from frescoes and mosaics to sculpture and poetry. Commodus seems to have resented people of learning and culture as effete snobs. Hercules didn't write poetry. He didn't sit in quiet contemplation, quill in hand, debating the relative merits of different schools of philosophy. No! Hercules was a man of action. He was a man of heroic strength and physical prowess. Not only did Commodus fail to patronize the arts, but he actively persecuted their practitioners. If Rome were to bow before his Herculean strength, then it needed to pay less attention to their brains and more attention to his brawn.

Hercules had carried a big club and wore a lion skin. So, of course, Commodus followed suit. Statues of him show this obsession manifest. It's as though he wanted to use that big club to bash in the brains of intellectuals and drag Rome back to a more primordial era, where man and beasts were locked in a mortal struggle, and only strength and sheer will would lead to man's supremacy.

Commodus's executions were beginning to cause serious trouble for the empire. Dedicated public servants being systematically wiped out created a power vacuum filled by people of devious ambition. In 185 CE, one of Commodus's top officials was accused of plotting to overthrow the emperor. Predictably, he was executed. This is the one and only time Commodus seems to have been contrite for the actions of his imperial

Commodus donned a lion skin and club in emulation of his hero, Hercules. But despite the outward bravado, he had none of the bravery of the legendary strongman. *Wikimedia Commons.*

administration. He laid all the blame for his bad actions on his disgraced adviser and vowed a more just and peaceful administration. He kept his word, too, and really tried—for a few days. And then the bloodshed began in earnest again.

In place of the fallen retainer was a man of insatiable avarice, Cleander. This guy did anything to embellish his own wealth. His principal method of fund-raising was to sell anything and everything, even things that weren't his to sell. He sold commissions in the military. He sold rank in society. He sold the high offices of the land. Anyone who wanted to cut the line and jump to the top of either society or the military, or both, wrote a big, fat check to Cleander, and voilá! Riches, prestige, and influence galore. Cleander's corruption spread to the courts. Convictions could be overturned with bribery. For a little extra, you could even have the conviction taken from you and applied to the individual who'd brought the charges against you in the first place. The soul of Rome itself was for sale.

Cleander got away with this by kicking back a big portion of the proceeds to Commodus. Enjoying his bottomless checking account, Commodus let Cleander run roughshod over the empire. The emperor didn't ask any questions; he just laughed all the way to the bank. But for Cleander, the good times couldn't last. He had his own fall from grace. When Cleander pushed things too far, Commodus had him decapitated and tossed his head to a rioting crowd. It mollified them for the time being, but Commodus's killings continued nonetheless.

As the cold blade of the death squads' knives and swords sliced their way through the flower of Roman society, Commodus got busy. Literally. In every way and with everyone possible. He is said to have had a harem of three hundred beautiful women and three hundred young boys, essentially kept in a state of sexual slavery, to be available at all times, depending on whatever whim struck Commodus. They had been gathered from across the empire so Commodus could have his pick of the best and most beautiful creatures on the planet. Can you imagine being forced to give a young son or daughter to the emperor to be used as a sex toy? It's not just gross; it's horrifying, and it was the shared fate of six hundred Roman families.

Between orgies, the only thing Commodus seems to have taken seriously was his martial training. If he was to follow in Hercules's massive footprints, then he had to hone his craft. Prowess with a bow and arrow, precision with a sword, skill driving a chariot. If it was martial in nature, Commodus worked hard to put himself in the same class as his hero Hercules. It must be said: he seems to have been a specimen. He was a great shot, too, but he was a poor sport. There was a paradox in Commodus's character. For all his bravado with feats of hunting and fighting, he was a coward.[9]

To show what an exceptional marksman he was, Commodus had the finest and most exotic animals gathered from across the empire and sent to Rome. The first time most Romans saw these animals was when Commodus was slaughtering them in arenas. Panthers, elephants, rhinoceros, ostriches. You name it: he killed them. But Commodus didn't put much at risk. He stood from the safety of the stands and loosed his arrows at the poor animals. He was a good shot, though. But if anyone was impressed by that, then they were downright embarrassed when Commodus did set foot on an arena floor as a gladiator.[10]

Although gladiators certainly were the rock stars of their day, they were at the bottom of the social rank. For an emperor to degrade himself by fighting as a gladiator was to degrade the dignity of Rome itself. But that didn't matter to Commodus. He was a warrior. A primal being. Maybe Hercules himself. He stepped bravely onto the arena floor and took up his sword. Well, maybe not so bravely. He gave opponents lead weapons. He had them maimed and wounded before the start of the match. He used every trick to make the fight unfair, then cut down his poor victims, one after another. In a particularly sadistic addition to his repertoire, Commodus made a habit of deliberately maiming victims, cutting off and keeping as trophies noses and ears.[11] As a reward for his gladiatorial bravery, he paid himself a gladiator's salary. Well, thousands of times a gladiator's salary. After lining his pockets from the funds, next to nothing was left for all the people who did risk life and death to fight for the entertainment of the masses.[12]

Lots of emperors ordered deaths. None personally killed more people by his own hand than Commodus. These poor people were sacrificial victims on the altar of his megalomania. And when Commodus did come out from behind the safety of the stands to confront animals in his hunts, he generally only approached them once they had been safely tied down with nets. He coldly slit the poor beasts' throats and lauded his unrivaled prowess.[13] Neither man nor beast was a match! Commodus, in the most literal way possible, bathed in blood. Animal and beast alike. Romans could be forgiven if they'd prefer to avoid such charnel slaughter. Whether or not they wanted to, Rome's elite had to watch the awful spectacle. To skip the festivities wasn't just an offense to the emperor, it was—you guessed it—grounds for execution.[14] They were forced under pain of death to bear witness to the awful spectacles.

Commodus used the machinery of the imperial courier service to send word of his accomplishments to the corners of the empire. His boastful dispatches made their way through Rome's legendary road system. Roman citizens were used to imperial propaganda. But instead of declaiming great acts of generalship, or grand building projects, Romans heard about Commodus's historical winning streak in the gladiatorial arena.[15] But Commodus didn't just revel in blood in the arena. He occasionally slipped into surgery, pretending to be the surgeon so he could open up the veins of the patients and watch the unfortunate victims bleed to death in front of him.[16] He probably skipped that part in his imperial dispatches.

Commodus was very sensitive that he, and only he, be seen as a legendary warrior and huntsman. He ordered the execution of a notable citizen because he had successfully taken down a lion with a javelin thrown from horseback. This feat of hunting prowess filled Commodus with an envious rage. He had the man killed, indirectly slain by his own javelin, as it were.[17]

In 189 CE, Mother Nature decided to get in on the act and started to wipe out Romans. A plague swept through the lands. In one terrible day, two thousand people died. In response, Commodus did what no Roman emperor had ever done: nothing. He lifted not a finger to alleviate suffering, instill hygiene, stop the spread of the pestilence . . . nothing. He and death seemed to be very good friends. Who was he to stand in the way?

As his megalomania reached new heights, Commodus decided to recast the whole Roman world in his name and likeness. The two most important aspects of the Roman Empire were the capital city itself and the legions that projected its military might into all corners of the known world. As befitting such a godlike warrior king as himself, the old names of these things just wouldn't do anymore. Rome was to be renamed Commodiana. The legions were to be called the Commodian legions. The poor, much-persecuted Senate was to be the Commodian Senate. Even a day of the week was to be changed to Commodiana. The empire itself got a new handle. It was henceforth to be called "Immortal, Fortunate Colony of the Whole Earth."[18]

After all, if he was in charge, of course the people were fortunate. The Romans themselves weren't to be called Romans anymore. No, they were "People of Commodus."[19] From now on, any reference to his rule was to be called a "Golden Age." To match this declamation, he poured cartsful of money into erecting golden statues of himself.[20] Sometimes he just saved time by having statues of glorious Romans from history recarved in his likeness. He was to be everywhere and everything. As his coffers began to dry up, Commodus did one thing in keeping with a certain Roman tradition: he denounced rich people as traitors so that he could appropriate their estates and wealth.[21] Eventually, though, he skipped the formalities and just ordered people to hand over their money on his birthday.[22] "Happy birthday, Commodus! Here's my life savings. Please don't kill me."

Commodus. It was a nice enough name, but was it really appropriate to such a magnificent, godlike superhuman warrior such as himself? Obviously, no. Accordingly, Commodus took a new name. One more appropriate to his magnificence. His new moniker was Amazonius Invictus Felix Pius Lucius Aelius Aurelius Commodus Augustus Hercules Romanus Exsuperatorius. That's more like it. If you add them up, you'll find twelve names in this new and improved handle. Twelve names . . . twelve months. Hmmmm. Commodus (and we will still call him Commodus because if we use that full name from here on, this book might never end) reassigned the months of the calendar, with one month per each name. January became Amazonius, February became Invictus, and so on.

Clearly paranoid *and* deluded, Commodus eventually decided to just kill everyone. Literally. Convinced that the people were making fun of him, he ordered the city burned and the people slaughtered. He was only deterred at the last minute through the heroic intervention of an adviser who managed to change the emperor's mind.[23] This level of crazy couldn't go on forever. Indeed, over the course of his reign, there had been a few assassination attempts, but none ever got very close to succeeding. For a psychopathic megalomaniac such as Commodus, you'd think the end would be dramatic, an explosion of light and sound. He didn't deserve to die a glorious, showy death, though.

And so it was, Commodus met his end not in drama, but ignominiously. A mistress slipped him some poison. In his stupor, he went to bathe. A wrestling partner wrapped his hands around Commodus's neck and squeezed until his life ebbed away. Commodus likely was not conscious of what was happening. He lived a coward's life. Despite covering himself in so much blood, he died without a fight. Good. Freaking. Riddance. He was thirty-one years old and had ruled alone for a dozen years. He took Rome from the height of its power and prestige to its absolute depths in the blink of an eye.

Finally, free of the bloodthirsty lunatic, the people rose up in an outpouring of pent-up fury. They wanted to desecrate his corpse and toss it into the Tiber.[24] His successor, fully aware of just how awful Commodus really was, nevertheless showed deference, if not exactly to Commodus but to the office of emperor, had Commodus cremated and his ashes interred in the Mausoleum of Hadrian (today known as Castel Sant'Angelo). Commodus had no respect for the traditional institutions of Rome and offered nothing but contempt and death for anyone or anything. Even in death, he was granted a measure of respect and dignity by those very same people—a measure of respect he most certainly did not deserve. Commodus might have done more to degrade the dignity of the Roman Empire than any ruler in the previous thousand years, but Rome itself was not yet utterly devoid of dignity.

It's easy to shudder when you consider his age at death: thirty-one. Had he lived to be as old as Marcus Aurelius, he would have had another twenty-seven years on the throne. It's almost certain Rome would have been in ashes, depopulated and ruined. Commodus had no redeeming characteristics. His death gave the empire a fighting chance to regain its footing. It had a lot of work to do. Commodus's life nearly spelled the empire's death.

So, what are we to make of this guy? For those familiar with the movie *Gladiator*, the biggest issue with the portrayal of Commodus, at least as far as the author sees it, is not the historical embellishments and inaccuracies. It's that it makes Commodus too smart, too calculating, even too tormented. Commodus doesn't seem to have been particularly bright. And for all of his epic feats of hunting and gladiatorial prowess, he was devoid of personal courage. He was self-absorbed enough to let himself believe the fake image of demigod heroism he projected and that he demanded others believe. By lying to the people, he was lying to himself. He wasn't cunning. He wasn't calculating. He didn't plot schemes requiring patience.

He was a brutish boor, a lazy, self-indulgent, dimwitted narcissist, violent and brooding. To be near him was dangerous. Far from the hero he convinced himself he was, Commodus was the opposite, a deplorable human being who abused his power and neglected his responsibilities. He didn't even die a heroic death. He was strangled to death by his wrestling partner in the bath while in a poisoned-induced stupor. He was probably not even conscious of what was happening. Some brave hero. Commodus was so bad, in fact, that many people point to his disastrous reign as the point at which Rome's long decline toward collapse began. That might be overstating things a bit, but if nothing else, the contrast between the wisdom and dedication of Marcus Aurelius, and the exact opposite of Commodus, might just be the biggest gap between "good" and "bad" in two successive reigns in Rome's long history.

6

THE BODYGUARDS

After members of the Praetorian Guard did everyone a favor and pulled off the plot against Caligula, Rome was briefly left without an emperor. The plot had focused more on how to put plenty of steel into the emperor and less about who would succeed him. As Caligula's German guards went on their murderous rampage, the Praetorians stumbled into the imperial palace. One of them found a cowering, trembling member of the imperial family hiding behind a curtain. They coaxed the poor guy out and told him it was going to be OK. In fact, they said, *you* should be emperor. This solution appealed to the Praetorians. The guy behind the curtain was the dead Caligula's uncle, Claudius.[1] He certainly had the credentials; Claudius was a brother of the beloved Germanicus. But from the Praetorians' point of view, he had one virtue that set him apart as a candidate: he was stupid. Or so they thought.

Claudius had managed to survive in the cutthroat world of the imperial palace largely because no one thought he was worth killing. Claudius suffered a childhood illness that left him with a limp and partial deafness. He also had difficulty speaking, fighting a stammer, and endured involuntary physical ticks. He was assumed to be stupid. His own mother called him a monster. His family banned him from any role in public life. As the power players in the imperial family murdered their rivals, Claudius kept his head low. Actually, he kept his head in a book. He read and read and read. He spent time with the renowned historian Livy. He wrote dozens of books. Despite his literary accomplishments, the rest of his family just kept assuming him stupid, and so he just kept living.[2]

When he was pulled from behind the curtain by the Praetorians, the guards thought they had pulled off a score. By proclaiming him emperor, they thought they had a simpleton they could manipulate for big cash bonuses and easy treatment. They could exercise power through their puppet. He would be the face, but they would hold the reins while he did their bidding, wrote their checks, and settled their scores. They whisked him from the palace to their fortified barracks and demanded that the Senate acknowledge him as emperor. The Senate, meanwhile, looked around and saw, for the first time in nearly a century, no strongman to lord over them, an actual ability to return to the good old days of the republic, and senatorial rule. Debates raged inside the Senate as to whether they should reject Claudius, declare the republic restored, and assume the mantle of leadership, or yield to the Praetorian demands and place Claudius on the throne.

After a brief standoff, one thing settled the argument: the cold steel of the Praetorian's swords. They were the only armed soldiers allowed in Rome, and as a result, their influence on key events was outsized. They had power they could project when they wanted to assert their will. Just ask Caligula, whose bloody corpse was still lying where it fell in the tunnel beneath the theater. Cowed by the paramilitary guys down the road, the Senate put their aspirations aside—permanently, it would turn out—and proclaimed Claudius emperor. They brought him to the palace, invested him with the purple robes of the emperor, and congratulated themselves on their quite literal coup.

Claudius duly paid them a nice cash bonus but then surprised everyone by being a pretty great emperor. Historians seem to agree that his afflictions subsided after his elevation. He had been playing up all his maladies to make himself less of a threat. Now safely on the throne, he could drop the pretense and get down to business. Although he'd had no experience with public office, he had spent a lifetime in scholarly pursuits and he had ideas, lots of ideas. He put them to work with zeal and stabilized an empire that Caligula's madness had upended.

But before he did all of that, he had a measure of revenge. He tracked down the conspirators who assassinated his lunatic nephew and had them executed. Yes, their actions had put him on the throne. And yes, they did everyone a favor by ending the Caligulan reign of terror. But it would have set a bad precedent to let someone kill an emperor and live to tell the tale. Claudius asserted himself, and the Praetorians backed down. If they had counted on ruling by proxy through a weak, feeble emperor, then they had badly miscalculated. To be fair, everyone had. No one saw Claudius's excellence coming. Except, perhaps, Claudius, who had known from a young age what he was doing. He would go on to rule for more than a decade, and in the end, prove to be among Rome's most competent, energetic, and accomplished rulers. What did him in was not Praetorian pretensions, but his love life, which we discussed in our chapter on Nero.

You cannot tell the story of Claudius without including the role of the Praetorians. They were a group of people who had outsize influence on Roman history over the entire span of the empire. Sometimes, they used their positions of power for good, or at least to prevent bad things from happening. But too often, their status as the only armed soldiers in Rome provided too much temptation, and they put their swords to nefarious use. In addition, the captain of the Praetorians, called the prefect, gained influence as a confidential advisor to the emperor. With a direct channel to the boss, and an armed gang at his back, a Praetorian prefect could bring destruction and horror.

They had the ability to make or break an emperor. They could march through the streets and cut down anyone who stood in their way. They had power over the life and death of everyone, from the imperial family to the poor plebs on the streets. They were kingmakers, assassins, thugs, and executors. They ruled in their own way, and they did so for hundreds of years.

Over the history of the Praetorians, some of their most horrid deeds warrant mention in this treatment of murderers, tyrants, and lunatics. With Claudius, the Praetorian actions were toward one end, a very narrow and selfish power grab, but resulted in another, the elevation of someone who turned out to be excellent. The Romans were lucky. It was the exception where the devious Praetorians were concerned. At times previous, and in many times subsequent, the Romans weren't so lucky. Thanks to the Praetorians and some truly psychopathic prefects, they left a path of death and destruction in their wake.

The first time the Praetorians appear on the radar as among the worst rulers of Rome is a few decades earlier, in the reign of the emperor Tiberius. Tired of the viper pit of Roman politics, Tiberius semiretired to his pleasure palaces on the island of Capri. Part of the reason he felt confident in his ability to do so was that he wholly trusted his Praetorian

The only armed soldiers allowed in Rome, Praetorians had uncontested power, which they repeatedly used for their own enrichment and all sorts of other evil ends. *Wikimedia Commons, b y Historien spécialiste du bassin minier du Nord-Pas-de-Calais JÄNNICK Jérémy Louvre-Lens, GFDL.*

prefect, Sejanus. He called Sejanus "the partner of my labors" and gave him enormous latitude to look after things and make decisions.

It would be understandable if you read the description of Tiberius in the chapter on Caligula and wondered, "Why isn't Tiberius on this list?"

A big part of the answer is that many of the actions that beg the question were really undertaken by Sejanus.[3] It's tough to overstate just how sick this guy was. He whispered rumors and made-up conspiracies in Tiberius's ear, manipulating the aging emperor, who was always a bit inclined toward paranoia. Sejanus had informants fan out across the city, listening for anyone to say even the slightest thing against Tiberius. He put spies in attics and on the streets. He had associates say malicious things just to see if an individual agreed. He sowed fear, suspicion, and acrimony. Anyone heard to say anything bad against the emperor, or even rumored to have done so, was put on trial and executed. Sejanus was responsible for a lot of death.

Sejanus turned Tiberius against his family. He was the reason Tiberius slowly eliminated Caligula's immediate family. Sejanus made up conspiracies, whipped Tiberius into a frenzy, then calmly told the boss he would take care of things and killed off everyone, one by one. But why? What was his motive? It appears that Sejanus was deeply seduced by power, and certainly he had strong sadistic tendencies. He also seemed to want to hold the reins of power himself. He wasn't just content to rule by proxy; he seems to have been trying to position himself to be a successor candidate in his own right. By turning Tiberius against his own family, Sejanus was eliminating *his own* rivals to power. Sejanus also controlled all information to and from the emperor in exile. He thereby prohibited Tiberius from knowing what was happening back in the capital. As Sejanus's reign of terror progressed, Tiberius only heard the warped version of the truth that Sejanus filtered to him. Tiberius glibly nodded and let Sejanus run roughshod over everyone in the capital.

In his quest for power, though, Sejanus had two big problems: he wasn't a member of the royal family, and he wasn't a member of the patrician order. Ever calculating, Sejanus saw these as temporary obstacles, not permanent roadblocks.[4] He convinced Tiberius to make him consul, cementing his bona fides. Now, if he could just marry into the royal family, then all would be good.

Tiberius had a young son, Drusus. Drusus was one of the few people who saw Sejanus's villainy for what it was. The two clashed constantly, and it is said that Drusus struck the older man, knowing Sejanus could not hit him back. In this feud, the calculating Sejanus saw not an obstacle but an opportunity. Sejanus seduced Drusus's wife, Livilla, and together they poisoned Drusus. Tiberius was distraught over the death of his son and heir but suspected nothing. Livilla was herself a member of the imperial family; she was sister to Germanicus and Claudius, the daughter of Tiberius's brother (also named Drusus). After the appropriate mourning period, Sejanus approached Tiberius for permission to marry the widow. Although Tiberius was generally susceptible to Sejanus's suggestions, this went too far. Tiberius rejected the proposal. Sejanus had to find another way around this obstacle. He was calculating and patient; he would stay at it. Eventually, he succeeded in convincing Tiberius to allow the marriage. He was just inches away from his goal of complete power. Or so he thought.[5]

Unfortunately for Sejanus and his followers, his time was just about up. Antonia, the widow of Tiberius's long-dead and beloved brother Drusus, had been watching events unfold in stoic silence. She and Tiberius maintained a great and trusted relationship over the years, and she was one person insulated from Sejanus's machinations. In 31 CE, Antonia decided that Tiberius needed to know the truth of what was happening with the Praetorian prefect Sejanus running the show. Sejanus had usurped the power of the emperor. Whether or not he was trying to make himself emperor officially was beside the point. He was acting as though he was, in itself a violation of the majesty and dignity of the emperor. Enough was enough, and she resolved to act. She secreted a messenger off to Capri with a letter detailing the truth. When Tiberius received her letter, he read it with a growing sense of horror. He had to act, but Sejanus had spies, informants, and coconspirators everywhere. In Tiberius's absence, Sejanus held all the power and was nearly omnipresent. Tiberius had to act carefully.[6] His actions proved that the old man was still formidable, even so many years into his self-imposed exile.

Word went out. Sejanus was to be lauded in the Senate for all his accomplishments. A grateful Tiberius called a special meeting of that body to grant Sejanus even more power, this time fully legal and sanctioned. With his chest proudly puffed out, a cocky Sejanus strode into the Senate House and took his seat, patient to hear the words in the letter Tiberius had written and instructed to be read out loud. Sejanus's loyal Praetorians waited outside, standing guard and controlling who could enter the building. But as Sejanus settled in to accept the congratulations of the senators, a new Praetorian commander, appointed by Tiberius, strode up, showed the official paperwork to the troops on duty, and dismissed them all. This prefect, Macro, then replaced Sejanus's troops with his own. Unknown to Sejanus, his loyal guard was gone, and a new cohort of armed soldiers waited outside with orders to obey a previously unknown rival.

When Tiberius's letter began to be read out, everyone was surprised by its contents. Rather than lauding Sejanus, Tiberius denounced him, heaping anger and vitriol on the man in whom he had invested so much trust. As the nervous senators edged farther and farther away, Tiberius dropped the hammer: Sejanus was to be executed. Macro arrested Sejanus and led him away.[7] He was dead within hours, strangled, and his corpse tossed into the streets for the people to violate. They obliged by tearing it to pieces. Statues of him were torn down. His memory was damned. His name was cursed. Such was the fury against Sejanus, that his children were also condemned. His youngest was a small girl named Junilla. Roman law forbade the execution of a virgin. Given her tender age, the soldiers tasked with carrying out the orders debated what to do, finally raping the poor child before strangling her to death.

In the aftermath of the fall of Sejanus, and to reassert his imperial prestige, Tiberius initiated a counter-purge, where anyone suspected of association with Sejanus was rounded up and slaughtered. Sejanus's downfall and death didn't end the terror. It simply started another wave of it.

Praetorian prefect Sejanus had parlayed his position of chief imperial bodyguard into de facto ruler of Rome. He introduced the treason trials that left so many dead, tore families to pieces, and tried to murder his way to the top. He created an air of fear and suspicion that permeated Rome and destroyed the way of life for countless citizens. His purge of political opponents also led to the Tiberian counter-purge and unleashed a whole new wave of bloodletting across the city.[8] If this was an isolated incident, it would be easy to sum up as the actions of one man, not condemn the entire Praetorian Guard. Unfortunately for history, these guys were just getting started. In fact, they were directly responsible for one of the most shameful moments in all of Rome's history, an incident that permanently stained Rome's honor and showed history just who these guys really were.

After the bizarre and disastrous reign of Commodus, a decent and competent man was acclaimed emperor and duly ascended to the throne. Pertinax was an unlikely emperor. He was the son of a freed slave. Rather than building his career in the hallways of power politics, he was in the field, serving with the army. He rose through the ranks of the officer corps, distinguishing himself in the campaigns against Rome's long-standing, bitter rival, Parthia. He went on to serve as provincial governor and eventually found his way into the Senate.[9] While earnestly working for the betterment of Rome in the Senate, Pertinax ran afoul of Commodus's Praetorian prefect, Perennis.

Perennis had gained enormous influence over Commodus. Much in the same way that Sejanus sought to rule from this command post, Perennis had tortured, murdered, and manipulated himself into a position of proxy ruler of the Roman Empire.[10] He was every bit as evil and detestable as Sejanus, and, eventually, he met his end in a similar way. Denounced by Commodus, he was unceremoniously executed in a spectacular fall from grace. Pertinax breathed a sigh of relief. He also noted the lesson: the Praetorians had too much power and were a threat to the stability of the empire. They held the power of life and death in their hands and used this power to ill means time and time again. Despite his lowly origins, or perhaps because of them, Pertinax had a clear view of changes that needed to happen in the empire. All he needed was an opportunity to put them into action.

His time came after the assassination of Commodus. Recognized by politicians as the most competent man in the Senate, and by the soldiers as one of them, Pertinax was uniquely poised to appeal to all sides of the Roman power structure. He was proclaimed emperor on January 1, 193. Like Claudius, he had been in the care of the Praetorians in their fortified barracks at the time of his acclimation. Like Claudius, his path to the throne had only been possible by the Praetorians' assassination of his predecessor. Once again, they had killed one emperor and were instrumental in crowning the next. But this time, Pertinax knew that the Praetorians had too much power and were too capricious in their use of it. For their part, the Praetorians expected gratitude. They made this guy emperor. He'd better pony up with a nice, fat bonus for their effort.

But bribing the Praetorians was low on Pertinax's to-do list. The empire once again found itself reeling in the after-effects of a catastrophic rule. Before Commodus, Rome had been blessed with what historian Edward Gibbon, he of the *Decline and Fall of the Roman Empire* fame, called "The Five Good Emperors." Nerva, Trajan, Hadrian, Antoninus Pius, and Marcus Aurelius had led Rome to the zenith of its power, and, at times, great periods of peace and prosperity. Commodus had derailed a century of wise administration in just a few years. Reform was needed everywhere, and Pertinax was very busy. In fact, one of the reforms Pertinax sought to implement was to the Praetorians themselves. They'd grown lazy, ill-disciplined, poorly led, and disorganized. They were violent, unpredictable, and held too much power with too little accountability. The Praetorians didn't want to be reformed. They didn't want some insufferable moralizer telling them about duty and responsibility. What they wanted to do was be paid. Now. [11]

The Praetorians wanted fat cash bonuses. Pertinax had given them some money, but far less than they wanted or demanded. Frustrated at the stance of the new emperor, they took events into their own hands. Less than three months into his rule, they realized that once again, they held power of life and death over the emperor. Several hundred angry Praetorians armed themselves and marched on the imperial palace. An angry Pertinax bravely went out to confront the unruly mob. [12] They drew their swords and shouted at him. He argued back, shaming them for their actions and reminding them of their sworn oaths and duties. His courage, and his conviction, gave the mob pause. They equivocated and considered backing down. The call to honor their oaths of duty and loyalty was strong. But the call for riches and lax discipline was stronger. After a brief standoff, one soldier stepped forward and butchered Pertinax where he stood. They decapitated him, put his head on a lance, and marched back to their barracks in triumph. [13]

Now, the legitimate emperor was dead, leaving an opening for the top job. Not only did the Praetorians get rid of the curmudgeonly Pertinax, they created an opportunity to enrich themselves. As the only troops in the city, the path to the throne ran through them. What mattered was not credentials, legitimacy, or experience. What mattered was who the Praetorians backed, and against whom their steel was pointed. They had all the keys. They knew it. The senators knew it. And every aspirant to the throne knew it. Accordingly, they devised an insidious and shameful way to exploit their power. They marched back to their barracks and proclaimed that they would back as emperor the individual who promised the highest cash bonus. They then barred the gates and opened the bidding. [14]

Rival claimants rushed to their barracks and shouted their bids through the gates. As the bids went higher and higher, the Praetorians inside were dizzy with glee. Not only was the stingy Pertinax gone, but they were all about to be rich for their troubles. Their fortunes had swung dramatically.

For now. Eventually, two bidders remained, going back and forth, offering literal blood money for the chance to rule. In an auction, only one winner emerges, and eventually Didius Julianus, a soldier, administrator, and officer offered the highest bid at 25,000 sesterces per soldier, an amount equal to more than a decade's pay for a Praetorian. Smugly satisfied with their work, the Praetorians opened the gates, welcomed in Julianus, and proclaimed him emperor.[15]

Magnanimously, one of Julianus's first acts was to forgive his rival, stating no ill will toward the other finalist. To complete the terms of their sale, the Praetorians donned their armor, brandished their weapons, surrounded their new cash cow, and marched him through the streets. With their spears pointed to drive home the demand, they commanded the Senate to convene and recognize Julianus.[16] Despite the backing of the Praetorians, things fell apart for Julianus quickly. He wouldn't have long to enjoy his bought-and-paid-for office. He didn't just buy the empire. He sowed the seeds of his own death.

The Praetorians' assassination of Pertinax and subsequent actions kicked off a civil war that brought Rome to its knees. Rival claimants did battle in the provinces and in the city, with Roman fighting Roman in a bloody conflict that left the empire mentally exhausted and drained its resources. The greed and avarice of the Praetorian guard nearly crippled the empire. The eventual winner in this civil war, known to history as The Year of Five Emperors, was a general named Septimius Severus. Nine weeks after Julianus bought the throne, he bought the farm, with Severus's troops running him through with swords of their own.[17] All his fortune had secured was sixty-six days on the throne.[18]

Severus declared that Pertinax was the last legitimate emperor, had him deified, and took part of Pertinax's name into his own. He ordered the Praetorians to assemble unarmed. He marched them out into a field, surrounded by a corps of troops loyal only to him. The Praetorians were summarily dismissed, stripped of their treasure, and banished under pain of death to stay at least one hundred miles from Rome.[19] Those responsible for Pertinax's assassination were rounded up and executed. This wasn't high-minded reform. Severus didn't dismantle the Praetorian Guard. He simply dismissed the current ones and replaced them with his own men. In almost no time, the reconstituted Praetorians would again menace the well-being of the empire . . . and the emperors.

Severus founded an imperial dynasty that ruled for a couple of generations, including some rulers who are featured in upcoming chapters.
Through his change of guard in the Praetorians, he came close to disman-
tling one of the elements that undermined Roman society but instead
allowed it to live on.[20] Consequences would follow. The Praetorians were
front and center as Rome entered the most significant period of decline
and instability at the end of the house of Severus. Dubbed the "Crisis of
the Third Century," it saw a remarkable twenty-six different emperors
and claimants in the fifty-year span from 235 to 285.

Splinter kingdoms broke off. The empire began to fracture. Discord
and acrimony took hold, and the empire nearly died a premature death.
Barbarian hordes invaded. Civil war, rebellions, and plague all broke out.
Rather than work to restore the stability of the empire, the Praetorians
took an active role in the chaos, killing many of the emperors who strug-
gled to regain Rome's footing in those tumultuous years. The Praetorians
killed three emperors in the year 238 alone. Some of the emperors needed
to go. No one looks back on the death of Caligula with lamentation. But
more often than not, pursuit of their self-centered greed helped usher
Rome to the brink of destruction.

The tide began to turn with the rise of the emperor Aurelian. Through
a series of brilliant military campaigns, he subdued rebellions and
brought huge swaths of territory back into the fold. He stitched the empire
back together through energetic campaign, for which he took the title
Restitutor Orbis, or, Restorer of the World.[21] Also struck by the growing
sense that the capital itself was vulnerable to foreign invasion for the first
time in a thousand years, he ordered the construction of the massive city
wall that largely rings the Eternal City to this day.[22] Despite his initial
successes, he had much work to do to bring about sustained stability. Just
as he was starting, and after only five brilliant years on the throne, he
was—you guessed it—assassinated by the Praetorian Guard.[23]

Fortunately for Rome, Aurelian's successors would pick up where he
left off, closing the terrible chapter of the Crisis of the Third Century and
setting the scene for the next two centuries of Roman rule. When one
looks at their pattern of action, it's amazing that the Praetorians were
allowed to exist for so long. Edward Gibbon sums it up nicely when he
says, "The Praetorian's [sic] . . . licentious fury was the first symptom and
cause of the fall of the Roman Empire."[24] They had centuries to devastate
and destabilize until they were finally disbanded by Constantine the Great

Few emperors did more to stabilize the flailing Roman Empire than Aurelian. The massive walls that he built to protect Rome largely exist today, but he couldn't protect himself from the treachery of his Praetorians. *Wikimedia Commons.*

in 312 CE.[25] By then, the cumulative damage that they had done was incalculable.

When the doors to the Praetorian barracks were finally closed; so, too, was a terrible chapter in the story of Rome. The Praetorian legacy is one of intense brutality, regicide, purges, recrimination, and greed. As the only armed troops in Rome, they could be an effective bodyguard to the imperial family. But, increasingly, they became a force of their own, untethered by loyalty or duty to anything other than their own interests. Their loyalty was for sale, and to stand in their way was to put a target on one's back, or a steel blade to one's throat. The Praetorians gave us Sejanus and Perennis. They gave us the murder of Pertinax and the literal sale of the imperial throne. They brought about death, destruction, and dishonor. They also gave us terrible but fascinating stories plus lessons about the nature of power and its effect on the behaviors and actions of mankind. Whether or not in name, the Praetorians ruled through the sharpness of their steel and their willingness to wield it. They ruled, and they ruled poorly. So poorly, in fact, that they have to be considered among the most wicked rulers of Rome.

7

THE SCOWLER

Mother knows best. If these two boys weren't going to get along on their own, then she was going to have to get them in line. Despite their father's deathbed advice, the two sons had done nothing but shout and argue with one another. Then they stopped talking to each other. Then they split the house in two and kept to their own sides. Then they started trying to kill one another.

This was madness. Brothers shouldn't behave this way. And besides, these weren't too bratty little kids; they were co-emperors of Rome. Unlike some of their predecessors, this family took their responsibilities as rulers seriously. How could they run an empire when they couldn't even run a household? This could not go on. Mom resolved to intervene. She called a peace conference to clear the air and find a way to get along going forward. They would share a meal in her apartments. Just the three of them, no bodyguards or entourages, and critically, the boys were to come to dinner unarmed.

Heeding their mother's call, the boys agreed to put aside their differences for one meal and made their way to their mother's dining room. One brother went in good faith. The other did not.

The older brother was Imperator Caesar Marcus Aurelius Severus Antoninus Augustus, but we will call him by his historical nickname, Caracalla. The younger brother was Imperator Caesar Publius Septimius Geta Augustus, but we will call him by the more concise Geta. One name was destined to be officially damned by the Roman government, excised from all buildings, scratched out from all documentation, obliterated by the ruthless efficiency of state. The other name was to suffer a far worse fate, to be damned by history itself, cursed by hundreds of generations as belonging to one of the worst people ever to rule.

The immediate cause of mom's peace conference was Caracalla's attempted assassination of Geta during the religious festival of Saturnalia. This plot was the culmination of a deteriorating relationship that was both bad for their life expectancies and bad for the business of running an empire. Certainly, the empire was big enough for both of them, right?

As they gathered for dinner, Julia Domna sought reconciliation between her sons. Things had gotten bad. They had quite literally divided the imperial palace in half. They barricaded the hallways from one half to the other and put detachments of troops to keep their respective sides safe from incursions. They were like two little kids arguing over an imaginary line in the backseat of a car. It was wholly undignified, behavior unbecoming Roman emperors. Julia Domna knew that the Roman Empire needed rulers focused on running the empire, not throwing daggers at one another. So the two boys put down their swords, dismissed their bodyguards, and headed to a nice, family dinner. Isn't this great? Everyone together?

It was a trap. Calculating and ruthless, Caracalla saw in this dinner invitation a chance to off Geta once and for all. His soldiers burst into the dining room and rushed toward Geta. Julia Domna tried to shield her younger son from the assassins, but they had their orders and they were going to carry them out. Geta was butchered in his mother's arms. Their work done, the soldiers left, and a weeping Julia Domna held Geta in her arms, his life ebbing away as his blood spread across her dining room floor.[1] Caracalla made some feeble excuse about foiling a plot on his own life, and left the room, now the sole ruler of the Roman Empire.

The family had come to power following the civil war kicked off by the Praetorian Guard's assassination of poor old Pertinax. The brothers' father, the statesman and general Septimius Severus, had seized power in 193 CE, a chaotic year known to history as the Year of Five Emperors. When news of Pertinax's murder reached Severus's military camp, his troops and those of a few other generals proclaimed Severus emperor. With their swords bolstering his claim, he marched to Rome; saw the current emperor, Didius Julianus (the guy who "won" the auction in the previous chapter) offed; and placed himself on the throne. Severus replaced the Praetorians with troops loyal to him, deified Pertinax, added

Septimius Severus with his wife and warring sons, Geta and Caracalla. Caracalla would rule the world after murdering Geta in their mother's arms, then ordering the name and memory of his brother obliterated from the earth. *Wikimedia Commons.*

that emperor's name to his own, and marched back out to fight more battles.[2] It took him a few years to consolidate power and finish off all the rival claimants to the throne, but by the time he did, he was left in sole command of an empire of enormous scale and complexity. It was a lot of work, and he needed help. He got a lot of this help from his second wife, Julia Domna, to whom he turned for advice and to think through thorny situations.

After his first wife died of natural causes, Severus realized that he was in his forties and had no kids. He had big aspirations, including the ultimate prize of emperor. But he didn't have the job yet, and he was childless. Given the danger that came with being emperor—after all, to be emperor was always just one crazed assassin away from becoming one of the gods—Severus knew he needed a legitimate heir or two as part of his imperial aspirations. He got word of a beauty in a far corner of the empire whom soothsayers had said was destined to marry a king. He traveled to meet this woman, proposed a marriage arrangement to her father, and the two got hitched.[3]

They made an exotic couple. Severus was African, the first Roman emperor born on that continent. Julia Domna was Syrian. Her father was the scion of a house of local royalty and the high priest of a Syrian mystery cult centered on worship of the sun god, Elagabal. Their marriage was a microcosm of the breadth and scope of the Roman Empire. Despite their wildly different origins, Severus valued and respected his wife, her advice, and her wisdom.[4] She was a good partner to him. Severus and Julia Domna had a happy marriage, and, as you've figured out by now, came to have two sons who would grow up to hate each other.

But Severus needed more than good advice from his wife. He needed to create legitimacy for his sons and heirs. His goal was not just to rule but to found a new imperial dynasty. He got more than he bargained for. In the year 198 CE, Severus made his older son, Caracalla, co-emperor. The lad was ten years old at the time. The idea was less about making Caracalla a true decision maker and more about getting people used to the idea that one day he would be in charge. But Severus knew that the job of emperor was too much for one person now, as it would be for Caracalla when his time came. Accordingly, in 209 CE Severus appointed Geta a third co-emperor. When Severus eventually died, not one but two Severan sons would be on the throne. This did not sit well with Caracalla.

Severus was constantly on campaign, marching his armies this way and that. Severus understood that the power of the emperor lay not in the capital, not in the people, and certainly not in the Senate. No, the power of the emperor lay in the troops. Nothing else mattered. If you have the army, you have the empire. Everything else is just noise. And no mistaking, Severus had the army. He lavished praise and donatives on the troops. He honored them, and they honored him right back.

With the army behind him, he could more or less do as he pleased, including, of course, condemning uppity senators and replacing them with his own cronies. But Severus's government, while ruthless, was efficient and free of the brazen corruption of Commodus. As such, he was pretty popular with the people. Severus was developing a blueprint for imperial rule, and he did everything he could to teach his young sons the right way to do things.

Under his firm, efficient, and autocratic rule, Severus pushed the Roman Empire to its largest extent. By the winter of 211 CE, he and his quarrelsome progeny were in Britain, warring against the highland tribes and trying to claim the unconquered northern territories for the empire.[5]

Caracalla was growing tired of sharing rule with the old man. While riding out to meet enemies and discuss terms on the field of battle, in plain sight of the whole army, Caracalla rode up to Severus, drew his sword, and made to assassinate his own father, who rode on in oblivion. People shouted warnings, and Severus spun his horse around in time to see his son's arm raised, sword in hand. Shamed by the eye contact, Caracalla lowered his sword.[6]

Back in camp, Severus called his son into his tent. He put a sword on the table between them and dared Caracalla to strike him down then and there. Caracalla didn't budge, and Severus strode away, satisfied that his eldest had been chastened.[7] The reality was that the ever-calculating Caracalla knew that the old man was on his last legs. A life of near-constant campaigning had worn Severus down, and what Caracalla couldn't bring himself to finish the cold British winter would. Aged and infirm, Severus retreated to his winter quarters in York and prepared for his death. As he lay dying, he called his sons to his bedside. He distilled his life's lessons to three succinct pieces of advice. "Be harmonious. Enrich the troops. Scorn all other men."[8] If you have family and soldiers on your side, nothing and no one else matters. Caracalla was pretty convinced that at least one of those things was not necessary.

With Severus dead, the number of emperors went from three to two. Each brother would have been content for that trend to continue as long as he was the last one standing. They hastily made a peace treaty with the tribes Severus had been fighting and pointed themselves south toward Rome. The two argued all the way back to the capital. They had very different personalities, ideas, styles, everything. They were oil and water, incapable of finding common ground. At first, they decided to just split the empire. One would go east, the other west, and they would stay the heck out of each other's way. Julia Domna realized that this would guarantee civil war, as it would only be a matter of time before the two led armies against one another. She talked them out of this scheme, but the infighting only accelerated.[9]

As Caracalla angled for ways to be Cain to his brother's Abel, he considered how he might flex his new imperial muscles. He began to order executions almost right away, and the much-maligned senatorial class, just beginning to regain its footing from Commodus's bloodshed a generation earlier, came straight into the crosshairs. The wave of death preceded Caracalla as he made his entry into the capital.[10] Senators weren't the only victims of this first purge. Caracalla had his own wife and father-in-law seized and executed. Keep in mind, she was the empress of Rome. The first lady, and, not to mention, his second cousin.

He was not safe to be around. Family ties meant nothing. All that mattered was his own power. As long as he had the troops as the finely honed steel point of his will, nobody could do anything to stop him. It took him no time at all to be feared by the nobility, which was good for him because he went out of his way to be feared. The one lesson he'd taken to heart from his father was to win the hearts and souls of the troops. He kept the cash flowing, and they never wavered in their support. Honor the troops. Scorn all other men. And, just as his dead wife demonstrated, he had no problem scorning women either.

He ran into trouble when he perpetrated fratricide. Geta was the son of Severus, and Severus had carefully promoted the brand and reputation of *both* of his sons. Both were loved by the troops. Besides, where Caracalla was dark and brooding, Geta was affable, a much nicer and more generous young man. People actually liked him. Granted, it's easier to be nice when you know the rest of your family is ruthless, and Geta seems to have played up the difference between his brother and himself whenever he could. To the troops in their barracks, they had two great patrons, and many had a strong affinity for Geta. When he died, these troops were nonplussed. They had sworn fealty to both emperors.[11] One had been assassinated at the hands of the other. Just because Caracalla was left standing didn't mean the troops were OK seeing the other son of Severus hacked to death. But how were they supposed to react? Some grumbled. Others kept their thoughts to themselves.

The troops weren't the only ones put in a bad spot by Geta's murder. Like any young, charismatic politician, Geta had numerous followers and adherents in the capital and across the empire at large. They were furious at the loss of their beloved. Tens of thousands of Geta's supporters expressed their outage. With the troops restive and the people riotous, Caracalla was on thin ice. So, he did the thing that every leader does in times of scandal: he lied. [12] Caracalla claimed that he had been the victim. Geta, Caracalla claimed, had been trying to kill him. Caracalla only acted in self-defense. Praise the gods, his life had been spared at the last minute.

The number of people buying this bald-faced lie? Exactly zero. Caracalla was a psychopath, but he wasn't stupid. He knew he couldn't let the soldiers grow restive. Honor the troops. They were his base of power. Caracalla went to the barracks and told the men he had survived Geta's plot, only killing his brother in self-defense. There was a silver lining, he asserted. "Rejoice, fellow soldiers, for now I am in a position to do you favors." [13] When a few troops started to speak, he cut them off and showered them with winning words and promises of riches and glory beyond their wildest dreams. If their loyalty was split before he entered the camp, it was fully concentrated in his hands before he left. The army was his now, no matter how laughable his conspiracy theory was proving to be. [14]

More confident in his power, Caracalla stuck to his story. He forced the Senate to pass the decree of *damnatio memoriae*, which not so surprisingly means that one's memory is to be damned. Geta's name was to be erased from history. It was to be scratched out of official inscriptions. Any images of him were to be destroyed. Statues of him were to be smashed. To this day, visitors to Rome can see the results of this edict. In the forum is the arch of Septimius Severus, which he erected to laud the accomplishments of his family and to pave the way for his sons to rule. All references to Caracalla are intact, but any mention or likeness of Geta has been chiseled away. Gone. Like he never existed. Except you can still see the scars in the marble. History is not changed so easily.

Because Geta had been "plotting to murder his brother," his death was justified. Accordingly, mourning was prohibited. Even his mother, in whose arms poor Geta had been killed, was not allowed to show any sadness. She had to go out in public and be seen by all as laughing and smiling, carrying on as though she had not a care in the world. Otherwise, as Caracalla made clear, she would meet the same fate as Geta. [15] So to sum up the last few months, aside from the ho-hum, run-of-the-mill purges of senators and wealthy citizens, Caracalla had raised a sword to his father, had his wife and father-in-law killed, had his brother hacked to death in the arms of his mother, and threatened that poor woman with the steel of an assassin's sword if she didn't act happy enough for all the world to see. He was racking up quite a body count. And he was just starting.

As Caracalla promoted the lie of Geta's foiled plot, he thought he would try another page in the imperial playbook. He thought that maybe he should just try acting like a nice guy. You know, just to see what happened.[16] Caracalla went to the Senate, full of humility and contrition. In his speech, he declared an amnesty for all political opponents, granted pardons, and recalled disgraced citizens from exile. He lured as many people back to the capital as he could. This all was, of course, a ruse. Caracalla was biding his time, figuring out which people had been followers and supporters of Geta.[17] He made his list. He didn't check it twice. Anyone he perceived to be naughty got sliced. Caracalla's death squads had come to town.

Once he was ready, the killings began in earnest. Caracalla didn't care anymore whether people believed his lie. He drew a line in the sand. To have been Geta's supporter, have been associated with him in any way, spoken positively of Geta or ill of Caracalla, or just generally been suspected of any of these things, was to be marked for death. Caracalla ordered the bloodiest purge in Roman history. The killings swept across the city like a plague. Doors were broken down as innocent people were cut to pieces. Entire families were wiped out. The killing was indiscriminate. Men, women, young, elderly. Hour after hour. Day after day. Death after death. The death toll was staggering. Twenty thousand people were killed in Caracalla's orgy of death.[18]

At this point, it would be fair to ask, why didn't some people just stay in exile? A quick glance at Roman history showed that recalled exiles usually didn't have too long to enjoy their newfound return to good graces, or, for that matter, their lives. It seems the call home was too much to resist.

Caracalla didn't just order death: he sanctioned it as an instrument of terror for others to wield as well. He set out to prove to his Praetorians that he meant it when he said they would enjoy his sole rule. He gave them a license to kill. They fanned out across the city, settling old scores and killing their own enemies.[19] This was next-level stuff. It was one thing for an emperor to order the death of his own enemies, real or perceived. It was another entirely for the emperor to let his soldiers do as they wished and kill as they wished, no approval required.

The one thing Caracalla didn't want was to be called a god. So many of his predecessors either projected divinity to cow the masses or convinced themselves that they genuinely were divine. Caracalla wasn't having any of it. He didn't want to be called a god, referred to as a god, or treated as a god. But this wasn't humility. He didn't want to be compared to gods because he didn't want to have to emulate their virtues.[20] Even the strangest gods in the Roman pantheon had certain obligations to mankind. Caracalla was beholden to no man. And vice was a lot better than virtue.

His justice had no rhyme or reason. He made it a habit of not having any habits, at least in terms of his decision making. He did one thing one day, then contradicted himself the next. He changed his mind at a drop of the hat. No one ever knew what to expect.[21] Everyone was liable to be rounded up and killed, "Both guilty and guiltless alike," according to Dio Cassius.[22]

Previous emperors at least had pretended that their victims had been guilty of something. Even when the charges were absurd, far-fetched, or farcical, at least there were charges. Caracalla skipped such formalities. A point, a nod, a whisper, and people were just murdered. As long as the fat cash bonuses kept coming in, the soldiers were happy to do his bidding. Life was cheap. Their loyalty was not, but it was paid in full. The soldiers loved him.

His love of human bloodshed even spread to the arena. Where Commodus loved all kinds of spectacle, Caracalla cared not for the animal hunts. What he loved were the gladiators, not because of the life or death struggle. Just the death. He reveled in watching gladiators die.[23] In one example, a gladiator won. So, Caracalla sent in another adversary. The man won again. Another adversary. Another victory. Caracalla kept sending in opponents to face the stalwart champion until one finally cut him down.[24]

Aside from death, Caracalla's true obsession was Alexander the Great.[25] He might not have wanted to be considered a god, but he let it be known that he wouldn't mind people suggesting that he was the reincarnation of the ancient world's greatest general. He emulated Alexander in every way he could think of. A historical rumor had it that Alexander's tutor, none other than Aristotle himself, might have had a hand in plotting Alexander's death. Just to prove that absolutely no one was safe, the emperor had the school of Aristotelian philosophy suppressed and its adherents added to his hit list.[26] Keep in mind, five hundred years had passed, and it was all hearsay. But in Caracalla's mind, time fell away and he was destined to walk in the footprints of his long-dead hero. He set up a new army modeled on Alexander's, sixteen thousand strong, equipped them in period armor, and trained them in period tactics. Never mind that half a millennium had passed, and weapons and tactics had evolved. Caracalla could pretend that he was leading an ancient Macedonian army, with himself as the incarnate Alexander. In fact, to even be named Alexander was grounds for imperial favor. Caracalla promoted men of the name through the ranks, independent of any talent or ability.[27]

He didn't neglect his "normal" army either. He kept raising their pay. The imperial taxes went straight from the people to the soldiers. Caracalla gave them so much cash that he nearly bankrupted the empire in enriching the soldiers. But he had other ways to keep the cash flowing as well. Caracalla used his troops as an implement of terror all over the known world. Previous Roman emperors led campaigns for conquest and territorial expansion. Occasionally, Romans fought to prevent incursions or harassment from barbarians. Caracalla just fought to fight. He turned his army loose when and where he could, with the express goal of raping and pillaging. Caracalla wanted his army to fight not for territory but for plunder. He kept them ravaging towns and villages wherever he could.[28] They destroyed everything in their path, an apocalyptic, insatiable horde of locusts, growing fat and rich off of the suffering of innocents. To keep feeding the beast, he poured every cent he could into the army. He spent and spent and spent, every payment furthering their loyalty and tightening his grip on absolute power.[29]

In 212 CE, Caracalla did the one thing historians mark as a positive for his reign.[30] Roman citizenship was a complicated institution. It carried rights with regard to property, marriage, voting, legal protection in the courts, and the ability to hold public office. At first, only free-born males from the city itself enjoyed the full benefits of citizenship, while anyone else got only partial benefits, or none at all. As Rome expanded its powers, it fought wars with ostensible allies over whether to grant them full citizenship. Roman citizenship was worth fighting for. It was much better to be a full citizen than not. Eventually, as the empire projected to its greatest extent, it was a checkerboard of who had citizenship status. With a stroke of the pen, Caracalla extended Roman citizenship to all free-born males in the empire, and all free-born women were granted the same legal status as Roman women.[31] Wherever they were and whatever their historical relationship with Rome, Caracalla extended the highest degree of legal rights and privileges to a wide swath of people living inside the empire.[32] So nice of him to be inclusive and fair-minded, right? Wrong.

Although the outcome of his edict strengthened the empire, his motive was purely self-serving. Roman citizens had to pay for all their rights through taxes. Caracalla wasn't celebrating Rome's great cultural and ethnic diversity. No, he was simply trying to increase the number of hard-working people he could fleece through his parasitic tax collectors. It all came down to pouring money back into the army.

Caracalla didn't limit his extortion to tax schemes. He was constantly on the move, visiting the provinces, checking on the frontiers, crisscrossing the empire. Naturally, as emperor, he expected to be put up in style when he paid a visit. He checked his schedule, figured out where he would be staying and when, and ordered the locals to build elaborate, opulent houses and palaces for him. The locals, already bled dry by Caracalla's insatiable taxation, scrounged every cent they could and left themselves destitute to meet his demands. And then, he would be a no-show, or only stop but very briefly.[33]

As if this wasn't bad enough, he ordered towns to construct theaters, racetracks, and stadiums in town where he might spend the winter. They needed to be ready to entertain him. Then, he'd simply change his plans and order the buildings demolished, unused.[34] If he wasn't going to enjoy them, then no one was. He didn't stop there. If, when scanning a map, Caracalla found blank spots in places he thought he might stop, he would order entire cities constructed.[35] Of course, refusal or delay in building these houses, cities, and places of entertainment was a certain death sentence. For Caracalla, these actions were less about the building projects and more about his projection of power onto the poor people who had no choice but to comply.

Caracalla was a nasty guy. He wanted people to be scared. He fed off of fear. He deliberately wore a vicious expression on his face, practicing his scowl until he found the most menacing visage.[36] The statues of him that survive are unlike any other empirical statues. Most portray emperors with a serene and wise gaze. Caracalla looks like he's trying to kill you. To be fair, if you'd lived back then, then he probably *was* trying to kill you. Like Commodus, Caracalla had no interest in intellectual pursuits. Unlike Commodus, he was intelligent and cunning, not dumb as a brick.

But he had no interest in cultivating his mind. He was a soldier, or so he thought. He did everything he could to be beloved by the troops and to be seen as one of them. He shared in the hardships of camp, their meals and rough living. To cement his place in the hearts and minds of the troops, he added his own comradeship to the big cash payments. The irony was that for all of his camp bravado, he was a subpar general.[37] He might have thought himself one of the troops, but his poor decision making and lack of tactical abilities unnecessarily endangered the lives of the men.

Perhaps if he'd spent a little more time developing his brain, he might have been a better general. However, he eschewed all intellectual efforts and focused instead on his physique. In this way, he broke with his hero, Alexander, who was insatiably curious about everything. With the absolute power of uncontested rule of the world's most powerful empire in his hands, whether or not he meant to, Caracalla skipped the preferable example of Alexander for the loathsome one of Commodus. He exercised frequently, building up his body. He put himself through vigorous workouts, honing his strength at every opportunity.[38] We can almost imagine the obnoxious guy strutting around in the gym, trying to intimidate everyone he sees. It didn't matter that he wasn't getting much done. Like Commodus, Caracalla didn't need to actually accomplish anything. He just needed to say he did. He broadcasted edicts to all corners of the empire proclaiming the runaway success of his administration.[39]

Actually being good mattered less than simply being able to say it was so. He was an accomplished propagandist. But, above all, Caracalla's true craft was death. He relied on tried-and-true ways to off people. Still, to simply say the name "Geta" was to be dead on the spot. One unlucky victim was the son of the dead emperor Pertinax. He made a clever but, in retrospect, highly costly quip about Caracalla's fratricide. It cost him his life. Father had deified and honored Pertinax. Son murdered Pertinax's son.[40] He could be awfully unimaginative, tossing out simple death sentences wherever he went. But he also found interesting and novel ways to condemn people. For example, if a magistrate was in ill health, Caracalla would "promote" him to a foreign posting in a climate that would hasten his demise.[41]

Commodus came back to haunt Caracalla. Literally. In 213 CE, Caracalla grew ill. In his stupor, he was taunted by visions of his dead predecessor. Commodus paid him a delirium-induced visit, in which the dead emperor told Caracalla to prepare for judgment before the gods.[42] Around

Caracalla wanted the whole world to know that he was not to be messed with, even practicing his scowl so he could be more menacing. *Wikimedia Commons, by Marie-Lan Nguyen (2011), CC BY 2.5.*

this same time, Caracalla seems to have become impotent.[43] He vented his fury—one could say impotent rage—in predictably awful ways. He accused some vestal virgins, the sacred virgin priestesses, of adultery and had them buried alive.[44] People entering brothels were killed, as were those accused of adultery or any sexual crimes.[45] These were not moral punishments. Their true crime was being able to, ahem, act on their sexual impulses, when Caracalla could not. To be "able," when the emperor was not, was a death sentence.

Everything was a death sentence with this guy. People had to be very careful. Caracalla would tell his advisers and retainers to meet him before dawn, then keep them waiting all day.[46] They were stuck. He would go off, doing whatever he pleased, while the administrators of the Roman Empire sat on their hands, wondering if this guy would ever show up. If they gave up and left the meeting place, and Caracalla suddenly appeared and found them gone, well, you know by now what fate likely awaited them. Caracalla went out of his way to humiliate Romans of high rank and responsibility and deliberately degraded traditional institutions. As the ranks thinned from his constant bloodletting, he replenished them, not with people of competence and experience, but with jugglers, petty merchants, and dancers.[47]

In 215 CE, Caracalla went to Alexandria, Egypt. It's impossible to overstate how important this port city was to the Romans. It funneled massive amounts of Egyptian grain to the empire and kept the Romans from starvation and rioting. The city was more than a conduit for grain. It was a wealthy, active port, generating huge volumes of commerce, as well as an artistic, religious, and intellectual hub. It was very much the second city of Rome and one of the ancient world's most important cultural centers.

The Alexandrians, like everyone else in the Roman world, were not fooled by Caracalla's claims of self-defense in the murder of Geta. They found these claims laughable, and so naturally, they laughed. The Alexandrians mocked Caracalla's claims. His visit to Alexandria was not to pay respect to the second city of the empire. His true aim was much more sinister.

Caracalla made a grand show of wanting to enroll the flower of Alexandrian youth in the Roman military juggernaut. His love and treatment of the troops was legend. Alexandrian families proudly rounded up their sons and presented them to Caracalla and his soldiers at the city walls.

But rather than evaluate these young men for lives in service of the army, they were condemned to a death at its hands. Seething over the city's mockery of him, Caracalla gave the nod, and his army pounced on the unsuspecting youth. Heavily armed, veteran Roman soldiers rushed forward against defenseless, unarmed, naive young men. It was outright slaughter.[48] The troops wielded their swords with apocalyptic precision. Thousands died in an instant.[49] But Caracalla's fury was not yet slaked. He gave the order, and his army was cut loose to savage the city.

From the temple of the chief Alexandrian god Serapis, Caracalla watched smugly as his troops desecrated the city, spreading rape, pillage, and slaughter to all corners. His troops stripped the city of all its wealth, piling up all the coins and riches into overflowing carts. They gathered more than they could carry. Rather than leave any money behind, lest the locals use it to try to fund the recovery of the city, Caracalla had the leftovers burned, the coins melted down and rendered useless.[50] As the fires his troops started were sweeping across the city founded by and named after his hero, Alexander, Caracalla called these acts rites of purification, cloaking his profane acts with a sacred veneer.[51] I doubt the Alexandrians felt closer to the gods. Well, those who were left. By the time the army hit the road and marched away, the city was in ruins, its people destitute, a whole generation of young men erased, and as many as twenty-five thousand people dead.

Caracalla seemed invincible. He was the sole, undisputed master of the Roman Empire, one of the most powerful people who had ever lived. He had cowed anyone and everyone. No one dared to speak against him, even in the privacy of their own homes. To do so could mean not only death for you, but for thousands of people around you. His army was an instrument of his will, his insane, violent, death-wielding will. They got paid two ways: from Caracalla's coffers and in the blood of their victims. The coins that fell into their outstretched, greedy hands were quite literally blood money.

Caracalla projected his power everywhere. It radiated outward and in every direction. People averted their eyes when he came by. Fear was everywhere. Caracalla placed himself at the center of the ancient world's most powerful army. These troops loved and venerated him. He paid them. He honored them. He let them do whatever they wanted. His power seemed to be unlimited. Everyone obeyed. But one woman could still issue a command that Caracalla had to obey: Mother Nature.

When you are in the constant company of someone who is a genocidal maniac, it doesn't take half a brain to realize that your time could be up at any moment. To kill such a maniac could be a proactive act of self-preservation. And that is how one of the bloodiest tyrants in Roman history met his long-overdue end. The head of Caracalla's imperial body-guard, Macrinus, got word that he might be next on the hit list. Resolving to act before Caracalla could give the word, Macrinus recruited a few conspirators and enacted his scheme. How do you kill an emperor who is surrounded by tens of thousands of fiercely loyal, violent, and ruthless soldiers? You wait for one of the few times when he would be alone and vulnerable, if only for a few seconds.

While Caracalla was marching from one place to the next, he stopped to answer nature's call. Ordering his rumbling army to take a brief pause, the emperor went down the road a few strides for a little privacy and started to relieve himself. Capitalizing on this brief moment of vulnerabil-ity, an assassin stabbed the emperor. He bled to death on the road. He was twenty-nine years old and had ruled solo for just six years.[52]

What to make of Caracalla's life and career? Clearly, he was a mur-derous lunatic who brought a reign of terror upon Rome, its enemies and allies alike. Plenty of emperors had been pretty loose with orders to kill, but Caracalla took this to a whole new level. Never before had death been so systematized. As long as the money kept flowing, his troops were more than happy to do his psychopathic bidding. He was obsessed with his own power, and those whom he didn't kill he sought to humiliate. His treatment of people, even of whole cities, ushered in a new high bar for degradation of the dignity of Roman institutions. He was as unpopular with the nobility as he was popular with the soldiers. They were, as one might imagine, furious at having their patron assassinated and the spigot of blood money turned off. As will be seen in an upcoming chapter, their loyalty to Caracalla would extend even in death. There would be grave consequences for his successor, an opportunity to manipulate the troops' anger to the advantage of one cunning noblewoman, and the entrance to the stage of one of the weirdest and worst people ever to rule.

8

THE UNHOLY PRIEST

Fortunately for everyone, absolute power doesn't come into the hands of fourteen-year-olds very often. A kid of that age hasn't had much life experience or education to rule with the nuanced perspective so important to good judgment. Wisdom, moderation, and judiciousness, ideal traits in a ruler, generally take the better part of a lifetime to cultivate. Plus, your average teenager has a lot going on . . . hormonally. All that impulsiveness, those urges, it's almost like teenagers are at the mercy of the chemical soup swirling around in their heads. Handing absolute authority to a child and all that comes with it—control over life and death, no checks on personal whims and impulses, and so forth—is a recipe for disaster.

Yes, it's a good thing that in history, such power rarely is held by those so young and unprepared. Unfortunately for the Romans trying pick up the pieces in the aftermath of Caracalla, a fourteen-year-old emperor is what they got. No one could have predicted what was to follow. Before we get to know the kid, we need to understand the events that led the Romans to hand him the keys to the kingdom and to meet the person behind the scenes who made it all happen.

Macrinus did the whole world a favor when he offed the genocidal Caracalla in April of 217 CE. Depending on your point of view, that is. If you were a Roman noble, a senator, a member of the administration, a governor, or even a rank-and-file everyday citizen, basically anyone but a soldier, then you were better off with Caracalla dead. But if you were a soldier, this was not exactly an ideal turn of events. Caracalla had doted on the troops, making them rich. When their patron died, so, too, did their cash cow. They seethed but waited to see what the new guy would do with his office. Maybe he would continue Caracalla's generosity. After all, angering all the guys with the swords was never a good idea.

Macrinus had a lot of work to do. Following Caracalla onto the throne meant things were in shambles. The empire was broke, its institutions fractured, and it was at war on several fronts. He sought to pick up the pieces, but bringing order back to the Roman Empire would take a lot of blood, sweat, and tears. The blood would be forthcoming. Unfortunately, for Macrinus, the blood would be his own.

Upon taking office, Macrinus did not indulge in a bloody purge of the prior administration. Neither officials nor relatives of the dead Caracalla were visited by imperial executioners. Macrinus also sought the consent of the Senate to rule, paying homage to the nobility. He sent them a letter full of vows and promises, stating, "It is my intention to do nothing without your approval."[1] He promised them a restoration of their rights and honors. Although they were certainly glad to hear it, mostly they were just relieved that Caracalla was gone.[2]

Caracalla's mother, Julia Domna, died shortly after her son, apparently from suicide.[3] Domna's story was larger than life. Tracked down by an aspirant to the throne for her beauty and ties to local royalty, she became empress of Rome. Both her sons had been emperors. One murdered the other, only to be murdered himself a few years later. Left without immediate family and in failing health, Domna took her own life. She left behind more than an incredible story; she had a sister, Julia Maesa, who was ready to make her mark on the world.

Upon Macrinus's accession, Maesa had been sent away from the imperial court at the key city of Antioch. However, trying to prove what a nice guy he was, he left her in possession of the considerable fortune that she had amassed in her twenty years as a member of the imperial family.[4] She packed up, gathered her fortune, and left Antioch, making her way to the family's home base, the Syrian city of Emesa. This intact fortune was the root of Macrinus's downfall.

Macrinus was trying to put out fires everywhere. He blundered badly when he kept the core of Caracalla's army together up on the eastern border over the first (and only) winter of his rule. The army, comfy amid all the eastern luxury, got to talking. We can imagine them saying things such as, "Remember the good old days of Caracalla? When all we had to do was to not kill him and pretend he was one of us, and he would give us piles of cash? That was the best."[5] Macrinus had cut down their patron but left them together as a unit. He should have broken up this army and spread the troops all over the empire. That way, they couldn't feed off of one another's disaffection. But he didn't. Distracted by other matters, Macrinus left Caracalla's favorite army together to while away the winter season in idle luxury. As if this wasn't bad enough, the chosen city for their winter quarters was none other than Emesa, home of Julia Maesa.

Maesa got word of their grumblings and began to scheme. She had two grandsons who could be her path back to rule. This time not as sister-in-law to the emperor, but as regent, using her grandsons as her tools to be the ultimate power broker. Besides, what good is a huge pile of cash if you don't use it to bribe an army? Having Caracalla's loyal army delivered to the city of her exile, almost exactly on her doorstep, was a coincidence too good to pass up. Or perhaps a sign of divine favor. But how to make her move?

The troops began to notice that the young priest of a local god called Elagabalus bore an uncanny resemblance to their beloved Caracalla. He might have; the young teenager was Caracalla's cousin, Maesa's older grandson. This, she knew, was her ticket back to the big time. Maesa began to take the boy around the soldiers' camp, showing him off, playing up the resemblance, and claiming that he was Caracalla's natural son.[6] If true, then the troops would see the boy as Caracalla's rightful successor. If not, then, well, who cared? Maesa was there to shove fistfuls of coin on the troops to make sure everyone saw things her way.[7] Her machinations did the trick, and the troops declared for the teenager and rebelled against Macrinus.[8]

At first, Macrinus didn't take the revolt too seriously.[9] But when he finally realized the severity of the rebellion, Macrinus scrambled to quell the revolt. He gathered up his own army and marched them toward a confrontation. When the big moment arrived, Macrinus failed to inspire his own troops. Swayed by the prospect of another Severan on the throne, Macrinus's men deserted him and flocked to the pretended son of Caracalla. Inevitably, Macrinus was killed, as was his nine-year-old son, whom he had elevated to co-emperor, thus saving all but the biggest history geeks from having to remember the name of Emperor Diadumenianus.[10] The army was elated. Another member of the House of Severus was back on the throne. This time, though, they would come to regret their actions. In this regret, the army and the people of Rome would be united.

At this point, you're probably wondering what any of this has to do with the awfulness of any ruler. So far, we've talked about Macrinus and Julia Maesa, but not the terrible deeds of an awful ruler. But as the fourteen-year-old Elagabalus is set to make his entry into the story, it's impossible to overstate just how much his grandmother facilitated his rise. Don't worry. From here on, we will get to know Elagabalus really well. Incidentally, Elagabalus was the name of the sun god for whom he served as a priest in Emesa. It's also the name by which the young man is referred. Of course, he took a proper empirical name upon his elevation, one befitting an emperor: Imperator Caesar Marcus Aurelius Antoninus Augustus. But Elagabalus would do nothing to honor all of the illustrious predecessors included in his regal name. He would disgrace all of them, the empire, and the institutions they fought so hard to build and maintain. To many Romans, his rule was a declaration of war on all the things the Romans held dear.

Normally, a claimant to the throne would at least give the Senate the opportunity to go through the charade of "selecting" the emperor. Elagabalus got off to a bad start with the elites back in the capital by simply announcing himself their lord and master.[11] His grandmother Maesa, who had done so much to secure his rule, urged him to begin by adopting Roman dress and manners. The people would be more likely to accept him if they saw in him a continuation of tradition. But eschewing her advice, he draped himself in the finest silk clothes, claiming that the traditional Roman wool was cheap.[12]

He also commissioned a massive portrait of himself, serving as priest to his beloved sun god, and had it shipped to Rome. If anyone was missing the point of who was in charge now, Elagabalus instructed that the portrait be hung in the most prominent spot in the Senate House.[13] Both he and his god were in charge now, Elagabalus the emperor in the temporal realm and Elagabalus the god in the spiritual one. If people were looking for indications that the teenage boy from the east would respect Roman tradition, these were very discouraging signs, and just the tip of the iceberg. Before making his way to the capital, Elagabalus set about to consolidate power.

Unlike Macrinus, who kept an eye on stability of the empire and retained people with skill and experience, Elagabalus demonstrated no such moderation. Regardless of the consequences to the empire, Elagabalus coolly had the associates of his predecessor killed for no reason other than their service under the prior administration.[14] Where Macrinus had had members of the royal family sent into dignified exile, Elagabalus had Macrinus's young son put to the sword. Macrinus had barely enough time as emperor for people to form an opinion about his abilities. Historians don't portray them as either great or terrible. But they all agree that the transition from him to Elagabalus spelled disaster for the Romans.

While Elagabalus systematically murdered Macrinus's advisers, he kept an eye out, or more precisely, an ear out, for declarations of loyalty. He demanded recognition from everyone that he was the rightful and true emperor. Those who failed to make such a declaration immediately were viewed with hostile suspicion and liable to find themselves dead before they knew what happened.[15]

In Elagabalus's initial purge, one guy died for giving a lavish gift to his mistress. He had a plate with his likeness gilded and gave it to her. Word got to Elagabalus, and he flew into a rage. He claimed that he was angry because this guy must be planning a revolt. Why else would he have made golden images of himself? It seems more likely that Elagabalus was infuriated that anyone else would be portrayed in such expensive, divine golden imagery, a right he wanted to claim exclusively for himself. Whatever the true reason of his anger, the result was the same. The poor fellow was dragged off for an appointment with the imperial killing squads.[16] No record describes the fate of the mistress, or, for that matter, the plate.

Generals were put to death simply for being competent. If they were competent, then they could lead a rebellion. If they could lead a rebellion, then they had to be killed preemptively.[17] Intention didn't matter. Loyalty didn't matter. What mattered was the sheer possibility that someone *might* develop disloyalty. People were killed simply for being good at their jobs. In fact, people were killed for all kinds of reasons. Or for no real reason at all.[18] It could have been Maesa orchestrating the purge, systematically eliminating anyone she saw as a threat to her family. Or it could have been Elagabalus, fourteen years old, invested with power he was way too immature to properly wield. It mattered little to the soldiers, senators, nobles, and administrators who died by the score in the spasm of violence.

The motivations for the killing went beyond clearing the path of enemies—real or imagined—of the new regime. One man found himself
summoned to the emperor, denounced for disloyalty, and killed. The
reason? He had an attractive wife, and the lusty teenage Elagabalus cov-
eted her. He forbade her to grieve and, instead, took her for himself.[19] It
didn't last long. As time would tell, he would marry and divorce so
often—both men and women—that it's nearly impossible to say how
many marriages he had.

Before Elagabalus even entered Rome, he had overseen widespread
violence and bloodshed and sown the seeds of discord in the hearts and
minds of the people he intended to rule. Once he got there, things would
shift from bloody to downright bizarre.

Elagabalus took his sweet time making his way from Emesa to Rome.
His entourage partied all the way, getting used to the newfound trappings
of luxury.[20] When he finally made his grand entrance into Rome, the
citizens were aghast. They had never seen anything like what now
streamed past their eyes. The teenage emperor wore long, flowing silk
and golden robes, necklaces, bracelets, and a tiara. He was covered in
gemstones from head to foot. He wore makeup, sporting eyeliner and
rouge on his cheeks. Roman emperors traditionally presented themselves
as conquering generals. Even those with little to no military experience
portrayed an image of manly, martial prowess. Now here comes this
weird kid from the hinterlands, dressed in what to Romans seemed to be
the height of effeminacy.

Elagabalus brought more than unorthodox fashion sense back to the
seat of the empire. His arrival marked the advent of a new level of
depravity and debauchery. Ironically, he would cloak his actions in a veil
of religious piety. As the priest of the local sun god from Emesa, he
worshipped a black, conical stone. This cult object had allegedly fallen
from heaven to bring divine favor to Earth, and Elagabalus believed that
it was responsible for his elevation.[21] This stone was the earthly embodi-
ment of the god of Elagabalus. This god, and the gods of the Roman
pantheon, were about to wage their own war for spiritual supremacy.

The Romans were very serious about their religion. The gods were a
presence in everyday life. The city was full of temples, to the principal
gods, Jupiter, Juno, Mars, Minerva, and so forth. The remains of the
soaring temples to these gods still impress. Rome also had a dizzying
array of lesser and local deities with their own temples, local altars, and

household shrines. Consider Terminus, god of boundaries; Averruncus, god of averting disaster; and Pilumnus, god of protecting infants at birth. You name it: the Romans had a god for it. And now, this teenage weirdo shows up with a black stone, and everyone is supposed to be awed and to offer supplication?

Elagabalus wasted little time in placing his god atop the Roman pantheon. He immediately ordered the construction of a massive new temple complex to give his god a proper home. While this construction project got under way, Elagabalus got to work on his own project: he sought to subjugate Roman gods to his own, degrading temples, demoting gods, and generally giving the middle finger (or whatever was the Roman equivalent) to the Roman religion. [22] He set up his god for adoration in the heart of the city. For the pious, god-fearing Romans, this was an invitation to disaster. We can only wonder if invocations to Averruncus shot through the roof.

Then Elagabalus took things one step further. He compelled army officers and civil officials to come forward. Reluctantly, they offered the weird black stone their best wishes. [23] It's easy to imagine them thinking "Forgive me, Jupiter!" in their heads as they committed this forced sacrilege. Those who kept such thoughts to themselves were fine. Some were not so discreet with their opinions, making fun of the strange ways and religion of the new emperor. Showing that his age did not mitigate the streak of cruelty that ran through the Severan family, Elagabalus had those who dared mock him rounded up and executed, confiscating their wealth for good measure. [24]

As he waged his war on Rome's spiritual values, he settled into a rule of depraved hedonism. Elagabalus threw himself into pleasure with reckless abandon. [25] He cast about the empire for the most well-endowed men and had them sent to him for his pleasure. [26] To these men, he lavished countless expensive gifts, draining the resources of state. [27] To some he gave high office.

The kid had absurdly expensive, often bizarre taste. He demanded only the best, most expensive furniture, gilding some of his pieces and casting others in solid silver. He only swam in perfumed pools. He had everything covered in jewels: his clothes, his hair, his shoes, his chariot. When riding in public, Elagabalus liked to have his chariot pulled not by horses, but by beautiful, naked women. [28] His extravagance was more than a snub to Roman tradition; it was expensive. To fund his decadent and bizarre lifestyle, Elagabalus needed cash. He turned to the old play-book: selling offices to the highest bidder.[29] The upper ranks of the Roman administration were increasingly populated by men with either big penises or huge checkbooks.

Elagabalus also began to appoint his friends and entertainers to offices. Charioteers, actors, and performers enjoyed his imperial patronage as a reward for their skills as entertainers.[30] Elagabalus prioritized an unusual set of criteria when naming people guardians and administrators of the empire.

He was just a teenager, but he indulged in food, wine, and, above all, sex, like no Romans could recall in their lifetimes. Elagabalus slept with everyone he could, man and woman alike. He took a series of wives in rapid succession, marrying and divorcing with dizzying rapidity. At one point, he married a man, and then declared himself to be not emperor, but empress. To the Romans, this was not socially progressive. This was a shocking violation of social norms. It wasn't so much the sexual relationship between two men. This was not uncommon in Rome. It was the adoption of the female role in the relationship, which was assumed to be subservient. He was an emperor! He was supposed to be the height of manly vigor. Virile, martial, aggressive, and daring. The soldiers who had placed him on the throne were disgusted.[31] You did *not* want to be on the soldiers' bad side. As discontent mounted, Elagabalus slept around with reckless abandon.

Genitals were an ongoing subject of obsession with Elagabalus. He wished to cut off his own but was either dissuaded from doing so or simply couldn't go through with it.[32] Instead, in an act of religious piety to his god, Elagabalus had himself circumcised. It was probably painful to endure as a teenager, but at least he was the one making the choice. Elagabalus being Elagabalus, he went a step too far and commanded that his retainers and companions endure the same procedure.[33] In another bizarre act, he locked a lion, a monkey, and a snake in the temple of his god and threw in offerings of mutilated human genitals.[34]

His sexual antics were more than just so much personal depravity. They were also horrifying and sacrilegious. Obsessed with elevating his god over the rest of the Roman pantheon, Elagabalus raped the head priestess of the vestal virgins—the sacred priestesses of the goddess of hearth and home, Vesta. He tried to justify his actions to the horrified

When reading the stories of Elagabalus, it's easy to forget that he was a teenager when he was dragged from his priesthood in Syria and made emperor in Rome. Maybe the pressure was too much, perhaps the stories are embellished by moralizing historians, or perhaps bad things happen when you give unfettered power to a teenager with raging hormones. *Wikimedia Commons, by José Luiz Bernardes Ribeiro, CC BY-SA 4.0.*

Roman people by saying, "I did it in order that godlike children might spring from me—the high priest, and her—the high priestess."[35]

Elagabalus decided that his god needed to get hitched and looked around for an appropriate match. He first settled on the goddess Pallas. The statue of this goddess, so the Romans believed, came all the way from Troy and was among the most sacred and protected objects of pious veneration.[36] But Pallas was a warrior goddess, which offended Elagabalus's grotesque sensuality. He banished Pallas and cast around for a better match for his god. He struck upon a Carthaginian moon goddess, Urania.[37] After all, who would be a better mate for the sun than the moon? He commanded that the statue of the goddess be transported to Rome, along with all the gold from her temple. He further demanded that huge amounts of additional money be gathered up from her home territory and sent as a dowry.[38] Elagabalus was forcing people into financial and spiritual bankruptcy.

Always up for an extravagant party, he offered shocking amounts of wine, animal, and incense sacrifices to his god. Countless cattle and sheep were slaughtered in homage. He had the best wines brought forward and poured out as libations. Blood and wine swirled together as Elagabalus delighted.[39] He and his retainers performed sensual singing and dancing while stoic Romans looked on in disbelief.[40]

Elagabalus's so-called religious fervor devolved into downright savagery. Ensuring that his god had all of the best sacrificial victims, Elagabalus had young children offered as human sacrifice.[41] He believed that the greater the suffering the sacrifice caused, the more favor he would curry with his god. As such, he ordered that the most beautiful children from Italy's noble families be sent to Rome to be offered up. He commanded that only children with two living parents be sent, to maximize the amount of pain the loss caused.[42]

Amid all this excitement, Elagabalus's new temple complex was completed. He needed to move his god into his new home and ordered the citizens to help make the move in style. When bringing his god to the temple, Elagabalus made a grand show of adoring and honoring the stone. He placed it in a magnificent chariot and walked before it, walking backward so that his eyes would never have to leave the sacred stone. The chariot, adorned with gemstones, was pulled by six white horses. Gold dust was sprinkled in front of the chariot to glorify the path.[43] Elagabalus made the people run alongside him, carrying torches and showering him with flowers and adorning the path with wreaths.[44]

Elagabalus wanted his god to take up residence in style. Once accomplished, he set to prove to the people his generosity. He climbed to the top of a tower and showered gold and silver cups down on the people. As the crowd surged to snatch up the precious vessels, he switched to the finest clothes and linens. With the crowd at a fever pitch, he began to toss down animals and livestock.[45] What started as a chance to grab a gift from the emperor turned into a struggle for life, as people sought to avoid being trampled. The festival turned into a riot as frantic citizens surged this way and that. To keep the crowd in line, Elagabalus's soldiers began to use their spears to deadly effect, cutting down the mob. The religious festival turned into a killing spree. Between those trampled and those cut down by soldiers, numerous Romans lost their lives. Elagabalus looked on with delight. He danced atop his tower while his citizens battled for life.

As the disaffection continued to mount, Elagabalus kept indulging in sexual depravity of all kinds. Aside from run-of-the-mill promiscuity, which he certainly elevated to new levels, the lusty young emperor invented new ways to satisfy his insatiable need for lovers. He dressed in drag and went out into the streets. Stopping in brothels, he drove away the female prostitutes and plied the trade in their place. He also stood naked in a doorway of his own imperial palace, calling on passersby to come in off the street for a tryst with the emperor.[46] It's one thing to be a horny teenager. It's another thing entirely to violate the dignity of the office.

Not just his sexual proclivities shocked his contemporaries. Everything he did was strange. His dining preferences were certainly unorthodox. He would only eat seafood when he was far from the sea.[47] He ate strange, expensive, or difficult-to-acquire foods such as cocks' comb, but only when cut from a living bird, of course, or peacock tongue, or the heel of a camel.[48] He even fed his pets exotic foods, giving goose liver to his dogs, the finest grapes to his horses, and parrots to his lions.[49]

Elagabalus commanded chefs to prepare new and exotic sauces. If he liked the results, he would offer rewards to the inventor. But if he didn't, then Elagabalus would order the chef imprisoned and forced to only eat the subpar sauce until he could invent something more palatable to the emperor.

Often, he commanded that the colors of all the food match. Meals were blue, green, yellow, and so forth. A different color for every day, for an entire summer.[50] He had serving pieces carved with lewd images to tickle his delights and shock his companions.[51] To ensure that he, as his god's earthy representative, was eating the food appropriate to the divine, Elagabalus commanded that gold and pearl dust be mixed into his food.[52]

But if his food preferences were strange, then his behavior *at* meals was downright bizarre. Sometimes, he would be the only one at a banquet who ate. While he was served all of the delicacies, his guests were served copies made of wax, wood, or ivory. At other times, while his courses were being served, his guests would receive paintings or embroidered representations of what he was eating.[53] They could only look on while he gorged himself.

To be his guest at dinner was to be subject to serious violations of privacy, even by Roman standards. Elagabalus would invite nobles to dinner and grill them about their sex lives and sexual preferences. He would go into great and graphic detail about his own exploits.[54] He frequently made obscene hand gestures throughout the course of his meals, a behavior he repeated when out among the people.[55]

On some occasions, Elagabalus seemed outwardly generous. At his dinner parties, Elagabalus would have drawings to determine which gifts he would bestow upon his dining companions. Some lucky people would win objects of great value, such as four-horse chariots, servants, gold, and silver. But some would receive from the emperor corpses of dead dogs, or a jar of flies.[56] One time, he stepped out of the dining room and barred the doors behind him, leaving his guests to wonder what scheme had had concocted for his enjoyment. His retainers began pouring violets from the ceiling above. The diners were probably amused at first. But then the flowers just kept coming and coming and coming. He had so many flowers rain down on his guests that some suffocated to death. That's a *lot* of flowers. What a way to go.[57]

His antics were not just reserved for his dinner guests. Elagabalus had snakes gathered up and unleashed on the people. One summer, deciding he wanted a reprieve from the heat, Elagabalus had carts of snow loaded up from the higher altitudes and carted to Rome so that he could enjoy a mountain of snow in the middle of the city.[58] Once, to degrade his slaves, he commanded that they gather up and bring him a thousand pounds of spiderwebs.[59]

Julia Maesa, Elagabalus's grandmother, watched with increasing horror at the monster she'd created. Ever calculating, she started to hedge her

A dinner invitation to join Elagabalus was a fraught proposition. On a good day, you could get wood painted to look like food. On a bad day, you could be suffocated by flower petals. *Wikimedia Commons.*

bet. She convinced Elagabalus to adopt her other grandson, his cousin Alexander.[60] Alexander was a very different person than his older cousin. Although only ten at the time of his cousin's elevation, he was from the start studious, serious, and mature beyond his years. As more and more Romans got a look at the character of Elagabalus, the contrast between the cousins, turned father and son, could not have been starker. The serious Alexander soared in popularity.

Elagabalus had his own plans for shoring up his imperial position. At this point in Roman history, to be the senior emperor was to be "Augustus," and to be a junior emperor or designated heir was to be "Caesar." Elagabalus tried to promote his favorite male love to Caesar. Julia Maesa was adamantly opposed, and she managed to thwart the scheme. This would have sent people over the edge, and the full, stark realization that she might lose her grip on power set in. Eventually Elagabalus's histrionics would get him killed. Without a backup plan, she would be out again and this time, the successor would likely not be so kind to the House of Severus. She kicked up her scheming against Elagabalus with a mind toward protecting her own power.[61]

Elagabalus grew jealous and paranoid. He wanted to kill his young cousin-turned-son, sensing a threat to his own rule. He plotted and schemed for different ways to eliminate Alexander, but Elagabalus couldn't keep his mouth shut and kept revealing the details of the various plots.[62] This had two effects. First, it gave Alexander plenty of time to protect himself. Second, it spread the word far and wide that Elagabalus was plotting against his very popular adopted son. This was bad news for Elagabalus, who was already unpopular with the guys with the pointy swords. Julia Maesa, however, sensed opportunity. If she could betray Elagabalus in favor of Alexander, she could ensure her hand in the succession and continue to sit at the center of imperial power. Ever the opportunist, she began her scheming.

Sure enough, with Maesa's encouragement, Elagabalus's Praetorian guards did everyone a favor and dispatched him to the afterlife. Well, everyone but Elagabalus. When word leaked out that they were hunting for him, the still teenage boy-emperor fled for his life. Determined to find their quarry, the troops found Elagabalus cowering in a latrine. They quickly cut him down. Venting their rage, they mutilated his corpse and dragged it through the streets. The troops' fury raged on all day, as they stuffed the dead emperor's body in and out of sewers, covering it with the filth they saw as appropriate. Eventually, they took his body to a bridge and tossed it into the Tiber. He was eighteen years old.

As the lifeless body of Elagabalus floated down the river, the soldiers surrounded the popular Alexander and proclaimed him emperor. Alexander was now the same age Elagabalus had been at the time of his accession, fourteen. They may have shared age and the family name, but the similarities ended there. In stark contrast to Elagabalus, Alexander, was serious, committed to solid policy, good governance, and moderate behavior. Well, they had one more common denominator: their grandmother. Maesa had sacrificed one grandson so that the other could rule, thus keeping herself as the central power broker in Rome. The Severans were getting one more shot at power. Time would tell how it would turn out.

9

THE GIANT

After Elagabalus was dispatched to the afterlife, the Severan dynasty got one more crack at power. It's fair to wonder why. Septimius Severus was competent but ruthless and autocratic, more of a military dictator than an emperor in the traditional sense. Then Caracalla took over, once he brutally murdered his brother, that is. And things only went downhill from there. Elagabalus had his run of lunacy in the big chair. Each Severan rule was worse than the one before it. And yet, another young Severan teenage prince was elevated to the role of emperor.

Alexander Severus was Elagabalus's cousin. But aside from their precocious age and kinship, the two could not have been more dissimilar. Alexander was studious and driven by an innate sense of responsibility. He was young on his elevation, about fourteen years old, but was surrounded by good administrators. His grandmother and mother exercised considerable power as regents. That these women had control over the young emperor may have miffed a few snobs in Rome's paternalistic society, but Alexander's administration was more efficient and less corrupt than the one that proceeded it. It was certainly more rational.

Things went more or less OK. As Alexander grew up, he grew into his role. As so often happened, Rome got entangled in wars against its great rival, the Sassanid Empire (think: Persians) and the great thorn in its side, Germanic tribes. His armies held up against the Sassanids, but when he eschewed open warfare with the Germans and opted for peace through diplomacy, his troops were disgusted. They saw Alexander as weak and vacillating. Rather than accept that the empire was stretched to its limits,

the troops rose up and killed him and his mother. With the soldiers playing kingmaker, they picked one of their own. Alexander had been a
decent emperor. He had reversed the trend of the Severans and had restored a measure of prestige to the dynasty and the family legacy. Although he didn't bring Rome back to the peak of its glory—that goal was
unattainable—he and his advisers had done a competent job at a time of
great instability.

And now, like so many previous emperors, he was dead. Assassinated
because someone with access to power thought he could do better, or
simply was lured by all the trappings of power. Given all that Alexander
and company had accomplished over the previous decade plus, the new
guy had big shoes to fill. But he just might have had the biggest shoes of
any emperor ever. You see, Maximinus Thrax was physically huge, a true
giant, an outsized man for an outsized job.

His path to power was as unlikely as any that had come before. Hail-
ing from Thrace on the fringes of the empire (thus the name Thrax, which
sounds super cool but simply means Thracian), Maximinus grew up as far
from the inner circle of imperial power as possible. Caracalla's edict of
citizenship might have granted him that status, but to the people in
Rome's snobby upper classes, Maximinus and everybody like him would
have been nothing more than uncouth barbarians. But his physical stature
created opportunity that he exploited to the fullest. Maximinus was of
gigantic proportions. Exactly how big is a matter of debate and impossible to know. One history puts him at more than eight feet tall.[1] This
seems unlikely, but no matter what, no one debates that he was head and
shoulders above everyone else in height and strength. He is said to have
drunk seven gallons of wine and eaten forty pounds of meat at a time.[2] He
could pull a fully loaded cart by himself. He could snap trees in half and
crush stones with his bare hands.[3]

It was his size that set him on his unlikely path to power. He came to
the attention of Septimius Severus during games thrown in honor of his
up-and-coming son Geta. (Remember poor Geta? He had a bright future
once.) Maximinus showed up and challenged anyone to best him in a
fight. None could. Not even a dozen at a time.[4] The hulking giant bested
all comers, and Septimius Severus, duly impressed, fast-tracked Maximinus's career. He began to work his way up the ranks. By the time Alexander Severus had been on the throne for a dozen years, Maximinus was a
general, widely respected by his troops. But his career hadn't been

The giant **Maximinus Thrax** towered over everyone. His bloody, autocratic rule ended when his troops turned against him, and his death plunged Rome into the Crisis of the Third Century. *Wikimedia Commons.*

smooth. He had a hard time shaking off the perception of barbarism that followed him everywhere.

Some people held out a hand to Maximinus on his ascent, whereas others showed him contempt. He seethed when he thought about his treatment at the hands of snobby nobles. When Maximinus paid them calls, he had been left waiting at the door, treated contemptuously, and then turned away by their slaves.[5] Remembering these instances filled him with embarrassed rage. He wanted revenge. All he needed was power. He got it when the troops offed poor Alexander and proclaimed their general Maximinus emperor. For the first time, a common soldier had risen through the ranks to become ruler of the empire.[6]

His first order of business was to distance himself from the past that had caused him so much embarrassment. He sought out anyone who had given him grief in his "barbarian" days. He had them all killed. Then he found all the people who had helped him along the way. He had them killed, too.[7] Friend and foe alike. He tracked down childhood friends who could attest to his roots and had them put to the sword.[8] Anyone who knew his true origins was targeted. Simply to know where the emperor had come from was a death sentence. With his massive hands firmly grasping unrestrained power, he killed anyone and everyone who knew his backstory. He used the blood of friend and foe alike to wash the slate clean.

He then looked around at Alexander's advisers and staff. He had known and worked with many of these people in his capacity, so he knew which ones had talent. Generally, Alexander's administration was efficient and honest, so Maximinus only dismissed a few. The rest he killed.[9] Simply having been associated with the prior administration was enough to send people fleeing for their lives, or to an early grave. Maximinus cared little for talent, administrative ability, or knowledge transfer from one administration to the next. The stability of the empire had been tenuous at best. Alexander Severus had taken difficult but important strides in bringing some semblance of order back to the Roman world. Maximinus sought out all the people who had played a hand in this challenging and important accomplishment and removed them from the picture, one by one.

Maximinus made haste to use another play in the tyrant's playbook. He "discovered" a conspiracy against his life and used it as an opportunity to eliminate a talented, charismatic contemporary. A senator named

Magnus was accused of plotting a coup. Without trial, witnesses, or evidence, Magnus was butchered. His supporters and adherents were granted leave and sent away from the army.

Oh, no, wait. They were killed by the thousands: four thousand, to be more precise. Whether or not they'd actually had any association with Magnus, simply being suspect was a death sentence.[10] The corpses piled up as Maximinus watched with smug satisfaction. This did little to endear Maximinus to the senators and the nobility. So far, he had done nothing to disprove their judgment of him as a savage barbarian. Not that he cared a bit what they thought. Or did he? By deliberately defiling the nobility and the administrative classes, Maximinus was proving that no matter how huge he might have been, he had remarkably thin skin. For a big guy, he sure was overly sensitive.

With his boulder-crushing hands firmly grasping the reins of power, Maximinus squeezed tight. He lavished bonuses on his army, of course.[11] In this, he wasn't particularly innovative. Giving cash to the troops, Praetorians and common soldiers alike, had become the industry standard. Time would tell if they would have the same loyalty and love for him that they'd had for Caracalla.

With the obligatory reward/loyalty bribe paid to the troops, Maximinus unleashed a horde of spies and informants, who fanned out across the empire to sow the seeds of fear and recrimination. It did not take long for this atmosphere of suspicion to spread across the empire, and with no one to stand in his way, Maximinus exacted his revenge on the nobility. He had enemies seized and sewed into the hides of dead animals. He had them torn apart by wild beasts. He had them bludgeoned to death.[12] Maximinus would not let anyone of noble birth or accomplishment near him.[13] He didn't want to be reminded of his origins. Surely they were OK with this arrangement, as it slightly increased their chances of survival.

To the rank-and-file Roman citizen, Maximinus's war on nobility didn't mean all that much.[14] Who cares if some rich snobs get their comeuppance? They started to care when Maximinus unleashed his army on the people. He ordered his troops to loot towns, strip temples, and melt statues of gods, heroes, and emperors, all to raise money to pay the troops. Keep in mind, these were *Roman* towns. When people rose up in protest, Maximinus had them massacred.[15] His army began to sour at these kinds of orders. It was one thing to savage a Germanic village. It was another thing entirely to attack your own kin.[16] Nevertheless, his wholesale confiscation of wealth continued. His spies and informants "uncovered" sedition, and the "guilty" parties had their estates and assets seized to feed the army behemoth.[17]

In addition to murdering Roman nobles and attacking Roman cities, Maximinus certainly did his fair share of savaging Germanic villages. Where Alexander favored diplomacy, Maximinus set out to prove himself in war.[18] Maximinus sent armies out in all directions, fighting anyone and everyone they could. He devastated German towns, fighting gruesome campaigns of total war. His troops destroyed crops in the fields.[19] He burned villages and towns to the ground, leaving the local population homeless, starving, and destitute.[20] It must be said: the guy was undoubtedly brave. He personally led charges and rallied his troops when their courage flagged. After one notable victory, he commissioned giant paintings of his exploits and sent them to Rome to be set up outside the Senate House, just to remind those snobs how awesome he was.[21]

Predictably, though, the Senate and nobility grew tired of Maximinus's histrionics, and revolts sprang up, far off in the provinces and in the Italian homeland alike. A series of claimants took their turn congratulating themselves on being emperor. Not for nothing is the year 238 CE known as the Year of Six Emperors. When word of the rebellions reached Maximinus, he flew into such a violent rage that everyone fled as he threatened to kill everyone in sight, even his own son.[22] When his boiling rage settled into smoldering fury, Maximinus turned his army south, intent on marching on Rome and taking his vengeance directly on the Senate. He would put those priggish bastards in their place once and for all.

The first city he came to in Italy was Aquileia (somewhat near modern-day Venice). Knowledge of his savagery fortified the resolve of the citizens. They closed the city gates and prepared for a long siege.[23] Fate had other plans, as disease and famine quickly swept through the army.[24] The troops, fully aware of Maximinus's legendary temper, knew that he wouldn't take kindly to their lack of progress, endangering their lives.[25] All the cash donatives in the world couldn't win them over if they didn't trust him to honor the relationship. With Caracalla, they knew that he vowed to "honor the troops." With Maximinus, the troops were not quite so sure. If he could threaten to kill his own son, then any one of them could find their lives forfeited. Besides, ravaging Germans was one thing. The constant warfare on fellow Romans was another. They'd had enough.

Certainly some other grasping autocrat would follow and heap cash upon them.

Accordingly, Maximinus's troops turned on him, just as they had on Severus Alexander, Elagabalus, Commodus, and so many more. In their camp outside the gates of Aquileia, the emperor's bodyguards murdered him and his son, impaled their heads on stakes, and waved them in front of the walls for the citizens of Aquileia to see, much to the relief of the besieged citizens.[26] The gates of the city were thrown open, the soldiers were welcomed in, fed, and cared for. In no time at all, the mood shifted from tense and fearful to a party atmosphere. In death, Maximinus brought Romans back together, creating a sense of common purpose and shared identity that he could not accomplish while among the living.

The Senate and nobility breathed a big sigh of relief. The man who had spent so much energy attacking them was dead. Unfortunately for them, and for all of Rome, the trouble was only beginning.

With the death of Maximinus, the Roman Empire tumbled headlong into the period known as the Crisis of the Third Century. The next fifty or so years would be very rocky indeed. This time also marks the transition to the period known as the dominate, when Rome became a true military dictatorship. Although Maximinus was the first soldier to rise through the ranks to become emperor, he certainly wouldn't be the last. Fortunately for Rome, at this point, some of the most talented and competent rulers are still in its future, but, unfortunately, some bad ones, too. The fun wasn't over just yet.

(DIS)HONORABLE MENTION #3: THE PRAGMATIST

As rebellious soldiers kept plunging knife after knife into emperor after emperor, the empire itself plunged deeper and deeper into chaos. When poor Alexander Severus was offed by the oafish giant Maximinus Thrax, all hell broke loose. Alexander had ruled for thirteen years and was just twenty-seven at his death. His studious, responsible administration was replaced by a succession of emperors more concerned with killing rivals and claiming power for its own sake than in wisely and justly guiding the ship of state. In the roughly fifty years following Alexander's death, a dizzying array of pretenders and claimants rose so fast that it's nearly impossible to keep track of them all. In that time, at least twenty-six different people claimed the throne. Most met violent deaths, not at the hands of a foreign enemy but as part of a palace conspiracy. Few ruled for years. Many ruled for months. Some ruled for days.

Barbarian hordes invaded. Italy itself was invaded. The city of Rome was threatened for the first time in centuries. Civil wars raged. The empire was locked in a life-and-death struggle for survival, while piles of claimants for the throne vied for the chance to be the next one to be assassinated.

While various rivals plotted and schemed against one another, the empire shattered. Taking advantage of the chaos gripping the empire, a client kingdom of Rome got tired of being subservient. Queen Zenobia of Palmyra decided to throw off the yoke, rebelled against Rome, and set up her own empire. The emperor Aurelian had taken over in 270 CE. After putting down the barbarian threat, he next resolved to break the Palmyrene rebellion. He marched his armies to the scene, annihilated the upstarts, and brought Palmyra to heel.[27]

Back in 260 CE, a general named Postumus had gone rogue, seized western territory, including much of modern-day France and England, and set up shop as an independent empire.[28] Attempts to unseat him were halfhearted and unsuccessful until two things happened. First, Postumus was challenged, of course, by a less talented but more ambitious rival who wanted control of the renegade kingdom. This kicked off a chain of events that led to his own assassination.[29] Second, Aurelian showed up and smashed the so-called Gallic Empire into submission. In his five-year reign, Aurelian drove off and defeated barbarian hordes and reconquered not one but two breakaway kingdoms. For his trouble, Aurelian was hailed as Restitutor Pactor Orbis, or Restorer and Pacifier of the World, and Deo et Domino Nato, or Born God and Master.[30] As mentioned in the chapter on the Praetorian Guards, he was, of course, assassinated.

Aurelian was one of a series of talented but short-lived emperors whose energy and drive slowly reversed the fortunes of the crumbling empire. But they were not yet out of the woods. Following Aurelian's assassination in 275 CE, the merry-go-round of emperors, rivals, and civil war continued. That is, until a cavalry commander with a decidedly Greek name made his move.

Diocles had risen through the officer corps to gain a senior military position. But he owed his success less to martial prowess and more to organizational genius. Diocles was methodical and calculating, always a step ahead of everyone else.[31] As he rose steadily through the ranks, he grew closer to the seat of power. After a while, he decided to make his move. True to the nature of the times, his seizure of power was chaotic, a confused mess. But Diocles was nothing if not clever, able to see through the confusion.

The emperor Carus rose to power in 282 CE. He lived just long enough to name his two sons, Numerian and Carinus, co-emperors and march off on campaign only to die after being struck by lightning.[32] In 284 CE, Numerian took his turn as senior emperor. While on campaign, he grew ill. His senior advisers claimed that he had an eye infection and needed darkness, drawing the curtains on his carriage. After a couple of days, people noticed the terrible smell, drew back the curtains, and found the dead emperor, rotting away in his darkened carriage.[33] Numerian's prefect, Aper, tried to garner support for his claim to the throne. Diocles had other plans. He bested Aper and won over Numerian's troops, then accused Aper of having killed Numerian. He had Aper bound in chains and brought before him. Raising his sword to the sky and denouncing Aper, Diocles plunged his sword into the bound and disarmed prisoner, killing him in plain sight and by his own hand.[34]

This was less a bloodthirsty act by a murderous maniac and more a calculated move by a shrewd operator, seeking to cement his persona in front of his troops and retainers. His seizure of power was almost complete. He took his new army, marched to confront Carus's other son, Carinus, dispatched him in battle, and took sole possession of the Roman Empire. Upon taking control of the throne, Diocles took a more Roman-esque name, and he is referred to from this point forward as Diocletian.

Once in command, Diocletian put the full weight of his administrative genius against the challenges of the empire. Not for nothing do historians mark his accession as the end of the Crisis of the Third Century. Everything he did was toward greater stability and harmony. Diocletian got to work reforming every corner of Roman society. He reformed the tax code, the market system, the money supply, the civil administration, everything. Some reforms were more successful than others, but he just kept working and working and working.[35]

The Crisis of the Third Century had taken a toll on the prestige of the emperors. How much genuine authority could an emperor wield if he was likely to be hacked to pieces by the next guy in line? How divine could one be if his time on earth was so tenuous? Diocletian sought to reverse the degradation of empirical prestige. He made himself less visible, more a rarely seen, godlike figure and less a man of the people. He surrounded himself with layers and layers of bureaucrats and retainers. He dressed in clothes befitting a god and wore a diadem, a type of crown only worn by eastern monarchs, and never previously by an emperor.[36] Diocletian brought back the monarchy in everything but name and in the process added a sense of divine mystique. He didn't do these things to gratify an outsize ego. Rather, they were calculated moves to awe everyone and cow would-be rivals.

Recognizing that his skill was bureaucratic, he brought on a co-emperor to add military might to the upper ranks. Maximian was a career soldier. Where Diocletian was refined and cunning, Maximian was a blunt instrument, unlearned and unabashedly martial.[37] He gathered up armies and went out to smash the various tribes that had been stressing the borders of the empire. Diocletian and Maximian might have had the same title, but everyone knew who ultimately called the shots. Diocletian ran things from the eastern half of the empire, while Maximian followed Diocletian's lead from the west. Ever calculating, Diocletian understood that stability was more than putting out fires, easing the pressure on borders, and reforming the administration. True stability could only come by planning for the future.

In perhaps his biggest stroke of genius, Diocletian subdivided the empire once again. In 293 CE he appointed two more junior emperors, Galerius and Constantius.[38] Galerius would be paired with Diocletian in the east, Constantius with Maximian in the west. Each of the four would have his own capital and zone of responsibility. They were to coordinate strategy and movement. They were to rule as a group. This administration was called the tetrarchy, or rule of four. Not only would this serve to keep a closer watch on all corners of the empire, but Diocletian and Maximian could train their successors through hands-on experience, hopefully ensuring a peaceful transfer of power and avoiding civil war when the time came.

To Diocletian, order and unity were the keys to stability. He wanted one set of rules, customs, and laws coercing the entirety of the empire. His junior partner, Galerius, agreed and started whispering that one big problem threatened the plan: religion. A strange cult was spreading like wildfire across the empire. Turning their noses up at the traditional Roman pantheon, these zealots would rather face death than renounce their fervent faith. They were called Christians, and they were undermining the goal of unified harmony. Galerius pestered Diocletian to do something about it. Off and on over the years, attempts had been made to suppress the weird religion, but, Galerius argued, now it was time for a systematic purge. The gods were restive. By allowing this cult to spread, the empire was tempting divine wrath. By deploying the administrative efficiency of the tetrarchy, they could wipe out Christianity, curry favor with Jupiter and all of his friends, and finish the task of creating unity across the empire.

Diocletian listened and considered the argument. He hesitated. Always seeing further, he understood the implications of Galerius's proposal.[39] This would be a lot more complicated than his junior partner suggested. But Galerius was insistent. He wore Diocletian down, and the senior emperor agreed to consult the Oracle of Apollo at the Greek city of Didyma to seek wisdom from the god directly.[40] Diocletian was told that the impious on earth were hindering the god's ability to dispense advice.[41]

Between the vague prophecy and the nagging of his junior partner, Diocletian gave in. In 303 CE, Diocletian began to issue a series of imperial edicts revoking the rights of Christians. They were to renounce their practices and observe the traditional Roman religion. Priests were arrested. Churches were destroyed. The administration and the military were purged of Christians. Scriptures and holy texts were burned. Citizens were ordered to sacrifice to the Roman gods. Refusal to do so meant death. And death was visited on Christians in scores. Stemming from these edicts, dozens, then hundreds, then thousands of Christians died. Heads rolled. Blood flowed. Diocletian might have been reluctant to initiate the persecution—known to history as the Great Persecution—but once committed, he stamped his name on it and pursued it with the inexhaustible efficiency that he brought to every challenge.[42]

But this was one attempt at reform that was out of reach, even for Diocletian. His co-emperors in the west weren't nearly as enthusiastic, only going through the motions of complying with his orders. Many pagan Romans had sympathy for the persecuted and offered protection. Some Christians simply lied about their faith or swore loyalty to the traditional pantheon, then kept on doing their Christian thing. Rather than being rigorous, systematic, and exhaustive, the Great Persecution was

Every move the shrewd Diocletian made was carefully calculated. His Christian persecution was born less of religious fervor and more with a mind to enforce the traditional Roman religion to create unity across the empire. *Wikimedia Commons, by Nino Barbieri (talk contribs), CC BY 2.5.*

spotty and ineffective. Christianity was too far rooted to be eliminated by imperial edict, even under the threat of martyrdom.[43]

As the persecution stumbled along, Diocletian pulled another shocker in 305 CE, wholly unprecedented for an emperor: he abdicated. He then compelled Maximian to do the same. Constantius and Galerius were promoted to senior emperors, and junior emperors were appointed in their place.[44] Galerius, now the senior member of the tetrarchy, put out his own edicts and ramped up persecutions while Diocletian retired to his palace to tend his cabbages. Galerius carried on the persecutions for another six or seven years until 311 CE before finally seeing the futility and calling them off.[45] The next time a big persecution would grip the empire, it would be a resurgent and now dominant Christianity leading the charge to triumph over Roman paganism.

At the end of the day, Diocletian's reforms breathed new life into a dying empire. The road ahead would be fraught and eventually crash, but that the empire survived another seventeen decades is testament to Diocletian's enduring genius. He is seen as one of the best emperors in Roman history, and he came at a time when he was sorely needed. But his legacy bore an ineradicable stain—the blood from thousands of martyrs, whose deaths did nothing to stem the rising tide of Christianity.

(DIS)HONORABLE MENTION #4: THE PENITENT

The Crisis of the Third Century seemed to be leading to collapse of the empire. Civil wars, internal strife, and financial hardships had taken their toll. The empire had been cleaved in three. Thanks to the likes of Commodus, Caracalla, Elagabalus, and Maximinus Thrax, so many competent administrators and nobles had been purged, it's amazing that anyone with half a brain to look after things was left.

But the succession of strong, competent generals in the latter half of the 200s CE began to bring things back in line. By the time Aurelian stitched the empire back together and took the title Resitutor Orbis, the Western Empire had another two centuries of life ahead. Diocletian's reforms and Constantine's consolidation of power further stabilized the situation. But the heady days of the *Pax Romana* were long gone. No more could an emperor while away the hours in idle luxury while things took care of themselves. Instead, the order of the day was a heavy dose of civil war, infighting, and betrayal. This was a serious job for serious people, which came with a short life expectancy.

By the time Theodosius I ascended the throne in 379 CE, he had been in civil and military administration for most of his life. He had traveled the breadth of the empire, gaining important experience and understanding the totality of the challenges it faced. Upon his accession, he inherited more than nice, purple robes. The empire, once again, was in crisis. The previous year, the Roman armies had suffered a humiliating defeat in the city of Adrianople at the hands of Gothic hordes. To make matters worse, the eastern emperor Valens died in the battle, leaving his nineteen- and four-year-old nephews, Gratian and Valentinian II (the sons of his dead brother and co-emperor, Valentinian I) as nominal emperors.

Desperate for help, Gratian appointed Theodosius as co-co-emperor. Upon taking up the call, Theodosius shouldered a very heavy burden. The army was shattered, its finances a mess, barbarian hordes running loose inside the borders, morale at an all-time low. His two co-emperors were just kids, one of them only four.

But he had one big ally, one person of incalculable power who loomed large over events: God. Theodosius was genuinely devout and God-fearing. Religiously, it was a confused period, with different Christian theologies and interpretations competing to take root as Christian orthodoxy. Many Romans still held tight to the traditional Roman pantheon. The cycles of religious tolerance and persecution had sapped the empire of strength and left a tangled mess.

To help guide his decisions, Theodosius relied on Ambrose, the archbishop of Milan, known to today's Christian world as Saint Ambrose. Ambrose prodded Theodosius, giving him communion, hearing his confessions. In Theodosius, Ambrose saw an opportunity to use the power of the emperor to be God's avenging angel, declaring war on any deviation from his version of orthodoxy and eradicating the last vestiges of ancient paganism. Theodosius listened but, at least initially, maintained a degree of independence, holding off on letting Ambrose fully dictate state policy. He had work to do that went beyond the wants and needs of a zealous bishop. Besides, Theodosius saw it as imperative to maintain the cult of empirical divinity. At least for the time being, God and Theodosius would be partners on equal footing.

One of Theodosius's boldest moves was signing a deal with the Gothic barbarians to let them live in the empire in exchange for their assistance in its defense. To some, this was unthinkable. How could Theodosius let these savages in? Hadn't they been marauding the borders and threatening the empire for centuries? Theodosius was a pragmatist. The Goths were too strong and the empire too weak. He acknowledged the situation and sought to turn it to his best advantage.

Theodosius was far from a dispassionate religious stoic. He had a violent temper. With that as a base ingredient, add religious zealotry, sprinkle in a little unconditional power. That was a recipe for disaster. It just took a match to light his short fuse. That moment came in 390 CE. The residents of the city of Thessalonica (modern-day Greece) didn't embrace the new Gothic reality with much enthusiasm. When a local Gothic commander imprisoned a beloved charioteer, the people rioted. In the chaos, the commander, one of Theodosius's trusted inner circle, was killed along with several of his men. When word reached the emperor, he flew into a rage. He sent word to the new garrison: at the next chariot race, let the people into the hippodrome, the large stadium that held as many as a hundred thousand fans. At a signal, the gates were to be barred, and the people were to be slaughtered.[46] As the imperial messenger left the capital with the orders, Theodosius took a deep breath and tried to calm down. As his blood pressure dropped, he felt a pang. Regretting the rashness of his actions, he sent another messenger to revoke his prior order.[47] It was a race: one messenger with orders to kill, the next with orders for clemency. Unfortunately for the citizens of Thessalonica, a head start was all the first messenger needed.

On the fateful day, the unsuspecting masses poured into the hippodrome, whipped into a fever pitch of excitement for a day of their favorite entertainment. Presumably, the messenger with the orders to call off the massacre was still racing toward the city. Too late. Once inside, the Gothic garrison, eager to avenge their fallen comrades, set to killing with reckless abandon. Once the signal was given, they drew their swords and slashed and hacked with deadly effect. Men, women, young, old: the soldiers drew no distinction as they slaughtered people by the thousands. Before the commanders called a stop to the killing, as many as seven thousand people lay dead.[48] Gothic or not, this was a Roman army slaughtering Roman citizens at the command of a Roman emperor. Some piety.

Back in the capital (Milan, at this point), Theodosius was ravaged with guilt. To mitigate against his own temper, he issued a decree: all death

Whereas Theodosius was racked with guilt over the slaughter of the Thessalonians, Ambrose, bishop of Milan, saw opportunity. Ambrose kept Theodosius from absolution to assert the Church's domination over the emperor and the empire. *Wikimedia Commons.*

sentences were subject to a thirty-day cooling off before the executions be carried out.[49] But this did little to abate his guilt. Ambrose sensed an opportunity. The bishop withdrew from the imperial court and threatened Theodosius with excommunication. A devastated Theodosius begged for absolution. Ambrose admonished the emperor, chastising, shaming, and cajoling him. Ambrose left Theodosius twisting in the wind for eight months, withholding absolution while the emperor grieved, sulked, and sobbed in the palace. Eventually, Ambrose pardoned Theodosius and brought him back into communion with the Church, but going forward, the balance of power would shift between the two men. God and the emperor were no longer peers. Theodosius, though emperor, was now a penitent, supplicant to the almighty, with Ambrose serving as His earthly vessel to help guide the empire. And Ambrose definitely had ideas he wanted Theodosius to act on.

Ambrose held sway over Theodosius in a way that fellow emperors and administrators did not. With Ambrose now firmly in Theodosius's ear, a new level of Christian fervor swept the empire. Fearing damnation, Theodosius set about to eradicate anything with pagan roots. For more than one thousand years, dating back to 776 BCE, the Greeks had celebrated the Olympic Games. With a stroke of his pen in 393 CE, Theodosius snuffed out the Olympic torch and with it the games.[50] He banned celebration of traditional Roman pagan religion, sacrifices, and observances. Theodosius condoned destruction of ancient temples of incalculable cultural heritage, buildings that even then were of great antiquity. Far and wide, across the empire from Greece to Egypt, these temples were pulled down, stone by stone.

For Theodosius, the return to divine favor couldn't come soon enough. He was beset with dire challenges on all sides, not the least of which was the struggle for control of the empire. A new challenger rose to claim his part of the prize. The children of Valentinian I and their regents vied for greater control. Just as Rome was emerging from the chaos and aftermath of Thessalonica, a new wave of civil war crashed over the struggling empire. The peak came in 394 CE.

Theodosius squared off against his rival, the pretender Eugenius. Both armies lined up. At first, Eugenius's troops got the better of things. At the end of the day, morale in Theodosius's camp was low. But he gave his men courage, reminding them that God was on their side. The next day, as a cocky Eugenius lined up for what he assumed was mop-up, a strong wind whipped up and blew straight at his forces. This gave Theodosius's men an opportunity that they seized with full advantage, routing Eugenius, winning the field and uncontested control of the Roman Empire for Theodosius. Perhaps he won with God on his side, or because he was the smartest, most accomplished, and clearest sighted of all the challengers. Either way, Theodosius triumphed, ending the civil war and restoring a tenuous peace to the empire.

Then again, maybe God wasn't yet mollified. Just after consolidating his power, Theodosius died of an inflammatory disease. He was forty-eight years old and destined to be the last emperor to have sole rule of a united empire. At the time of his death, his eighteen-year-old son, Arcadius, ruled the east, and his ten-year-old son, Honorius, sat atop the west. Both were weak, fated to be manipulated by powerful regents.

Theodosius enjoys a good legacy: historians dubbed him Theodosius the Great. He certainly brought a level of energy and drive at a time when it was desperately needed. For better or for worse, he not only consolidated political power, but also spiritual power. With Ambrose helping steer the path, the Christian Church took big strides in becoming the official religion of the Roman Empire and asserting itself as possessing a higher authority than even the emperors. Only God knows whether Theodosius ended up in heaven or hell.

10

THE BACKSTABBERS

In 1776, Edward Gibbon published the first volume of his epochal *The History of the Decline and Fall of the Roman Empire*. It took a dozen years and about a million words to conclude his magnum opus when the sixth and final volume was published in 1789. The book was so successful, so important, that it has inextricably linked the ideas of "collapse" and "Roman Empire" in the minds of so many, creating a sense of inevitability. But was collapse truly inevitable? Did it all have to end? Or could it have been avoided?

As the fourth century CE gave way to the fifth, things were looking pretty grim. Barbarians invaded left and right. Local tribes, with a burgeoning sense of determination, rebelled, attempting to throw off the Roman yoke. Economies suffered. Theological debates raged, sapping the empire of energy and unity. But the empire had come to the brink many times, only to be pulled back by brilliant leaders and competent administrators.

At the same time, from its earliest days, centuries before the age of the emperors, Rome had suffered through the indignity of countless murderers, tyrants, and lunatics. Two forces in opposition: awful rulers pushing Rome to the brink of catastrophe, people of talent trying to restore order. Rome at the dawn of the fifth century CE had both. Which would prevail?

Sometimes it's not how many people an emperor kills that warrants their inclusion in a book like this. It's who, and when. For an empire teetering on the edge of collapse, one death, one betrayal, one murder, could bring it crashing down.

* * *

Few could have known that when Theodosius kicked it in 395 CE, the Roman world would never be fully united under a sole ruler. His death does not mark the end of the Roman Empire, but it does mark an important transition. When trouble arose during the height of the empire, some noble or general or senator or member of the imperial family would decamp from Rome, march an army to the sore spot, snuff out the trouble, and return to the capital triumphant, smugly declaiming his invincibility for all to hear. When Rome descended into the hell of the Crisis of the Third Century, it wasn't leading figures from the capital who saved the day. People of talent and ambition from the provinces reversed the fortunes of the flagging empire. Even as the great generals and administrators miraculously stitched the broken empire back together and kept it from crashing, the axis of the empire began to tilt away from the old capital of Rome, toward the east.

The balance of power accelerated this shift to the east when Constantine the Great reconsecrated the ancient city of Byzantium as the *Nova Roma*, New Rome, in 330 CE. As the power of Constantinople grew, the power of Rome, and with it, the western half of the empire, was in terminal decline.

But like the old man in the beginning of *Monty Python and the Holy Grail*, the west wasn't dead yet. The latter Western Roman Empire still dominated much of its historical territory. History had shown that decline wasn't inevitable. Talented, energetic rulers and administrators could reverse flagging fortunes and restore the Eternal City to shimmering glory. It had happened before. Perhaps it could again. At the time of Theodosius's premature death at age forty-eight, Rome itself still awed visitors with its temples, markets, forums, and theaters. Crowds roared as chariots careened around the Circus Maximus, or as exotic beasts were hunted and butchered in the Colosseum. The city even had a magistrate called the *tribunus rerum nitentium*, the tribune of shiny things, to look after all the gilded statues, temples, and other embellishments that glittered in the blazing Italian sun.[1] Yes, Rome still was quite impressive. Although it may not have had as much power, it still claimed much of its glory, and Rome remained an important ceremonial and symbolic center—proud, maybe still a bit arrogant, but beneath it all, a shell of its former self.

But one important Roman wasn't impressed enough to call the Eternal City his home: the western emperor Honorius. Honorius ascended to control the Western Empire when his dad, Theodosius, died. Although the death was unexpected and the illness that killed him, edema, set in quickly, he had just enough time to make an important strategic decision that, in theory, could set up Honorius to be a successful ruler. Theodosius appointed his trusted general and administrator Stilicho to be guardian to his two sons: Honorius was one; his older brother, Arcadius, was the other. Honorius would rule the Western Empire; Arcadius, the east.[2] The house of Theodosius would continue to rule. Stilicho would look after things.

A man of great talent and ambition, Stilicho would prove to be one of the last bulwarks against collapse of the west. The goals of his actions were not always clear, and he definitely had a penchant for playing people off one another for his own advantage, but Stilicho brought drive and determination at a time when they were needed most. If Stilicho's actions didn't always render him the most trustworthy, traditionalists eyed him with further suspicion. For Stilicho was half Roman, half Vandal, one of the countless Germanic tribes that traditionalist Romans viewed with equal parts scorn and fear. While Stilicho was rushing from one crisis to the next, putting out fires, members of the imperial court eyed him with suspicion, resenting his power and nurturing their own schemes. Stilicho poured his considerable talent and energy into solving the numerous crises that beset the flagging Western Empire, while his charge, the boy-emperor Honorius brooded in the swamp-lined city of Ravenna.

To be fair to Honorius, it wasn't just that Rome lacked all of its formal grandeur that led him to reside elsewhere. It also wasn't as safe as it had been. Although the Western Roman Empire maintained a degree of control over its traditional territory, it was increasingly tenuous. Some Germanic tribes were allies. Some were adversaries. Some were both at the same time. At this time in Roman history, it was nearly impossible to define who was friend and who was foe. Although Theodosius made tentative peace with many of the more powerful tribes, his death left the situation uncertain. His younger son was ill-equipped to rule. But in that, he wasn't alone. His older brother, Arcadius, was in the same boat. Theodosius knew this. It is why he put so much trust in Stilicho. Theodosius wanted his sons to rule in name and Stilicho to guide the ship of state until they were mature and experienced enough to rule on their own.

Theodosius wanted to establish a new imperial dynasty. He did what he could to prepare his two sons. Proving the title was purely symbolic,

Honorius had even shared the consulship with his father at age two. Theodosius had elevated his sons to full corulers; Arcadius got the nod in 383 CE at the ripe old age of five. Honorius joined the fun in 393 CE at the downright ancient age of eight. Theodosius didn't have much time to mentor and groom his sons. When he departed this earthly realm in 395 CE, Arcadius was eighteen; Honorius, just twelve.[3]

Honorius ruled the waning Western Empire; Arcadius ruled the waxing Eastern Empire. The brothers were in way over their heads, partly due to their age and inexperience. But their shortcomings went beyond age. Neither had the drive nor talent of their dearly departed dad. They were generally brooding, sulking introverts. Any history that covers them describes the imperial brothers as "weak." Age, inexperience, and a lack of talent. What could go wrong?

At first, their rules went well enough because initially both were surrounded by competent advisers, chief among them Stilicho. But each brother had a cadre of people around him who wanted their half of the empire to be supreme. The tug of war between east and west began in earnest. At a time when coordinated action was more vital than ever, court advisers spent too much time figuring out how their half of the empire could achieve supremacy and not nearly enough trying to solve the bigger issues confronting the entire empire. Although not quite pushing things into open warfare, the imperial brothers' advisers sought to undermine and destabilize their rivals to the east or west.

Rather than a unified Roman Empire, it was cleaved in two, each half working against the other.[4] In many ways, Honorius had the upper hand, because he had the supremely talented right-hand man, Stilicho, close at hand. For his part, Stilicho cast his lot with the west, marrying his daughter to Honorius. Stilicho was many things Honorius was not: talented, ambitious, cunning, and experienced. He was a man of action, decisive, bold. He kept one eye on dealing with current issues and one eye on the chess moves to be made down the road. And a few years into Honorius's rule, Stilicho added father-in-law to the job description, marrying his daughter to the listless boy-emperor a few short years after his ascendancy.[5] Jealous court nobles and hangers-on whispered louder and louder about the uppity, untrustworthy barbarian strutting around like he owned the place. The whispers began to reach Honorius's ears. The weak young man, who was easily influenced, allowed suspicion to take root in his mind.

Stilicho's biggest challenge was to navigate the shifting alliances and rivalries with the various Germanic tribes, most especially the Goths. Roughly broken into two major tribes, the Ostrogoths and the Visigoths, they were more than the barbaric warriors the Romans considered them to be. They had art, language, jewelry, and so many of the hallmarks of advanced civilization. The Goths weren't to be dismissed or taken lightly. But an arrogant, isolated, weak young emperor was certainly liable to make that mistake. Especially with so many people around him sowing seeds of doubt about the one man who stood to do something about the challenge.

Stilicho was too busy to notice the smear campaign. He had work to do. The thorniest issue was the rise of the Visigothic king, Alaric. Alaric was a sometime friend, sometime foe of the Romans. Whichever side he fought on gained a formidable general and ally.

Alaric had befriended and fought for Theodosius, helping the then-emperor stem the tide of nativist uprisings in the province of Gaul in 394 CE.[6] The battle had been hard fought, and the Gothic troops allied with Alaric suffered heavy casualties. No one said thank you. Alaric was offended. In fact, the Goths believed that they were sent into battle first so they could bear the brunt.[7] Eventually, he took his troops and went off to pursue his own agenda. He broke his treaty with Rome and went a-plundering. Stilicho and Alaric squared off in 395 CE, and the Vandal vanquished the Goth, but Alaric escaped and lived to fight another day.[8]

It happened again in 397 CE.[9] They clashed again in Italy in the early 400s CE, with Stilicho getting the upper hand at each turn.[10] Eventually, the two settled their differences, and Alaric renewed his alliance with the Western Empire in 404 CE through Stilicho's deft negotiations.[11] The good times didn't last long, and it wasn't long before Alaric was again marching into Italy.[12] By 407 CE, Alaric and his army were looming. Stilicho was careening around the empire, trying to stem this invasion here, that rebellion there. Exhausted and overextended, Stilicho favored yielding to Alaric's demand of gold in exchange for peace.[13] Honorius waffled, his ears ringing with court invective against his only true champion. The fate of Italy rested on Honorius as he decided whether to follow the advice of his seasoned and experienced general, adviser, and father-in-law, or to yield to the chorus of jealous court nobles. Was he half Vandal? Sure. But he was also the only thing propping up the Western Roman Empire. Honorius sulked and brooded in his imperial palace. The petty jealousy, the whispers, the rumors, the conspiracy theories, all of them found resonance in the mind of the weak and still only fifteen-year-old boy-emperor.

Unfortunately for Stilicho, for Italy, and, ultimately, Honorius himself, the feeble emperor, gave in. In 408 CE, he accused Stilicho of treason and had him executed. The general met his downfall with stoicism, proving until the end that he was, according to Edward Gibbon, "the last Roman general."[14] Stilicho was beheaded. As Stilicho's blood drained from his lifeless body, the lifeblood of the Western Empire drained away with it. Decapitation was obviously a mortal wound for Stilicho, but would it be for the Western Empire?

Indulging in his bloodlust, Honorius unleashed a killing spree throughout Italy. Stilicho's son was hunted down, captured, and butchered. His followers were purged. Hundreds, possibly thousands, fell by the sword.[15] Thousands of Stilicho's multiethnic troops, some of the last tested veterans in the west, understood that by virtue of his Vandal blood, Stilicho had been cast aside and killed. Not wanting the same fate to befall them, these troops fled the Roman army, many switching sides and joining the ascendant "barbarian" tribes.

Quick to take advantage, Alaric brought the full weight of his burgeoning forces crashing deep into Italy. He didn't really want to destroy everything. He just wanted cold, hard cash, demanding massive payments to go away. Honorius, closed off in his palace in the swamp-lined city of Ravenna, vacillated. Weak, incompetent, and now without the one adviser who knew how to handle such things, Honorius sulked, wallowing in self-pitying indecisiveness. Eventually Alaric threw up his hands, marched his army to Rome, and put the Eternal City under siege. In 410 CE, his army poured into the city, sacking the symbolic center of the millennia-old Roman Empire. It was the first time in eight hundred years that Rome had suffered the horrifying indignity of sacking.[16] By ordering the execution of Stilicho and unleashing the bloody purge that followed, Honorius brought death and destruction to Rome itself. He didn't just have Stilicho's blood on his hands. He had that of Romans, too. The one bold decision he made in his reign proved to be cataclysmic. By murdering his father-in-law, Honorius sowed the seeds of Rome's destruction.

He would go on to live a sulking, secluded life in Ravenna for another thirteen years, dying in 423 CE of edema, or dropsy, as it was known.[17] Honorius ruled for thirty years, which sounds impressive, but for most of the time, he was just a child. When surrounded by good administrators, he could be kept on the right path. But once paranoia and suspicion took root in his mind, he made a series of blood-soaked decisions that proved to have awful consequences not just for the victims themselves but for the entire Western Empire. On his watch, the whole Roman project took one giant leap toward collapse.

Rather than remove a weak leader from the stage, the death of Honorius unleashed more chaos. Rivals fought for control of the fading embers of Roman power. In the midst of the struggle, Honorius's half sister sensed opportunities. A granddaughter of Theodosius the Great, as well as descended from the emperor Valentinian I, Galla Placidia had impeccable imperial credentials. She maneuvered through the churning course of events to place her young son at the center of palace politics. By 425 CE, he was sole ruler of the Western Empire, ruling as Valentinian III. He took the throne at the tender age of six.[18]

Here we go again.

Now we have a young prince, installed on the throne, with regents and advisers, both powerful and cunning, people using the small child to exercise their own power. This was a recipe for disaster. But again, one man had the talent, ability, and unquestioned devotion to the empire to stave off disaster, restore order, and begin to put things back together.

Flavius Aetius is the last towering figure of western Roman history. He was unquestionably loyal to the empire and brought enormous talent and energy to the unlimited crises that beset Rome. In the aftermath of Honorius's death, Aetius had dedicated his considerable talent to advance the cause of a rival claimant to the vacant throne. But once Valentinian III was in charge, Aetius devoted himself wholly to the cause of the little boy and his administration. It didn't seem to matter to him who was in charge. He served Rome. And if the emperor *was* Rome, then Aetius served the emperor, regardless of who it was. Once Valentinian III began his reign, Aetius got to work.

His path to power and influence was peculiar. Aetius had a strange childhood. His bloodlines were as Roman and noble as they came. Growing up in the imperial court, he was near the center of political power from his earliest days. As a child, he was held hostage by Alaric, then again by the kings of the Huns.[19] By spending so much time with what the average Roman considered to be "barbarians," Aetius understood more about the mind-set and motivations of Rome's foes than did any of his contemporaries. He learned to adapt their ideas and tactics as part of his emerging worldview. By the time his captivities ended and he entered military and political service to the empire, Aetius had a wealth of ideas and experience to draw on, combining in his person a powerful mix of creativity, innovation, and pragmatism. Once at service to the empire, Aetius would become a well-rounded, competent general and administrator.

His talents were desperately needed. Chaos was everywhere. Rome had withdrawn from Britain back in 408 CE, unable to defend the colony. Germany. Gaul. Hispania. Even in Italy. There were uprisings, invasions, rebellions, and coup attempts. Aetius took charge, pouring himself into solving the existential crises erupting across the depth and breadth of the land.

Amazingly, he began to lessen the chaos. Year after year, campaign after campaign, Aetius achieved a series of stunning victories. He drove back the Goths. He suppressed Gallic rebels and armies. He bested the Franks. His successes were hard won, and through his will, shrewd tactics, and leadership, he ground out an astonishing string of victories. Aetius asserted Roman authority and hegemony wherever he went. Unlike Stilicho, no one could use Aetius's bloodlines as a feeble way to undermine his nobility. He was Roman through and through.[20]

In 451 CE, Aetius confronted one of history's all-time great villains: Attila the Hun. Yes, *that* Attila the Hun. He had a well-won reputation for cruelty and ruthlessness. His ferocious warriors had been sweeping in from the east, terrifying all before them. He and they represented the apex of Roman fear and dread. In a fun historical footnote, some claim that Venice was founded on the islands in the middle of the lagoon by terrified Roman citizens fleeing before Attila and his Hunnic hordes.[21] But Aetius was not cowed. He did not waver in the face of the seemingly invincible might of what Romans saw as terrifying savages.

In June 451 CE, Aetius squared off against Attila. His army bested that of the terrifying Hunnic chief, and the Western Empire breathed a collective sigh of relief.[22] Unlike Aurelian, the brilliant emperor who had personally overseen reconstruction of the Roman Empire during the Crisis of the Third Century, Aetius was a commander subservient to the command of the emperor. He wasn't emperor; he was at the emperor's service. And what service it was. They might just get out of this mess yet. Aetius reached his apex in 453 CE when he betrothed his son to Valentinian III's daughter. All of his hard work and devotion brought him one step closer to cementing his legacy by merging his bloodlines with those of the imperial family.[23]

But not everyone was thrilled with Aetius's success. Once again, jealous nobles began to spin tales of conspiracy. Despite an unblemished track record of fervent devotion to the emperor, Valentinian III's coterie of retainers and hangers-on went to work pitting the emperor against his invaluable everywhere and everything number two. Unlike Honorius at the time of his fateful decision, Valentinian III was no teenager. In his mid-thirties at his betrothal, Valentinian III had done little to leave his mark on history.

While his general and armies devoted themselves to the cause of the empire, fighting campaign after campaign, Valentinian III devoted himself to decadence and luxury. Detached from the true state of affairs facing his domains, Valentinian III indulged in vice, sorcery, and astrology.[24] He was a spoiled, petulant brat, stunted from development by a world where he only knew sycophancy and unconditional power. Whereas the feeble Honorius was fifteen when he betrayed Stilicho, Valentinian III was in his mid-thirties.

But age is meaningless without emotional and intellectual development, and Valentinian III was stunted, incomplete, and deeply flawed. People craven for their own power tried to turn the emperor against his loyal general. "Remember thirty years ago, before you came to power? He supported the guy you deposed. He's probably been plotting your downfall all these decades," they said. "Oh, he wants your daughter to marry his son? He's probably trying to get rid of you so he can make his son emperor," they said.[25] And so on. Whispers. Rumors. Conspiracies.

A rational person could look at events, look at history, look at results, and toss aside this nonsense as petty jealousy. Aetius's track record was impeccable. He stood up against any figure from any period of Roman history. But Valentinian III wasn't a rational person. He was a jealous narcissist. The echoes rang in his ears and rattled around in his brain. Paranoia led to jealous rage. Egged on by a powerful senator, Petronius Maximus, and his chamberlain, Heraclius, Valentinian III made the only bold decision of his life: he resolved to kill Aetius.

In September 454 CE, Valentinian III made his move. When Aetius came before the emperor to report on the state of affairs, Valentinian III shocked his loyal lieutenant by launching into an unhinged denunciation.

One can only wonder what Aetius was thinking as his emperor accused him of this and that crime. As he began to defend himself against the accusations, Valentinian leapt forward, drew his sword, and aided by Heraclius, murdered his subordinate with his own hands. Convinced that he had saved himself from certain death, Valentinian III instead sowed the seeds of his own demise, the utter destruction of Rome, and the fall of the Western Empire. Asked of a noble what he thought of Valentinian III's deed, the noble's response echoes to this day: "I am ignorant, sir, of your motives or provocations; I only know that you have acted like a man who cuts off his right hand with his left."[26]

He didn't have long to enjoy his accomplishment. Valentinian III was right about one thing; there *was* a conspiracy against the emperor. He was just wrong about its origins. Within a year of Aetius's death, Petronius Maximus, the senator who had done so much to turn the emperor against his faithful deputy, killed both Valentinian III and his co-assassin, Hera-

The disastrous reigns of Honorius and Valentinian III robbed Rome of its most talented defenders at a time when they were needed most, opening the door to the sacking of the Eternal City for the first time in nearly a millennium. *Wikimedia Commons.*

clius. Maximus himself would be killed a few months later. The Western Roman Empire was in freefall. The last man who could do anything substantive about it was dead, a victim of plotting and scheming by petty, craven, jealous morons.

With Aetius out of the way, and the imperial house in chaos, the Vandal king Genseric nailed shut the coffin of the Eternal City. Just months after the deaths of Aetius and Valentinian III, Genseric marched his troops toward Rome. Nothing and no one was left to stop them. Genseric first ordered all of the aqueducts carrying fresh water into the city severed. In June 455 CE, his soldiers entered the city, looting and pillaging every bit of movable or material wealth. Whereas the sack of 410 CE under Alaric had been more symbolic than destructive, the Vandals plundered so completely, so remorselessly, that their name has become a synonym for theft and destruction.[27] In 455 CE, Rome was, in the most literal sense, Vandalized.[28]

Rome was irredeemably lost. The Western Roman Empire would limp along for another two decades, but Rome was gone. The Roman Empire collapsed. A long and storied chapter in the history of civilization was closed, forever.

The twin betrayals of Honorius with Stilicho, then Valentinian III with Aetius, robbed Rome of the only people who could stem the tide of Roman collapse. To address the rhetorical question asked at the beginning of this chapter, was collapse truly inevitable? Who knows . . .

History has a way of taking unexpected turns. But Stilicho and Aetius were men of true genius and ability. Neither was an emperor, but both were victims of emperors. Honorius and Valentinian III were different people with different legacies. But they have much in common. Each was weak, easily manipulated, spoiled, and decadent. Each turned over administration of the empire to a subordinate whose talents far exceeded his own. Each destroyed that subordinate for stupid reasons, wasting talent and leadership when it was most desperately needed and in short supply.

The Roman Empire declined and fell for many reasons. Centuries after Gibbon's work entered the scene, debate between scholars and armchair historians rages on. Theories and arguments abound. The collapse of an entire empire is so complicated and involves so many variables, so many factors, that identifying a definitive root cause probably is impossible, fun though it may be to try. At the end of the day one thing is crystal clear: both Honorius and Valentinian III, through parallel acts of betrayal and murder, hastened the demise of the empire. Nearly twelve hundred years of history came crashing down when the final curtain was drawn in 476 CE. Instead of leading with strength and conviction, Honorius and Valentinian III each took the empire one giant step toward the edge of the cliff. Contributing greatly to the collapse of the most powerful, most successful empire in human history does not do wonders for a legacy. Honorius and Valentinian III soaked themselves in the blood of the people they needed most, hastened the demise of the empire, and proved that right to its end, the story of Rome is the story of murderers, tyrants, and lunatics.

11

THE COUNTDOWN

So, who was really the worst? Before counting down the worst rulers of Rome, it's important to consider that Rome was blessed with some remarkable leaders and rulers. The Roman system produced rulers of historical talent: Julius Caesar, Augustus, Trajan, Hadrian, Marcus Aurelius, Constantine. Rome was the most powerful and largest empire of the ancient world. These and other rulers can claim credit for making Rome, well, Rome. It didn't happen by accident.

Even emperors at whom historians tend to look askance did some great things for the empire. Tiberius left massive cash reserves, and, despite his upbringing in the legions, opted for diplomacy over warfare, creating a more peaceful and stable era than what proceeded it. Domitian, though certainly autocratic and prone to execute a senator or two, was a prolific builder who stabilized the frontiers and reformed the military and judicial system. These two and others like them had their downsides and were excoriated by contemporary and later historians. As hated as Tiberius and Domitian were, they prove the point that few emperors were all bad. Some were great. Others had complex legacies.

Why mention this as prelude to a countdown to the worst ruler of Rome? Because only through the talent and energy of the good rulers did Rome survive the catastrophic reigns of the people we have met so far. When we consider all the worst emperors, it's understandable if you wonder, "How did this thing not fall apart sooner?" We do need to give a tip of the cap to the rulers mentioned above, for if it weren't for their talent, energy, and ambition, everything would have fallen to pieces much sooner—and we wouldn't have met the likes of Caligula, Commodus, and Caracalla. Those guys definitely made things interesting, and entertaining, in a twisted kind of way.

As we get to the top ten, we need to consider the ways we define "the worst." What makes a terrible ruler? We can look at this question in lots of different ways. Consider these variables: the impact of their rule on the stability of the empire, their treatment of others, their effect on Roman institutions, fiscal policy and responsibility, and overall sense of justice. And don't overlook the role of general intuition. Caracalla ordered his mom to pretend to be happy about Geta's murder. Did that ultimately affect the empire? No. But it sure is evidence we should consider when weighing his career and character.

How you and I weigh things like that may vary. Any such list has an inherent degree of subjectivity. That raises one last idea before we start. Thus far, we've been through ten chapters (not counting the Dishonorable Mentions), including grouping Honorius and Valentinian III into one. What follows is my ranking, counting down to the very worst, from ten to one. No obligation here, but you might put pen to paper and make your own list. At the end of this chapter, let's see how your list and this one compare.

Without further ado . . .

#10: THE SENATE

The Senate as an institution stretched from the founding of the city to the collapse of the Western Empire, even beyond. In some respects, it's unfair even to include the Senate on this list. As a governing body, senators ran the show for nearly five hundred years. That's a long time to pick the worst moments of their rule, tune out everything else, and hold up cherry-picked events as examples.

The last king, Tarquin, picked on them as a group; and after the rise of the emperors, they became a historical punching bag. For much of this story, the Senate is a more or less sympathetic victim. After the emperors consolidated power and dispensed with the charade of deferring to them, the Senate was little more than a social club, the place for the old noble families to hold offices of rank and prestige.

But again, and as discussed in the chapter about the Senate, we consider the Senate the ruler of Rome solely during the time when Rome was a republic, after senators ran off Tarquin and before the rise of Augustus. Before this time, they were subservient to the kings, and after this time, they were a shell of their former selves under the emperors. That sweet spot in the middle draws our scrutiny.

OK. First things first; let's give credit where credit is due. When it was their turn at center stage, the senators weren't all bad. Senators produced some great results with their power. Members of the senatorial class ran off the wretched Tarquin and his whole miserable family, for which Romans owe them a debt of gratitude. Perhaps more important, they established and developed institutions that set Rome up for regional, then continental, dominance. Under their watch Rome emerged as the dominant power in Europe and the Mediterranean. Rome reached new heights of power and prosperity when they called the shots.

Wait. If they did so many wonderful things, then why are they on this list?

First and most important, they refused to share power, prestige, and wealth. Early in their run at the top of the command structure, the senators' greed compelled the commoners to execute the first labor strike in human history. Rather than share, they hoarded, inadvertently creating organized labor. Don't take that as a slight against organized labor. Take that as evidence that they did such a bad job treating people fairly that they prompted its invention. With its grasp on power, the Senate turned Rome not into a democracy but an oligarchy. For all the senators' rhetoric about freedom and liberty, the senatorial policy generally demonstrated no thought about the lives and interests of the common folk. They were happy for everyone else to exist in servitude or slavery. As long as the senatorial oligarchs benefited, everyone else be damned. Of course, we are talking about thousands of people over a period of hundreds of years. This wasn't the attitude of each individual, but it does summarize the aggregate. When left either to look after a few rich people or everyone else, they took care of their own and left the masses to their fate.

As the republic entered its death throes, the Senate violently repressed reform movements and killed their leaders and adherents, often thousands at a time. As the need for reform reached a critical state, conservative senators refused any innovations. Rather than adapt to changing times and values, senators clung desperately to their crumbling power, lashing out at anyone who threatened their domination. This led to cataclysm, violence, and social upheaval. The bloody proscription of Sulla, where heads were nailed up as trophies in the Forum, was done in the name of preserving senatorial prerogative. Paradoxically, rather than protect their spot in the order, the senators sowed the seeds of their destruction. Populist reformers tried harder and harder, and senatorial repression grew more and more violent and pervasive. As the bodies mounted, the foundations of the republic crumbled.

The ultimate victim of the Senate was the Senate itself. By refusing to compromise, murdering reformers and their followers, senators hastened their own demise. Instead of becoming more democratic and inclusive, they closed ranks and convinced themselves of their inherent superiority. This gave rise to a series of increasingly charismatic populists, which in turn resulted in increasingly violent repression by the Senate. Once Caesar appeared, and the Senate had met its match, the Senate began a long slide into historical irrelevance. In the five hundred years following the rise of the emperors until the collapse of the Western Empire, the senators ceased to dictate the course of events. Although the senatorial class continued to churn out the highest magistrates in the empire, the scope of their power and policy-making abilities kept shrinking, and they were always liable to having their ranks thinned through bloody purges at the hands of megalomaniacal emperors. Had they been more open to reform, especially in the turbulent century from the rise and fall of the Gracchi to the rise of Augustus and the arrival of the emperors, their story could have been much different.

#9: HONORIUS AND VALENTINIAN III

Honorius and Valentinian III were objectively awful. Both came to power as comically young children, Honorius first making a claim to imperial rule at age eight, Valentinian III at six. Had they been surrounded by tutors, mentors, and regents to help foster their development, perhaps they could have been OK. Both had plenty of talented people in their family tree. The question would come down to whether they developed their own talents. Unfortunately for them, and for Roman history, they did not.

They two have so much more in common. In fact, they have so much in common that they share their place on this list. Both Honorius and Valentinian III were blessed with vigorous and competent lieutenants, but those deputies were so busy putting out fires everywhere, that the scumbags who accumulate around power gained imperial favor and used it to ill effect. Accordingly, these two emperors were surrounded by petty, jealous nobles who turned them against said lieutenants. They both betrayed and murdered these important people.

But wait: there's more! The causes and nature of these twin assassinations were a bit different. But a direct line can be tied from the death of Stilicho to the sack of Rome in 410 CE, the first time the Eternal City suffered that indignity in eight hundred years. Likewise, the course of events stemming from Valentinian III's cold-blooded murder of Aetius led to the Vandal sack of Rome in 455 CE. The first sack destroyed the illusion of Rome's eternal and perpetual glory, ripping out the symbolic heart of the dying Western Empire. The second ensured the empire's death knell and set up the city of Rome for centuries of backwater status.

Both Honorius and Valentinian III suffered from serious personality defects. They were weak, petty, indulgent, and paranoid. When the empire needed them, they did nothing noteworthy. Neither had courage, or even a desire, to take charge and lead. They sulked and brooded in luxurious isolation, either oblivious or apathetic to the state of the empire. In other words, they were the opposite kind of people needed to steer the ship of state through stormy weather. The single decision for which each is best known was utterly catastrophic.

So, why do the two come in at number 9? Because as bad as they were, the events in which they were embroiled were so much bigger than either of them. Each ruled at a time when Roman rule was collapsing everywhere. Although each had a brilliant lieutenant who tried to stop the flow, they were defined more by a failure to do anything useful than by a litany of awful deeds.

The respective murders of Stilicho and Aetius didn't so much cause the fall of the Western Empire as eliminate the people who could have stopped it from happening. The removal of those two brilliant men robbed the empire of talent when it was needed most, but it didn't change the broader issue: chaos and collapse lurked around every corner. It's impossible to tell how different events would have been if Stilicho and Aetius had lived out their lives in service to the empire. Thanks to the shortsighted and, ultimately, wasteful murder of these two great men, Honorius and Valentinian III earn their spot among the very worst ever to rule Rome.

#8: ELAGABALUS

What to make of this strange kid? His behavior was certainly aberrant. He flouted nearly every convention that Romans held dear. Overnight he sought to undermine Rome's religious institutions, which had evolved over a millennium. Temples were stripped of their relics; he raped a vestal virgin and violated their sacred cult. All were made to pay homage to Elagabalus's weird black stone/god. A later Roman emperor would come to be known as "Julian the Apostate." Julian was the last Roman emperor to try to stem the tide and switch the Roman world back from Christianity to its traditional pagan pantheon. But Elagabalus was the first and true apostate. He sought systematically to subvert Rome's traditions and replace them with a foreign mystery cult. In the process, he earned absolute scorn from historians, who needed little excuse to believe every scurrilous rumor or story, embellish it, and pass it along as absolute fact.

In the preface, we noted that some sources for these people and events can be a bit questionable. If any chapter in this book invites a degree of skepticism, it's this one. Much of the narrative is based on ancient sources written by historians who may have deliberately spun tales of horror to vilify a dead kid who couldn't defend himself. The unreliability of the sources is one reason why Elagabalus doesn't rank higher on the list. After all, he subverted the traditional Roman pantheon of gods. For a truly god-fearing people such as the Romans, such actions portended certain doom. Posthumous character assassination might have been a pious attempt to mollify the offended deities.

It's easy to dismiss this as so much ancient drama. After all, not many people pray to Vesta these days. Who cares what happened to some ancient pagans and their weird, defunct religion? It's not what religion Elagabalus practiced that earns his spot in this book. It's what he did in pursuit of that religion. But that was, of course, just the tip of the spear.

Regardless of the veracity of the sources, Elagabalus was little mourned when he died. In fact, his fall was cause for celebration; for many Romans, a deliverance from evil. Three things seem certain. First, his accession and his downfall were both engineered by his grandmother, Julia Maesa. Second, he was obsessed with elevating his local god to the top of the Roman pantheon and cared not a bit for the god-fearing traditions of his people. Third, he was oversexed, and his behavior was outside the norms of traditional Roman sexual mores.

In the Roman world, these add up to a ruler destined to be cut to ribbons, both by the swords of soldiers and the pens of historians. It's nearly impossible to tell what of their commentary is genuine historical discussion and what is so much post-facto piling on from people who wanted to portray the Syrian teenager as the devil incarnate. Even if the more outlandish stories were not wholly fact-based, particularly the second and the third reasons above would have more than enough to invite moralizing Roman historians to character assassination. The question is this: are they enough to earn Elagabalus's ranking on this list?

It is possible that the stories are no more embellished than those of any other emperor or ruler. Elagabalus was so young, just fourteen at his accession. He was invested with almost unlimited authority, and, at least initially, inherited a devoted army that made it very dangerous for anyone to defy his will. At the end of the day, he didn't do a tremendous amount of damage. The bloodletting that kicked off his rule was terrible. Thinning the ranks of experienced administrators might help someone feel secure on the throne, but it wasn't good for securing an empire. But once in Rome, Elagabalus seemed to want to indulge in sensual luxury more than unleash hordes of killing squads. Mostly, he was just weird. And because we must take the stories about him with a grain of salt, we need to see what followed his death to judge his impact.

After his death, the transfer of power was peaceful. It wasn't hard for the Romans to toss aside the black stone/god and restore order to their religious world. Fortunately for them, the next claimant to the throne, the studious young Alexander, took his responsibilities much more seriously. Alexander might have been the last ruler from the House of Severus, but at least he recovered some of the family's dignity after the disastrous reign of his cousin Elagabalus.

If this was a list of most incompetent Roman emperors, then Elagabalus would be ranked higher, likely in the top three. He is where he is less because he was truly evil and more because he was truly weird. Not that he doesn't belong on the list, and he certainly had his fair share of awful actions to attest to his ranking. It's just to say that his worst was a bit milder than some of the people who follow.

#7: MAXIMINUS THRAX

After the catastrophes of Caracalla and Elagabalus, Rome needed stability. For a time, it found it in the administration of the young Alexander Severus and his regents. But rather than play his part in the administration and solve some of the empire's dire challenges, Maximinus engineered the murder of the responsible, efficient young emperor and claimed power for himself. He took the throne and began anew the cycles of purges and recriminations that did so much to weaken Rome and its administration. Just as Rome was getting its footing, Maximinus did much to plunge it back into chaos.

For a guy so massive, he really was insecure. He seems to have been ashamed of his low birth status. Rather than being a confident emperor, he couldn't shake off his childhood insecurities. Six feet, seven feet, eight feet tall. It didn't matter. He was the giant man with a social Napoleonic complex. It was too bad, for Rome and for him. Maximinus seems to have been a talented general. He left the empire with its enemies cowed and its borders secure. But just as he wanted revenge on the nobility for their treatment of him, so, too, would the "barbarians" want revenge for his treatment of them.

By systematically eliminated people of rank, talent, and experience, Maximinus set the stage for decades of trouble. But his fury was not bound to the nobility. His sacking of Roman towns and citizens was unprecedented in scope and savagery. He destroyed anyone and anything that stood in his way, Roman friend or foreign foe alike. He consolidated all the power of the empire into one set of massive hands and weakened everything else in order to do so. This set the stage for wholesale instability, which would almost destroy the empire in the decades to come. He exhausted the empire with constant warfare, destabilized its institutions, preyed on his people, and drained the treasury to keep his armies in the field. This is all in addition to his personal cruelty, which ranks among the very worst of Roman rulers. When he died, he was little mourned. Why would he be? He had so many people—including childhood friends and supporters—put to death. Maximinus died an ignoble death. Thanks to him, the empire almost did, too.

#6: TARQUIN SUPERBUS

Lucius Tarquinius Superbus had a cool name. But Superbus didn't mean "superb." It meant "proud," as in arrogant. He was that and so much more. Tarquin was easily one of the worst people ever to hold the reins of Roman rule. He was ruthless and grasping, and his path to power was cleared by murder of the people to whom he should have been most faithful. In order to claim the throne, he killed or had killed his own brother, his sister-in-law, and his father-in-law, from whom he seized the throne in a bloody coup. Tarquin had a craven thirst for power. He didn't want the power to pursue a political agenda. He had no policy platform. Even if he had had such an agenda, even awful or devious, at least it would have been *something*. He sought nothing more than power for its own sake. He murdered a good and wise king, then proved himself to be the opposite.

Once on the throne, Tarquin created a culture of fear and intimidation in Rome. He allowed his family to rape and pillage at will. There was no justice. There was no moderation, no wise rulings from a benevolent king. Just tyranny, plain and simple.

Tarquin seized the throne at a time of Roman ascendency. It tussled constantly with its neighbors as it sought to project its power outward from its spot on the Tiber. At the same time, it defined its militaristic and civic institutions and began to develop its sense of identity. Tarquin's base lust for power and creation of a culture of fear and tyranny threatened to stop Rome's ascent to greatness before it even had a chance to get going. Another couple of years of his rule, and Rome may have crumbled, failing to reach the point where history took notice.

Tarquin was so bad, in fact, that kings were outlawed; to be accused of aspiring to become one was a death sentence. Not just Tarquin was banished. So was the whole concept of monarchy. It would take five centuries before it would come back, but not in name. Kings were gone forever, the idea of kingship scorned, the name of Tarquinius Supurbus cursed for all eternity. On the other hand, the Roman who led the overthrow, Lucius Junius Brutus, went down in history as one of the greatest

Romans ever. In fact, an obsessive desire to live up to the family legacy, nearly half a millennium later, led the more famous Brutus, Marcus Junius Brutus, to join a conspiracy and plunge a dagger into Julius Caesar.

If Tarquin had quietly left the stage after his deposition, perhaps he would not rank so high. But after being thrown out, he flailed about in a desperate attempt to get his throne back. For the rest of his life, he tried, and failed, to place himself back in charge. He was gone, but until he died, he remained a thorn in Rome's side, drawing away manpower, energy, and resources. He didn't even have to be king to be dreadful. Only when Tarquin finally died could Rome get on with the business of building its empire.

#5: THE PRAETORIAN GUARDS

As with the Senate, the story of the Praetorians is less about one person and more about an institution. It is a story told over half a millennium and involving many people. Unlike the Senate, there's little to add to the credit side of the ledger. Whereas the Senate helped Rome grow and prosper, the Praetorians were leeches, sucking power and wealth from the body politic. They did little to make Rome better and a lot to make it worse.

The Praetorians got their start under Augustus. Ostensibly, they were the emperor's bodyguard. The reality is that as the only armed troops allowed in the capital, they were in a unique position to project power and influence events. Too often they used this power for evil. Unlike the Senate, which contributed to Rome's rise to empire, it's hard to find much redeemable in this group of guys. Assignment to the ranks of the Praetorians was a sweet gig. They had no competition. They were loyal to the emperor only as long as the cash kept rolling in.

Some prefects were good, honest public servants who drilled discipline into their men and served the emperor faithfully. But too often they did the opposite. If a ruthless, lazy, or incompetent Praetorian was named commander, bad things followed quickly. No one could stand in his way, unless a commander in the provinces willingly marched troops to the city to cow the overweight, greedy slobs. When that did happen, they sacrificed the emperor, the one person they were duty bound to protect, and just switched sides, usually collecting another big cash donative for their trouble.

Time and again, their self-serving, myopic actions worked in direct contradiction to the best interests of Roman society. Rather than get in shape, they lounged in their barracks, coming out to intimidate people or eliminate opponents, either theirs or the emperor's. Increasingly, they cared less about their orders and duty and more about their self-interest. Time and again, the Praetorians abused their power and played kingmaker. The assassination of the emperor Pertinax and the subsequent auctioning off of the empire to the rich but otherwise hapless Didius Julianus was a disgrace of the highest order.

Too often, the story of emperors is told through the actions of their ruthless, evil Praetorian prefects. Sejanus, during the reign of Tiberius, is the starkest, most bone-chilling example. Sejanus wrote the script for how the Praetorian prefect could manipulate an emperor and spread a culture of fear and death through the capital and the empire at large. The paranoia of Tiberius's later years can be traced back to Sejanus's manipulation and evil schemes. Sadly, this was not limited to Sejanus. Nero had Tigellinus. Commodus had Perennis. Eventually, Praetorians began to make direct claims for the throne. Macrinus did the world a favor when he offed the genocidal maniac Caracalla, but he did nothing with his office and died a short time later, relegated to the footnotes of history.

The legacy of the Praetorians is stained with lots of imperial blood. Their near-constant regicide in the mid-200s was a major contributor to the Crisis of the Third Century. Their greed nearly destroyed the empire. What's amazing is not that they did all they did but that it took more than three hundred years for an emperor—in this case, Constantine—to get rid of the whole lot. By the time he did, they got credit for more than their fair share of evil, tyranny, and bloodshed. The Praetorians definitely must be counted among the worst rulers in Rome's long history.

From this point forward, a solid case can be made for all of the final contenders to be listed as the very worse. Each was profoundly terrible, but in a surprising variety of ways.

#4: CALIGULA

Sometimes legends drift far from reality. In the case of Caligula, the legend is just the tip of the iceberg. His very name evokes a shudder. Even people who don't know the details know that Caligula was a depraved lunatic. Or was he?

The true character of Caligula is a fascinating subject of debate. Some defend him as being warped by a horrific childhood. His dashing, heroic father died young under mysterious circumstances. His mother and brothers were starved and murdered by his uncle Tiberius. Then he was summoned to live by Tiberius's side as the old man indulged in every manner of sadistic and sexual depravity. Other historians paint the picture of a brilliant but cynical young man, whose actions exposed the fraud at the heart of Roman society, only being spun into tales of lunacy after his death, posthumous revenge by those he shamed. Finally, some say he was swell, off to a great start before he fell gravely ill, only emerging as a madman after his recovery, never quite the same.

All of this misses the point. It doesn't matter *why* he threatened to make his horse a consul. He threatened to do it. It doesn't matter *why* he marched an army to the sea to make them collect seashells; he did it. It doesn't matter *why* he turned the palace into a brothel. He did that, too. The debate over the psychological underpinnings of his actions risks missing the bigger picture: Caligula killed, raped, stole, debased, and bankrupted.

Historians reached consensus about one thing: his intelligence. Caligula had a quick and energetic mind. The issue was how he applied that energy.

In the end, it doesn't matter. Whether he was an unstable, mentally ill psycho, or a cold, calculating, brilliant but ruthless psycho, he was still a psycho. In any scenario, he was determined to humiliate and degrade Roman institutions, was wildly profligate, free flowing with death sentences. Caligula raped a bride on her wedding day, humiliated his own troops, brought back the treason trials of his predecessors, and so much more.

Caligula inherited an empire whose treasuries were overflowing, an empire that enjoyed peace and stability on the frontiers. In four short years as emperor, he left the empire broke, its defensive strategy incoherent, its nobility shaken. Distrust and paranoia were rampant, the connection between the imperial palace and the Senate House shattered.

Rome would face big problems in the years to come. Trust and cooperation between the emperor and nobility were important to civic governance. Before Caligula, emperors and the nobility had at least shared the pretense of civility between them. After Caligula, the dynamic was broken forever. From this point forward, the fate of the empire, more than ever, was in the hands of one person. The consequences would be disastrous.

Besides, the arguments over Caligula's sanity miss the point. He was evil. And he was a terrible emperor. The army hated him. The people hated him. The Senate hated him. Although the nature of his character may be up for debate, he is not historically misunderstood. His was truly one of the evilest Roman rulers.

#3: NERO

Which is worse? A terrible emperor who does minor damage year after year but who lives long enough for the impact to add up to horrible outcomes? Or one who does a ton of damage but exits the scene relatively quickly?

Lunatics such as Caligula and Elagabalus and vicious tyrants such as Maximinus Thrax flamed out relatively quickly. They aren't at this place in the rankings precisely because they died too soon to do even more damage. Someone killed them before they could destroy the empire. But Nero wasn't a lunatic. He wasn't violently unhinged. He certainly had a bad temper: just ask Poppea Sabina. But his reign is marked less by obscene spasms of blood and violence and more by a crippling, unrelenting incompetence, a chronic wound that just bled and bled. Part of why he's so bad is because he was just bad enough to last and last and last. Along the way, he indulged his narcissism, his grudges, his lusts, his basest character flaws. By the time someone got around to stopping him, the damage was done. It wasn't that the damage happened too quickly. It's that it happened too slowly so that by the time people noticed, things were *really* bad.

Over the span of his reign, the cumulative impact of Nero's just-bad-enough behavior added up considerably. Less flashy than Caligula, Nero nevertheless did more damage over a period and accumulated considerable deeds that argue for his position. He had his own mother killed. He had one wife executed on trumped-up treason charges and kicked another one to death while she was pregnant. His final "wife" was a castrated boy dressed up to look like the previous wife. The "ick factor" with Nero was off the charts. But his rule was more than a series of spectacularly failed personal relationships. Nero unleashed waves of religious persecution, devastated the finances, provoked rebellions across the empire . . . the list goes on and on.

Most egregiously, Nero nearly brought the empire to its knees in pursuit of his own vainglory. Convinced of his artistic genius, instead of governing, Nero sang, strummed the lyre, and strutted around onstage. He didn't fiddle while Rome burned, but he *was* out of town for a performance he made other people sit through and pretend to love.

In the aftermath of the Great Fire, Nero cemented his terrible legacy. He seized every bit of wealth he could to pour into his building program. That might have been OK if that program had benefited the masses, but it was all for one person: Nero. His disastrous response to the Great Fire bankrupted the empire, and the massive financial strain he put on the provinces to pay for his monstrous Domus Aurea fueled revolt. His oblivious self-absorption went unchecked as all came crashing down.

Nero ruled for nearly fourteen years. His death exposed the faultiness that had been slowly spreading across the Roman Empire and kicked off a civil war that would rage in Rome and across the empire, pitting Roman against Rome, denuding the provinces of troops, and tearing apart the fabric of Roman society. His megalomania was exceptional. It almost led to the destruction of the empire.

Nero didn't burn down Rome in the Great Fire. But he did burn down the House of Caesar. His legacy would never rise from the ashes, never have a historical renaissance. He died alone and unloved, and today he is detested and reviled. Unfortunately for Rome, the worst was yet to come.

#2: CARACALLA

Caracalla likely has the highest body count attributed to any emperor. He killed selectively. He killed indiscriminately. He killed in ones and twos.

He killed wholesale. He eliminated individuals. He eliminated entire populations. Caracalla's reign was soaked in blood.

He was ruthless, vicious, utterly contemptible. But he wasn't crazy. The method by which Caracalla approached his reign had a chilling logic to it. It was all about his own power. Everything he did, even the murder of his brother, came down to consolidating and projecting his own power. The slaughter of Geta's supporters, the annihilation of the Alexandrian youth—as historically savage as these actions were, they make a certain sense. Caracalla wiped out anyone he suspected might oppose him. This doesn't make these actions less awful. If anything, that rational logic fueled his murder sprees is all the more chilling.

Those he didn't have killed, he humiliated and degraded. His ordering that theaters and palaces be constructed for his entertainment, then demolished, unused, was a projection of power intended to put his boot on the throats of the local populace and their leaders. Making senators and magistrates meet him at dawn, then not appearing and leaving people to wait all day, was a way to assert his domination.

If anything positive can be said about Caracalla, it's that he accidentally stumbled into one big positive. By granting citizenship and rights across the entire empire, he brought more people into the Roman system, increasing cultural diffusion and integration. He also bolstered the tax rolls. Because he poured that money back into his insatiable soldiers—he was going to pay them, come hell or high water—at least his edict prevented the empire from being in even worse shape.

His doting on the army went way too far. Before him, the army existed for two principal reasons: to expand Roman borders and to protect the people living inside them. Caracalla's army became insatiable, a swarm of locusts more concerned with their own riches than their duty to the empire.

He left the empire at war on multiple fronts. His lack of strategic vision and his shortcomings as a general exposed the empire to enormous pressure on several borders. But the army was strong, loyal to his commands, and certainly well financed. He left a knotty mess, but Rome was not yet devoid of the ability to fight and defend itself. His citizenship edict and propping up the army might have been by-products of his single-minded, relentless consolidation of personal power, but they had benefits that can't be overlooked. Caracalla was an evil, megalomaniacal mass murderer, but even that wasn't enough to make him the worst that Rome had to offer.

#1: COMMODUS

Hand a self-indulgent, dim-witted oaf control of the most powerful empire in the world. Make his very wish everyone else's undisputed command. Surround him with vicious, scheming people. Allow him unfettered ability to indulge his delusions of grandeur.

What could possibly go wrong? As is turned out, almost everything.

Everyone's seen *Gladiator*, right? Commodus certainly is a villain. Joaquin Phoenix's portrayal has one problem, though: it shows the emperor as deceitful and unstable, but it also makes him look cunning, calculating, even smart. He was none of these things.

Commodus was the first person in Rome's history born into a world his father ruled as emperor, "born to the purple." He never had to develop his intellect or his character. All he had to do was wait. Even in pursuit of power, he was lazy and devoid of ambition.

His father, Marcus Aurelius, was of a world where sons inherited from fathers. He must have known that his son was a lout, but traditions were traditions, and the best Marcus could do was to surround his son with good people. That worked OK at first, until his survival of the assassination attempt. Then Commodus took control of the day-to-day operations of empire from people of merit and gave them to sycophants, schemers, and incompetents. Things fell apart quickly.

As his reign progressed, his character slid further and further into darkness. He went from a dull, lazy prince to a cruel, twisted emperor. The more violent and erratic he got, the deeper he spiraled. He became worse every day. He invented new ways to be horrible, new ways to express his evil. His bloodletting was unrelenting. Wild animals in the arena and senators alike, his thirst for blood was unquenchable. He was sick, cruel, sadistic, deluded.

Commodus inherited Rome at the peak of its power. He left it insolvent, its foundations crumbling, its nobility shattered. The disaster of Commodus set the stage for civil war, conflict, and strife that would dominate the third century.

Commodus has not one redeeming feature, not a single thing to his credit. Nothing. Not one thing that makes you pause for a moment. Everything about him was a disaster. Even Nero, Caligula, and Caracalla brought *something* to the table. Insufficient as those things might have been, at least you can find the germ of something useful in those guys. Commodus is all the bad without even a shred of good. Nearly two thousand years later, nothing speaks in his favor. When you compare him to his father, the gulf between one of the greatest emperors and the very worst is all the more appalling. Not a single thing about his assassination is tragic except that it didn't happen sooner. Some of his successors would try to put the pieces back together, but the sheer destructive force of Commodus was head and shoulders above everyone else. The cracks in the foundations of the Roman Empire take on a new seriousness, a new significance, in the twelve-year reign of the bloody tyrant.

After Commodus, the empire would endure unprecedented instability. Civil war. Foreign war. Domestic strife. The Year of Five Emperors. The Year of Six Emperors. Breakaway kingdoms led by renegade generals. Autocracy. Religious persecution. And, of course, more evil rulers exploiting this instability to the detriment of everyone else. You name it. The case has been made that the line from the height of the empire to its collapse starts with Commodus, that he was so bad that he almost single-handedly sowed the seeds of destruction of the ancient world's most powerful empire. It had its ups and downs along the way, but in the reign of Commodus, we find the beginning of the end. Maybe this is unfair: a lot happened after Commodus, so he can't be blamed for the end that came nearly three hundred years later.

Perhaps. But it doesn't matter.

The fact that the case can be made at all speaks volumes. And besides, he was terrible enough in his own lifetime to earn his spot. Equal parts murderer, tyrant, *and* lunatic, Commodus's blood-soaked reign was the nadir of Roman rule. Considering how many awful rulers Rome knew over the course of its history, to be the very worst that Rome ever produced is a pretty ignominious distinction.

* * *

So. Did you keep a list? How did it compare? Do we agree? The debate is always fun. History—even from events millennia ago—has a way of changing. One reputation improves; another sinks. The people on this list are objectively bad. But who knows what stories or scholarship

EPILOGUE

The End Is Just the Beginning

In 476 CE, the Gothic king Odoacer invaded Italy and deposed the teenager sitting on the imperial throne. Little more than a figurehead for his father, Romulus Augustulus was fated to be the last in a long line of emperors dating back centuries. Odoacer deposed the boy, but in an unexpected twist, let him live, sending the young man to live under house arrest in a castle near modern-day Naples. His father, the real power behind the throne, was not so lucky. Odoacer had him executed. It is this epochal event that most historians point to as the fall of the Western Roman Empire. Rome itself had long since ceased to be the seat of power, though it continued to have enormous symbolic importance. But while the power in the west crumbled, the Roman world continued to thrive, albeit farther east and with a decidedly Greek influence.

With the deposition of Romulus Augustulus, the Roman Empire now centered entirely on Constantinople, the city built for and by Constantine the Great. Constantinople had been waxing while western power was waning. History labels the Eastern Roman Empire the Byzantine Empire. Even as Gothic kings set up shop in the west, the Byzantines carried on the Roman traditions, including suffering through the lives and reigns of some truly dreadful people.

They weren't all bad. In fact, some were downright brilliant. One, Emperor Justinian, managed to reconquer most of the "old" empire, stitching it back together and reuniting east and west for one glorious swan song. It wasn't fated to last. Just as Justinian and his generals congratulated themselves on restoring the glory of the mighty Roman Empire, a plague swept through the lands, devastating the population, sapping the empire's military might, and causing the whole thing to crumble to pieces . . . again.

Justinian's successors would never achieve the same soaring feats. But, in carrying on the Roman traditions, some Byzantine emperors were good, just, and competent; others were murderers, tyrants, and lunatics. One that fell into the former category was Maurice. He rose through the ranks as a soldier, then general, eventually becoming emperor in 582 CE. His accomplishments were significant. Maurice successfully bested Rome's centuries-old enemy, the Sassanians (think: Persian Empire), restoring dignity in the face of a bitter adversary. He fought back incursions from hostile tribes up and down the Byzantine borders. Their armies once again reigned supreme. Maurice's successes extended beyond the battlefield, as he showed strong administrative talent, reorganizing the governance of the empire with wisdom and foresight. With a few consecutive emperors of talent, who knows how far things could have gone. But as the 600s CE rolled around, Maurice was old, and his armies were tired of fighting all the time. They wanted a break. Phocas, one of their officers, won them over with words about how much better things would be if he were in charge. They listened, revolted, and declared for Phocas.

They had one last battle to fight. They marched on Constantinople, intent on tossing the old man aside. Maurice, undeterred, carried on as usual. Even with a rebel army coming for him, he hosted lavish games and races, all smiles as he interacted with his people.[1] His people failed to return his kindness, pelting him with stones and shouting curses at him.[2] When serious, driven leaders tackle big problems, sometimes people tune them out. No matter how much the citizens of Constantinople needed Maurice's reforms, they much preferred to hear that they didn't need reform anymore. Ignorance is bliss. They turned on their emperor, drove him off his throne, and hailed the upstart Phocas. It was a bad move.

By now, Maurice was aged and infirm; his body was worn out from a lifetime of service to the empire. He awaited his fate stoically, and it wasn't long in coming. Phocas had the now-deposed emperor seized, along with five of his sons. Just to prove what an awful guy he was, the new emperor had those sons beheaded in front of their father, Maurice, one by one. That was Maurice's reward for his just and energetic rule: to endure a horror that defies contemplation. Phocas made poor Maurice watch as his line was wiped out, then put the old man out of his own misery. He had Maurice beheaded, too. Their bodies were cast into the sea, and their heads were put on pikes around town, lest anyone miss the lesson about who was now in charge.[3]

For his part, Phocas took sole possession of the imperial throne. He sent the images of his wife and himself to the Senate and clergy so that the new royal couple could enjoy appropriate veneration from the religious leaders and top magistrates alike.[4]

Unfortunately for the empire and its citizens, Phocas was not cunning, just ruthless. He was a boor, uninterested in anything but naked power and satisfying his lustful passions.[5] Lacking diplomatic grace, in short order he resparked the war with Persia that Maurice had just successfully concluded. This would last nearly three decades and prove disastrous to the long-term health and stability of the empire. But he wouldn't live to see it. He would die an inglorious death long before that, just not soon enough.

Fearful that Maurice's wife and daughters could become the focal point of a revolt, he had them dragged from exile and beheaded on the same spot as Maurice and his sons. Phocas was the archetype of the paranoid tyrant, and the blood began to flow. He indiscriminately rounded up victims, whether they were real enemies or only enemies in the mind of the deranged emperor. Setting a new bar for cruelty, Phocas had prisoners blinded, their tongues torn out, shot full of arrows, whipped to death . . . any savagery that can be imagined, and many that cannot. According to Edward Gibbon, "The hippodrome, the sacred asylum of the pleasures and liberties of the Romans, was polluted with heads and limbs and mangled bodies."[6] The capital itself was turning into a charnel house. Phocas skulked in the imperial palace, jumping at shadows and ordering the next waves of killing.

As Phocas lost his grip on reality, he also lost his grip on the empire. It was only a matter of time before rebellion threatened to topple the blood-thirsty tyrant. When the time came, those closest to him were all too happy to aid and abet the rebels. Those who equivocated took bribes to sway their support. In 610 CE, a revolt that began in the African provinces made its way to the capital. The ringleaders seized Phocas. Friendless and unloved, he was put in chains and dragged to his death. Like so

The Column of Phocas was the last monument erected in the Roman Forum. The collapse of the Western Empire in 476 CE didn't end the bloodshed wrought by Roman emperors; things just shifted east for the next thousand years. *Wikimedia Commons.*

many who had met the same fate at his capricious command, Phocas was beheaded and his body desecrated.[7]

His reign had been an unmitigated disaster. Focused on putting down imagined internal conspiracies, Phocas neglected the real threat to the empire. He failed to protect the borders against invasion. Wave after wave of invading armies poured in, even as wave after wave of citizens met a cruel end at the hands of Phocas's killing squads. By the time someone finally separated his head from his neck, the empire was in serious trouble. Successive emperors fought to put out the flames and bring back stability where they could, but immeasurable damage had been done. As had happened so many times before, Phocas's killing denuded the capital of many of its leading citizens and magistrates. Not only were the crises at hand severe, the threats existential, but the pool of talented people needed to rise to the challenge was drained.

Instead of installing competent people to look after things, he gave senior posts to relatives, the empire's most important positions to people devoid of talent. His terrible administration went hand in glove with his terrible character. Incompetence, nepotism, violence, and paranoia are rightly counted among the worst traits among rulers.

The Western Empire had collapsed a century and a quarter before Phocas seized power and unleashed his killing spree. But, just because the western half of the empire had collapsed, it didn't mean that the Romans were immune from bad, crazy emperors. The end of Phocas was not the end of the Eastern Roman Empire. In fact, it had more than eight hundred years left in its run. Along the way, the citizens of the empire in general, and those of Constantinople in particular, would have to endure more murderers, tyrants, and lunatics. For all the fuss about the "decline and fall" of the Roman Empire, the death knell of the Western Empire wasn't the end; it was only the beginning. Just ask Maurice.

APPENDIX

Cast of Characters

Roman history is full of thousands and thousands of important figures. Those outlined below stand out for their contributions to the stories told in this book. It's not an index, nor is it a list of every important Roman, just a list of the main characters central to this book's stories. From the introduction to the epilogue, we cover about fifteen hundred years of history—and a lot to keep straight in this story of murderers, tyrants, and lunatics.

Aetius

Roman general, administrator, and de facto ruler of the late Roman Empire. Of considerable talent and energy, Aetius stemmed the tide of the decline of the Western Empire. Like Stilicho before him, Aetius was betrayed and murdered, this time at the hands of the emperor himself, with Valentinian III personally striking the mortal blow. His death paved the way for the destruction of Rome itself and the Western Roman Empire.

Agrippina the Younger

The daughter of the legendary Germanicus, sister of the infamous Caligula, niece and fourth wife of the stuttering Claudius, and mother of the bratty Nero, Agrippina certainly had a front-row seat to imperial power. Grasping and cunning, her ambition got her to the very top of Roman society, but she was done in by her own son, who engineered her murder. She knew full well who was responsible for her impending death. As the death squad drew their swords, she pointed at her belly and said, "Smite my womb."

Alaric

Sometimes friend and sometimes foe, the Gothic king Alaric had a complicated relationship with Rome and its various emperors and generals. Once Honorius betrayed and executed Stilicho, no one left was competent enough to steer Rome through its various crises. Alaric took advantage of the talent vacuum, marched his troops on Rome, and sacked the Eternal City for the first time in eight centuries.

Alexander Severus

Normally, handing the empire to untested youths was a recipe for disaster, such as with his weirdo cousin Elagabalus. However, the last emperor from the Severan dynasty was surrounded by competent people and took his responsibilities seriously. Unfortunately for him, and for Rome, his grasping lieutenant Maximinus Thrax overthrew and killed young Alexander, plunging Rome deep into the Crisis of the Third Century.

Ambrose

The bishop of Milan in the late fourth century CE, Ambrose had considerable influence at the imperial court. When Theodosius repented his slaughter of the citizens of Thessalonica, Ambrose held out absolution, tormenting the emperor with threat of damnation. When he finally accepted Theodosius's confession, Ambrose accomplished a significant consolidation of the Church's power and the final ascendancy of Christianity.

Augustus

The first emperor, Augustus's career was nothing short of exceptional. Cast into the spotlight after his posthumous adoption by his great uncle, Julius Caesar, the man who would become emperor began his career through violence and bloodshed. Mellowing as he matured—and as threats to his power diminished—he eventually demonstrated a life of shrewd, farsighted policy.

Aurelian

A brilliant emperor who rose to power amid the Crisis of the Third Century, Aurelian's sheer competence and unrelenting energy began the process of stitching a shattered empire back together. After stringing together a series of remarkable victories, he was killed by his own Praetorian guards, cutting short a remarkable career and denying Rome a brilliant emperor at a time when brilliance was in short supply.

Caracalla

The older son of the emperor Septimius Severus, Caracalla killed his brother Geta rather than share rule of the empire. That was just the start, as his blood-soaked reign chalked up tens of thousands of victims across the empire. He died by the assassin's sword at only twenty-nine years old, likely saving untold thousands from his genocidal impulses.

Claudius

The uncle and successor to Caligula, Claudius was the brother of the beloved and legendary general Germanicus. Suffering from a stutter and a limp, Claudius survived the bloody inner circle of the imperial palace by pretending to be stupid, fooling everyone into thinking he was no threat and thus not worth eliminating as a potential rival. Once he became emperor, he fooled everyone again by proving to be one of Rome's best.

Cleander

Rising to prominence under Commodus, Cleander was an intimate of the maniacal emperor. Stoking Commodus's fears and suspicion, Cleander brought out the worst in an already terrible ruler. Cleander cleared the way to power by accusing his rival, Perennis, of plotting against Commodus, but eventually Commodus had the unpopular Cleander beheaded to appease the crowds.

Didius Julianus

Rich and anxious for power, Didius Julianus "won" the ignoble auction put on by the Praetorian guards to gain the job of emperor following their assassination of Pertinax. One of his first acts was to grant clemency to the runner-up in the bidding, showing a mild, tolerant disposition. It didn't do him much good though; all that cash bought him nine weeks as emperor before he was assassinated himself. His death cleared the way for the rise of the House of Severus.

Diocletian

A general who rose to power in the tumultuous era of the Crisis of the Third Century, Diocletian had a gift for administration unrivaled in the ancient world. His reign as emperor was widely successful but scarred by his decision to persecute Christians. Though based on a pragmatic goal of empire-wide unity, the Great Persecution accelerated the cult of martyrdom and strengthened the resolve of the Christians. Diocletian's unexpected abdication stands out as unique in Roman history.

Elagabalus

Rising to power at the machinations of his grandmother Julia Maesa, Elagabalus won over the army by way of the rumor that he was Caracalla's son. The fun didn't last, as the fourteen-year-old offended just about every Roman sensibility. Decadent, depraved, and committed to subjugating the Roman religion to his own eastern mystery cult, his popularity plummeted. Ever the opportunist, Maesa engineered Elagabalus's overthrow so she could replace him with her other grandson, the more studious and pliable Alexander Severus.

Gaius

More famously known as Caligula, Gaius was the third emperor of Rome. He ascended to the throne following the death of the reclusive and stingy old Tiberius. His rule started with great fanfare and joyous acclaim from the people, but then things became weird and bloody pretty quickly. The first truly awful emperor, Gaius invented all kinds of ways to degrade, humiliate, murder, and marginalize everyone around him. For good reason, he was also the first emperor to be assassinated.

Gaius and Tiberius Gracchus

Reform-oriented brothers, they hailed from a family with impeccable aristocratic credentials. Genuinely concerned about the plight of the common citizen, they were seen as traitors to their class. Rather than consider reform and firm up the shaky foundations of the republic, angry senators led violent suppression of the Gracchi and their followers, murdering people by the thousands.

Galba

The first to kick off the tumultuous Year of the Four Emperors, Galba rebelled against Nero and marched his troops on Rome. By the time he reached the capital, Nero had committed suicide, and the transition of power was reasonably peaceful, that is, until Galba started acting like a stingy, moralizing old man. Otho had Galba murdered and seized control himself. It wouldn't be long before Otho committed suicide just like his old friend Nero.

Genseric

Like Alaric before him, the Vandal king Genseric had a fraught relationship with Rome that ultimately culminated in open war. Echoing prior events, Valentinian III's murder of this top general and adviser, Aetius, opened the path to Rome. Unlike Alaric, when Genseric sacked Rome in 455, his Vandals showed no restraint in pillaging the city, making the name Vandal synonymous with wanton destruction.

Geta

The younger son of the emperor Septimius Severus, Geta inherited corule of the empire upon his father's death. Everyone seemed to like the genial young man, except for his brooding and violent older brother, Caracalla, who had Geta hacked to death while in the arms of their mother. After Geta's death, Caracalla tried to wipe the name and memory of his dead brother from the historical record.

Honorius

Son of Theodosius the Great, Honorius came to sole rule at a young age. He is portrayed as weak and indecisive, a sulking child ill fit to lead a powerful empire. His top general and adviser, Stilicho, worked tirelessly to reverse the fortunes of the flagging empire, but Honorius betrayed Stilicho and had him executed, all but sealing the fate of Roman power in the west.

Julia Domna

Wife of Septimius Severus and mother of the feuding Caracalla and Geta, Julia Domna was at the center of Roman power for two generations of the empire. Her older son had her younger son hacked to death as she tried in vain to shield him from the assassins. As if holding her dying son in her arms wasn't awful enough, Caracalla threatened her with a similar fate if she didn't act happy in public.

Julia Maesa

The power behind the throne of two emperors, Julia Maesa was the sister of Julia Domna, the wife of Septimius Severus. Maesa engineered the overthrow and deposition of Macrinus and installed her seriously unqualified grandson Elagabalus on the throne. When he proved to be a disaster, she had Elagabalus eliminated and replaced with another grandson, Alexander Severus.

Lucius Junius Brutus

Considered to be the founder of the Roman republic, Brutus led the expulsion of the Tarquins and the overthrow of the monarchy. His familial legacy of courage, virtue, and decisive action weighed heavily on his descendant, Marcus Junius Brutus, who followed the example of his ancestor when betraying his friend and patron, Julius Caesar.

Lucius Tarquinius Priscus

The fifth king of Rome, Tarquin Priscus was murdered by the sons of his predecessor, who felt that he had deprived them of their rightful place on the throne. His wife, Tanaquil, engineered the regal succession not to their own sons, but to a better, more qualified man, Servius Tullius. But after several decades of scheming, one of those two sons, Lucius Tarquinius Superbus, would murder his way onto the throne and bring the whole Roman monarchy crashing to the ground.

Lucius Tarquinius Superbus

The seventh and final king of Rome, Tarquin would seize power in a bloody coup, then go on to the most violent and ignominious reign of any Roman king. His son's rape of the virtuous Lucretia spurred the citizens to action, and the whole family was driven off. Tarquin lived out his days scheming to reclaim his throne and died in exile, still fuming at his deposition.

Lucretia

A noblewoman of unsurpassed virtue, Lucretia was raped by Sextus Tarquin, son of Tarquin Superbus. She went before her father and husband, told them what happened, and made them swear revenge. Once they did, she pulled out a knife and killed herself on the spot. Whipped into a fury by these actions, her husband and his friend Brutus would topple the monarchy and establish the republic.

Macrinus

A short-lived and little-mourned ruler, Macrinus didn't do much notable as emperor, as he was betrayed and murdered by his troops after just a few months on the job. His great contribution came before ascending to rule, as he engineered the assassination of the genocidal Caracalla.

Marcus Aurelius

The last of Edward Gibbon's "Five Good Emperors," Marcus was well-loved and respected. Dedicated to the ideal of the philosopher-king, he devoted considerable time to his own self-improvement. His biggest failing was turning the empire over to his lout of a son, Commodus. Many people point to his death and Commodus's accession as the start of the decline of the Roman Empire.

Maximinus Thrax

His stature wasn't the only thing gigantic: Maximinus Thrax also had massive insecurities. After murdering Alexander Severus, Maximinus turned his army on any perceived foe, including Roman towns and cities. His toppling of Severus and subsequent reign of terror plunged the empire headlong into the Crisis of the Third Century.

Otho

The best friend of the emperor Nero, Otho was "promoted" to a far-off province to clear the way for Nero to steal his wife. When fellow governor Galba rose up in revolt, Otho turned on Nero and supported Galba's cause. Upset at not being named heir to the aged Galba, Otho murdered the older man, seized the throne, and became emperor himself. Otho was, in turn, overthrown by another usurper. Otho's suicide in the face of looming defeat was seen by contemporaries as noble, an attempt to end civil war and save Roman lives.

Perennis

Praetorian prefect under Commodus, Perennis held great influence over the deranged emperor. The voice of Perennis whispering in Commodus's ear led to many of the worst acts of his long and twisted rule. Eventually Perennis got a taste of his own medicine when a rival convinced Commodus that Perennis was plotting against him. Perennis was arrested and executed.

Pertinax

Inheriting an empire in complete disaster, Pertinax took over after the catastrophic reign of Commodus. He was well respected and competent and understood that the empire was in serious financial trouble. When he tried to instill some discipline in the ranks of the Praetorian guards, they assassinated him and offered the job of emperor for sale to the highest bidder. He ruled just three months.

Poppea Sabina

Rich and beautiful, Poppea Sabina drew the eye of many admirers, notably Otho and his best friend, Nero. Once Nero "promoted" Otho to govern a province on the fringes of the empire, the lusty emperor claimed Poppea for himself. All was well until he kicked the pregnant Poppea in the stomach, killing both her and their unborn child.

Praetorian Guards

First organized by Augustus, the Praetorians were the emperor's bodyguards. As the only armed troops allowed in Rome or in the presence of the emperor, they could—and often did—use this power to ill ends. They killed lots of emperors. When they weren't killing emperors directly, they were often killing citizens on behalf of them. Their frequent assassinations contributed to the Crisis of the Third Century.

Remus

Legendary twin brother of Romulus. They shared an epic life together, including being abandoned as infants in a basket by the river and nursed by a she-wolf. They careened from one adventure to the next until a petty boundary dispute pitted them against one another. Romulus killed Remus to become the founder of the city and empire that would bear his name.

Romulus

Legendary, and likely mythical, founder and first king of Rome, Romulus had a life and career full of adventure, rarely letting scruples get in the way of accomplishing his goals. He murdered his twin brother, populated his colony with rogues and thugs, stole women from a neighboring tribe, and generally let nothing stop him from building his city on the Palatine Hill.

Sejanus

Praetorian prefect under Tiberius, Sejanus was cunning, devious, and ambitious. Playing to Tiberius's inherent paranoia, Sejanus was able to murder potential rivals, turn Romans against one another, and sow fear and hatred across the empire. He seems to have had plans to inject himself into the imperial family but was toppled before he could do so.

The Senate

Legend has it that the Senate was founded to serve as an advisory body to Romulus, the first king of Rome. It was an institution of Rome from the dawn of its history to its close. Subservient to kings and emperors, for nearly five centuries senators called the shots directly. Under their watch, Rome became an oligarchy and the Senate both violently suppressed and murdered reformers and oppressed common citizens.

Septimius Severus

An effective but autocratic emperor, Septimius Severus marked the start of the transition from civil to military control of the empire. On his death, he left the empire to his two sons, intending them to rule as co-emperors. The shared rule of the two, Geta and Caracalla, neither went well nor ended well.

Sextus Tarquinius

The son of the contemptible Tarquin Superbus, Sextus Tarquinius helped his father scheme, murder, and generally terrorize everyone. His own vicious behavior led him to rape the virtuous Lucretia. This horrid act and her subsequent suicide whipped the Romans into a frenzy of revolt. They drove off the Tarquins, banished monarchy forever, and established the republic, the era of direct senatorial rule.

Stilicho

Half Vandal, half Roman, Stilicho was a key figure in the late Roman Empire. Appointed to serve the imperial administration by Theodosius the Great, Stilicho navigated the shifting sands of geopolitics, fought great battles, and generally kept the Western Empire hanging on, albeit by a thread. Betrayed and executed on the orders of Honorius, Stilicho's premature death had great consequences for the empire.

Sulla

A member of the senatorial class, Sulla hailed from one of the most prestigious families in Rome. He resented serving under the commoner Marius until he finally got his own command. When populist agitation tried to put Marius back on top, Sulla marched his army to Rome, evicted all opposition, and ruthlessly slaughtered countless Romans. His proscription—done in the name of the Senate and the republic—was state-sponsored terrorism.

Tanaquil

Wise and quick-thinking wife of Tarquinius Priscus, the fifth king of Rome, Tanaquil's clever actions following her husband's assassination secured the throne for Servius Tullius over Priscus's and her own two sons. One of those sons went with the flow. The other, Tarquinius Superbus, fumed and plotted revenge.

Theodosius the Great

The last emperor to rule a unified Roman Empire, Theodosius died early and left the teetering empire in titular control of his two sons, Arcadius and Honorius. Although Theodosius earned his moniker "the Great," he ordered the bloody massacre of thousands of citizens. In repentance, he yielded greater control of the empire to the early Christian Church, thus accelerating Rome's centrality as the center of the Catholic Church.

Tiberius

The second emperor of Rome, Tiberius had none of the charm of his stepfather, Augustus. Paranoid and withdrawn by nature, he quit Rome to live in his pleasure palaces on Capri, trusting things to the care of his Praetorian prefect, Sejanus. Sejanus initiated a reign of terror until his own downfall, which led Tiberius to a bloody counter-purge.

Tigellinus

Praetorian prefect under Nero, Tigellinus rose to power through family associations. He curried favor with the petulant, self-indulgent emperor by encouraging his bad behavior and generally by sucking up. After the great fire of Rome, Tigellinus drew the suspicion of the public, and his popularity plummeted alongside Nero's. He was put to death by Otho during the Year of the Four Emperors.

Tullia

The wife of the vile Tarquin, Tullia helped him murder his way to the top. Together they killed her sister, also named Tullia; her father, the aged king Servius Tullius; and his brother, the gentle Arruns. When the citizens finally rose up and overthrew Tarquin, the whole family fled, except Tullia, who chose to commit suicide over losing power.

Valentinian III

One of the last western Roman emperors, Valentinian III was also the last emperor from the Theodosian dynasty. Ascending to the throne at age six, he knew nothing but luxury and indulgence. Jealous courtiers turned him against his trusted general Aetius, whose murder had such terrible consequences for Rome and the Romans.

NOTES

PROLOGUE

1. M. Cary, *A History of Rome* (London: Macmillan, 1954), 34.

2. Titus Livius and T. J. Luce, *The Rise of Rome* (Oxford: Oxford University Press, 1998), 14–16.

3. Dio Cassius, Earnest Cary, and Herbert Baldwin Foster, *Roman History*. 9 vols. (Cambridge, MA: Harvard University Press, 1927), 1:23.

I. THE PROUD

1. Titus Livius and T. J. Luce, *The Rise of Rome* (Oxford: Oxford University Press, 1998), 24.

2. Phillip Barlag, *The History of Rome in 12 Buildings* (Newburyport, MA: New Page Books, 2018), 20–21.

3. Livius and Luce, *Rise of Rome*, 43.

4. Livius and Luce, *Rise of Rome*, 48.

5. Dio Cassius, Earnest Cary, and Herbert Baldwin Foster, *Roman History*. 9 vols. (Cambridge, MA: Harvard University Press, 1927), 1:53.

6. Cassius, Cary, and Foster, *Roman History*, 1:40.

7. Anthony Everitt, *The Rise of Rome* (New York: Random House, 2012), 40.

8. Everitt, *The Rise of Rome*, 41.

9. Everitt, *The Rise of Rome*, 41.

10. Livius and Luce, *Rise of Rome*, 55.

11. Everitt, *The Rise of Rome*, 46.

12. Livius and Luce, *Rise of Rome*, 56.
13. Livius and Luce, *Rise of Rome*, 56.
14. Livius and Luce, *Rise of Rome*, 56.
15. Livius and Luce, *Rise of Rome*, 58.
16. Livius and Luce, *Rise of Rome*, 59.
17. Livius and Luce, *Rise of Rome*, 63.
18. Livius and Luce, *Rise of Rome*, 66.
19. Mary Beard, *SPQR* (New York: Liveright, 2015), 121.
20. Beard, *SPQR*, 122.
21. Beard, *SPQR*, 123.
22. Livius and Luce, *Rise of Rome*, 70.

2. THE OLIGARCHS

1. Anthony Everitt, *The Rise of Rome* (New York: Random House, 2012), 358.
2. Everitt, *Rise of Rome*, 364.
3. Everitt, *Rise of Rome*, 366.
4. Dio Cassius, Earnest Cary, and Herbert Baldwin Foster, *Roman History*. 9 vols. (Cambridge, MA: Harvard University Press, 1927), 1:119.
5. M. Cary, *A History of Rome* (London: Macmillan, 1954), 79.
6. Mary Beard, *SPQR* (New York: Liveright, 2015), 146.
7. Beard, *SPQR*, 147.
8. Everitt, *Rise of Rome*, 380.
9. Beard, *SPQR*, 267.
10. Beard, *SPQR*, 241.
11. Beard, *SPQR*, 227.
12. Everitt, *Rise of Rome*, 388.
13. Cary, *History of Rome*, 338.
14. Cary, *History of Rome*, 338.
15. Cary, *History of Rome*, 431.
16. Anthony Everitt, *Augustus* (New York: Random House, 2006), 82.
17. Adrian Goldsworthy, *Augustus* (New Haven, CT: Yale University Press, 2014), 128.
18. Tom Holland, *Dynasty* (New York: Doubleday, 2015), 42.
19. Holland, *Dynasty*, 42.
20. Holland, *Dynasty*, 45–46.

3. THE LITTLE BOOTS

1. M. Cary, *A History of Rome* (London: Macmillan, 1954), 524.

2. Suetonius, Robert Graves, and J. B. Rives, *The Twelve Caesars* (London: Penguin, 2007), 151.

3. Stephen Dando-Collins, *Caligula* (Nashville, TN: Turner, 2019), 1.

4. Suetonius, Graves, and Rives, *Twelve Caesars*, 155.

5. Aloys Winterling, *Caligula* (Berkeley: University of California Press, 2011), 50.

6. Dando-Collins, *Caligula*, 61.

7. Dando-Collins, *Caligula*, 67–68.

8. Winterling, *Caligula*, 61.

9. Dando-Collins, *Caligula*, 75.

10. Suetonius, Graves, and Rives, *Twelve Caesars*, 156.

11. Dando-Collins, *Caligula*, 78.

12. Winterling, *Caligula*, 78.

13. Suetonius, Graves, and Rives, *Twelve Caesars*, 165.

14. Suetonius, Graves, and Rives, *Twelve Caesars*, 161.

15. Dando-Collins, *Caligula*, 93.

16. Dando-Collins, *Caligula*, 79.

17. Winterling, *Caligula*, 83.

18. Winterling, *Caligula*, 105.

19. Dando-Collins, *Caligula*, 97.

20. Dando-Collins, *Caligula*, 97.

21. Dando-Collins, *Caligula*, 97.

22. Dando-Collins, *Caligula*, 119.

23. Dando-Collins, *Caligula*, 108.

24. Suetonius, Graves, and Rives, *Twelve Caesars*, 167–69.

25. Suetonius, Graves, and Rives, *Twelve Caesars*, 169.

26. Dando-Collins, *Caligula*, 103.

27. Dando-Collins, *Caligula*, 143.

28. Dando-Collins, *Caligula*, 188.

29. Winterling, *Caligula*, 181.

4. THE LADY KILLER

1. Suetonius, Robert Graves, and J. B. Rives, *The Twelve Caesars* (London: Penguin, 2007), 232.

2. Edward Champlin, *Nero* (Cambridge, MA: Belknap Press of Harvard University Press, 2005), 89.

3. Michael Grant, *The Roman Emperors* (New York: Barnes & Noble, 1997), 34.

4. Tom Holland, *Dynasty* (New York: Doubleday, 2015), 337–38.

5. Barry Strauss, *Ten Caesars* (New York: Simon & Schuster, 2019), 86.

6. Matthew Dennison, *The Twelve Caesars* (New York: St. Martin's, 2012), 157.

7. Strauss, *Ten Caesars*, 88–89.

8. M. Cary, *A History of Rome* (London: Macmillan, 1954), 529.

9. Holland, *Dynasty*, 348.

10. Holland, *Dynasty*, 348.

11. Holland, *Dynasty*, 350.

12. Champlin, *Nero*, 57.

13. Holland, *Dynasty*, 357.

14. Holland, *Dynasty*, 26–27.

15. Holland, *Dynasty*, 359.

16. Holland, *Dynasty*, 351.

17. Champlin, *Nero*, 86.

18. Dennison, *Twelve Caesars*, 176.

19. Dennison, *Twelve Caesars*, 179.

20. Dennison, *Twelve Caesars*, 179.

21. Holland, *Dynasty*, 382.

22. Holland, *Dynasty*, 384–85.

23. Suetonius, Graves, and Rives, *Twelve Caesars*, 224.

24. Holland, *Dynasty*, 383.

25. Cary, *History of Rome*, 530.

26. Suetonius, Graves, and Rives, *Twelve Caesars*, 233.

27. Champlin, *Nero*, 145–47.

28. Suetonius, Graves, and Rives, *Twelve Caesars*, 236.

29. Suetonius, Graves, and Rives, *Twelve Caesars*, 236.

30. Suetonius, Graves, and Rives, *Twelve Caesars*, 237.

31. Suetonius, Graves, and Rives, *Twelve Caesars*, 239.

32. Will Durant, *Caesar and Christ: The Story of Civilization III* (New York: Simon & Schuster, 1944), 277.

33. Grant, *Roman Emperors*, 45.

34. Grant, *Roman Emperors*, 47.

35. Grant, *Roman Emperors*, 46.

36. Grant, *Roman Emperors*, 46.

37. Cary, *History of Rome*, 601.

38. Grant, *Roman Emperors*, 47.

5. THE GLADIATOR

1. Michael Grant, *The Roman Emperors* (New York: Barnes & Noble, 1997), 95.

2. M. Cary, *A History of Rome* (London: Macmillan, 1954), 702.

3. Grant, *Roman Emperors*, 96.

4. David Magie, *Historia Augusta*. 3 vols. (Cambridge, MA: Harvard University Press, 1921–1932), 1:267.

5. Edward Gibbon, *The Decline and Fall of the Roman Empire*. 6 vols. (New York: Knopf, 1993), 1:90.

6. Gibbon, *Decline and Fall of the Roman Empire*, 1:99–100.

7. Dio Cassius, Earnest Cary, and Herbert Baldwin Foster, *Roman History*. 9 vols. (Cambridge, MA: Harvard University Press, 1927), 9:81–83.

8. Magie, *Historia Augusta*, 1:285.

9. Cassius, Cary, and Foster, *Roman History*, 9:99.

10. Gibbon, *Decline and Fall of the Roman Empire*, 1:107.

11. Cassius, Cary, and Foster, *Roman History*, 9:105.

12. Cassius, Cary, and Foster, *Roman History*, 9:111.

13. Cassius, Cary, and Foster, *Roman History*, 9:109.

14. Cassius, Cary, and Foster, *Roman History*, 9:111.

15. Gibbon, *Decline and Fall of the Roman Empire*, 1:107.

16. Magie, *Historia Augusta*, 1:293.

17. Cassius, Cary, and Foster, *Roman History*, 9:101.

18. Cassius, Cary, and Foster, *Roman History*, 9:103.

19. Magie, *Historia Augusta*, 1:301.

20. Cassius, Cary, and Foster, *Roman History*, 9:103.

21. Cassius, Cary, and Foster, *Roman History*, 9:105.

22. Cassius, Cary, and Foster, *Roman History*, 9:103.

23. Magie, *Historia Augusta*, 1:301.

24. Magie, *Historia Augusta*, 1:313.

6. THE BODYGUARDS

1. Tom Holland, *Dynasty* (New York: Doubleday, 2015), 297.

2. Holland, *Dynasty*, 299.

3. Michael Grant, *The Roman Emperors* (New York: Barnes & Noble, 1997), 22–23.

4. Robin Seager, *Tiberius* (Victoria, Australia: Blackwell, 2005), 152–53.

5. Barry Strauss, *Ten Caesars* (New York: Simon & Schuster, 2019), 72.

6. Strauss, *Ten Caesars*, 73.

7. Seager, *Tiberius*, 183–84.

8. Seager, *Tiberius*, 190–92.

9. Grant, *Roman Emperors*, 103.

10. David Potter, *The Emperors of Rome* (New York: Metro Books, 2011), 136.

11. Edward Gibbon, *The Decline and Fall of the Roman Empire*. 6 vols. (New York: Knopf, 1993), 1:115.

12. Gibbon, *Decline and Fall of the Roman Empire*, 1:115.

13. Gibbon, *Decline and Fall of the Roman Empire*, 1:116.

14. Potter, *Emperors of Rome*, 138.

15. Gibbon, *Decline and Fall of the Roman Empire*, 1:120.

16. Gibbon, *Decline and Fall of the Roman Empire*, 1:121.

17. M. Cary, *A History of Rome* (London: Macmillan, 1954), 705.

18. Gibbon, *Decline and Fall of the Roman Empire*, 1:28.

19. Gibbon, *Decline and Fall of the Roman Empire*, 1:29.

20. Cary, *History of Rome*, 705.

21. Grant, *Roman Emperors*, 187.

22. Grant, *Roman Emperors*, 184.

23. Grant, *Roman Emperors*, 187.

24. Gibbon, *Decline and Fall of the Roman Empire*, 1:117.

25. Grant, *Roman Emperors*, 229.

7. THE SCOWLER

1. David Potter, *The Emperors of Rome* (New York: Metro Books, 2011), 144.

2. Michael Grant, *The Roman Emperors* (New York: Barnes & Noble, 1997), 108–9.

3. Edward Gibbon, *The Decline and Fall of the Roman Empire*. 6 vols. (New York: Knopf, 1993), 1:142.

4. Barry Strauss, *Ten Caesars* (New York: Simon & Schuster, 2019), 241.

5. Strauss, *Ten Caesars*, 253.

6. Dio Cassius, Earnest Cary, and Herbert Baldwin Foster, *Roman History*. 9 vols. (Cambridge, MA: Harvard University Press, 1927), 9:269.

7. Cassius, Cary, and Foster, *Roman History*, 9:271.

8. Strauss, *Ten Caesars*, 253.

9. Herodian and C. R. Whittaker, *Herodian*. 2 vols. (Cambridge, MA: Harvard University Press, 1969–1970), 1:389.

10. Potter, *Emperors of Rome*, 144.

11. Grant, *Roman Emperors*, 118.

12. Herodian and Whittaker, *Herodian*, 2:7.

13. Cassius, Cary, and Foster, *Roman History*, 9:283.

14. Grant, *Roman Emperors*, 118.

15. Cassius, Cary, and Foster, *Roman History*, 9:283.

16. Cassius, Cary, and Foster, *Roman History*, 9:285.

17. Herodian and Whittaker, *Herodian*, 2:11.

18. Cassius, Cary, and Foster, *Roman History*, 9:285.

19. Cassius, Cary, and Foster, *Roman History*, 9:287.

20. Cassius, Cary, and Foster, *Roman History*, 9:289.

21. Cassius, Cary, and Foster, *Roman History*, 9:289.

22. Cassius, Cary, and Foster, *Roman History*, 9:291.

23. Cassius, Cary, and Foster, *Roman History*, 9:291.

24. Cassius, Cary, and Foster, *Roman History*, 9:291.

25. Potter, *Emperors of Rome*, 148.

26. Cassius, Cary, and Foster, *Roman History*, 9:293.

27. Cassius, Cary, and Foster, *Roman History*, 9:295.

28. Cassius, Cary, and Foster, *Roman History*, 9:297.

29. Cassius, Cary, and Foster, *Roman History*, 9:297.

30. Strauss, *Ten Caesars*, 254.

31. Cassius, Cary, and Foster, *Roman History*, 9:297.

32. Strauss, *Ten Caesars*, 254.

33. Cassius, Cary, and Foster, *Roman History*, 9:297.

34. Cassius, Cary, and Foster, *Roman History*, 9:297–99.

35. Cassius, Cary, and Foster, *Roman History*, 9:309.

36. Cassius, Cary, and Foster, *Roman History*, 9:301.

37. Cassius, Cary, and Foster, *Roman History*, 9:313.

38. Cassius, Cary, and Foster, *Roman History*, 9:303.

39. Cassius, Cary, and Foster, *Roman History*, 9:315.

40. David Magie, *Historia Augusta*. 3 vols. (Cambridge, MA: Harvard University Press, 1921–1932), 2:13.

41. Cassius, Cary, and Foster, *Roman History*, 9:305.

42. Cassius, Cary, and Foster, *Roman History*, 9:317–19.

43. Cassius, Cary, and Foster, *Roman History*, 9:319.

44. Cassius, Cary, and Foster, *Roman History*, 9:321.

45. Cassius, Cary, and Foster, *Roman History*, 9:321.

46. Cassius, Cary, and Foster, *Roman History*, 9:325.

47. Cassius, Cary, and Foster, *Roman History*, 9:333.

48. Magie, *Historia Augusta*, 2:17.

49. Adrian Goldsworthy, *How Rome Fell* (New Haven, CT: Yale University Press, 2009), 73.

50. Cassius, Cary, and Foster, *Roman History*, 9:335.

51. Cassius, Cary, and Foster, *Roman History*, 9:337.

52. Potter, *Emperors of Rome*, 148.

8. THE UNHOLY PRIEST

1. Herodian and C. R. Whittaker, *Herodian*. 2 vols. (Cambridge, MA: Harvard University Press, 1969–1970), 2:9.

2. Herodian and Whittaker, *Herodian*, 2:11.

3. Edward Gibbon, *The Decline and Fall of the Roman Empire*. 6 vols. (New York: Knopf, 1993), 1:158.

4. Gibbon, *Decline and Fall of the Roman Empire*, 1:158.

5. Gibbon, *Decline and Fall of the Roman Empire*, 1:157.

6. Gibbon, *Decline and Fall of the Roman Empire*, 1:159.

7. Herodian and Whittaker, *Herodian*, 2:25.

8. Gibbon, *Decline and Fall of the Roman Empire*, 1:159.

9. Herodian and Whittaker, *Herodian*, 2:29.

10. Gibbon, *Decline and Fall of the Roman Empire*, 1:160.

11. Gibbon, *Decline and Fall of the Roman Empire*, 1:161.

12. Herodian and Whittaker, *Herodian*, 2:41.

13. Herodian and Whittaker, *Herodian*, 2:43.

14. Dio Cassius, Earnest Cary, and Herbert Baldwin Foster, *Roman History*. 9 vols. (Cambridge, MA: Harvard University Press, 1927), 9:445.

15. Cassius, Cary, and Foster, *Roman History*, 9:445.

16. Cassius, Cary, and Foster, *Roman History*, 9:445.

17. Cassius, Cary, and Foster, *Roman History*, 9:447.

18. Cassius, Cary, and Foster, *Roman History*, 9:447.

19. Cassius, Cary, and Foster, *Roman History*, 9:449.

20. Gibbon, *Decline and Fall of the Roman Empire*, 1:161.

21. Gibbon, *Decline and Fall of the Roman Empire*, 1:162.

22. Gibbon, *Decline and Fall of the Roman Empire*, 1:162.

23. Gibbon, *Decline and Fall of the Roman Empire*, 1:162.

24. Herodian and Whittaker, *Herodian*, 2:47.

25. Gibbon, *Decline and Fall of the Roman Empire*, 1:163.

26. Cassius, Cary, and Foster, *Roman History*, 9:465.

27. Cassius, Cary, and Foster, *Roman History*, 9:469.

28. David Magie, *Historia Augusta*. 3 vols. (Cambridge, MA: Harvard University Press, 1921–1932), 2:163.

29. Magie, *Historia Augusta*, 1:117.

30. Magie, *Historia Augusta*, 1:117.

31. Gibbon, *Decline and Fall of the Roman Empire*, 1:165.

32. Cassius, Cary, and Foster, *Roman History*, 9:457.

33. Cassius, Cary, and Foster, *Roman History*, 9:457.

34. Cassius, Cary, and Foster, *Roman History*, 9:461.

35. Cassius, Cary, and Foster, *Roman History*, 9:459.

36. Herodian and Whittaker, *Herodian*, 2:49.

37. Herodian and Whittaker, *Herodian*, 2:51.

38. Herodian and Whittaker, *Herodian*, 2:51.

39. Herodian and Whittaker, *Herodian*, 2:45.

40. Gibbon, *Decline and Fall of the Roman Empire*, 1:162.

41. Cassius, Cary, and Foster, *Roman History*, 9:461.

42. Magie, *Historia Augusta*, 1:21–23.

43. Gibbon, *Decline and Fall of the Roman Empire*, 1:162.

44. Herodian and Whittaker, *Herodian*, 2:53.

45. Herodian and Whittaker, *Herodian*, 2:55.

46. Cassius, Cary, and Foster, *Roman History*, 9:463.

47. Gibbon, *Decline and Fall of the Roman Empire*, 1:163.

48. Magie, *Historia Augusta*, 1:147.

49. Magie, *Historia Augusta*, 1:127.

50. Magie, *Historia Augusta*, 1:143, 1:147.

51. Magie, *Historia Augusta*, 1:143–47.

52. Magie, *Historia Augusta*, 1:147.

53. Magie, *Historia Augusta*, 1:157–61.

54. Magie, *Historia Augusta*, 1:129.

55. Magie, *Historia Augusta*, 1:127–29.

56. Magie, *Historia Augusta*, 1:149.

57. Magie, *Historia Augusta*, 1:47–49.

58. Magie, *Historia Augusta*, 1:51–53.

59. Magie, *Historia Augusta*, 1:159.

60. Gibbon, *Decline and Fall of the Roman Empire*, 1:165.

61. Cassius, Cary, and Foster, *Roman History*, 9:465.

62. Gibbon, *Decline and Fall of the Roman Empire*, 1:165.

9. THE GIANT

1. David Magie, *Historia Augusta*. 3 vols. (Cambridge, MA: Harvard University Press, 1921–1932), 1:327.

2. Magie, *Historia Augusta*, 1:321.

3. Magie, *Historia Augusta*, 1:327.

4. Magie, *Historia Augusta*, 1:317–19.

5. Edward Gibbon, *The Decline and Fall of the Roman Empire.* 6 vols. (New York: Knopf, 1993), 1:192.

6. Herodian and C. R. Whittaker, *Herodian.* 2 vols. (Cambridge, MA: Harvard University Press, 1969–1970), 2:155.

7. Gibbon, *Decline and Fall of the Roman Empire,* 1:192.

8. Magie, *Historia Augusta,* 1:331.

9. Herodian and Whittaker, *Herodian,* 2:153.

10. Gibbon, *Decline and Fall of the Roman Empire,* 1:192.

11. Magie, *Historia Augusta,* 1:329.

12. Gibbon, *Decline and Fall of the Roman Empire,* 1:192.

13. Gibbon, *Decline and Fall of the Roman Empire,* 1:193.

14. Gibbon, *Decline and Fall of the Roman Empire,* 1:193.

15. Gibbon, *Decline and Fall of the Roman Empire,* 1:193.

16. Herodian and Whittaker, *Herodian,* 2:175.

17. Herodian and Whittaker, *Herodian,* 2:171.

18. Herodian and Whittaker, *Herodian,* 2:155.

19. Herodian and Whittaker, *Herodian,* 2:161.

20. Herodian and Whittaker, *Herodian,* 2:163.

21. Herodian and Whittaker, *Herodian,* 2:167.

22. Gibbon, *Decline and Fall of the Roman Empire,* 1:202.

23. Gibbon, *Decline and Fall of the Roman Empire,* 1:204.

24. Gibbon, *Decline and Fall of the Roman Empire,* 1:205.

25. Gibbon, *Decline and Fall of the Roman Empire,* 1:205.

26. Gibbon, *Decline and Fall of the Roman Empire,* 1:206.

27. Will Durant, *Caesar and Christ: The Story of Civilization III* (New York: Simon & Schuster, 1944), 638.

28. Michael Grant, *The Roman Emperors* (New York: Barnes & Noble, 1997), 173.

29. Grant, *Roman Emperors,* 175.

30. Grant, *Roman Emperors,* 187–88.

31. Durant, *Caesar and Christ,* 639.

32. Grant, *Roman Emperors,* 195.

33. Grant, *Roman Emperors,* 199.

34. Grant, *Roman Emperors,* 199.

35. Durant, *Caesar and Christ,* 641.

36. Gibbon, *Decline and Fall of the Roman Empire,* 1:422.

37. Gibbon, *Decline and Fall of the Roman Empire,* 1:388.

38. M. Cary, *A History of Rome* (London: Macmillan, 1954), 730.

39. Durant, *Caesar and Christ,* 651.

40. David Potter, *Constantine the Emperor* (Oxford: Oxford University Press, 2013), 91.

41. Potter, *Constantine the Emperor*, 92.

42. Durant, *Caesar and Christ*, 651–52.

43. Cary, *History of Rome*, 768.

44. Grant, *Roman Emperors*, 210.

45. Cary, *History of Rome*, 768.

46. Stephen Williams and Gerard Friell, *Theodosius* (New Haven, CT: Yale University Press, 1998), 68.

47. Williams and Friell, *Theodosius*, 68.

48. Williams and Friell, *Theodosius*, 68.

49. Williams and Friell, *Theodosius*, 68.

50. Durant, *Caesar and Christ*, 486.

10. THE BACKSTABBERS

1. Steward Perowne, *The End of the Roman World* (London: Hodder and Stoughton, 1966), 10.

2. Stephen Williams and Gerard Friell, *Theodosius* (New Haven, CT: Yale University Press, 1998), 138.

3. Michael Grant, *The Roman Emperors* (New York: Barnes & Noble, 1997), 278, 282.

4. Grant, *Roman Emperors*, 277.

5. Williams and Friell, *Theodosius*, 149.

6. Williams and Friell, *Theodosius*, 134.

7. Williams and Friell, *Theodosius*, 144.

8. Williams and Friell, *Theodosius*, 145.

9. Williams and Friell, *Theodosius*, 149.

10. Williams and Friell, *Theodosius*, 154.

11. Edward Gibbon, *The Decline and Fall of the Roman Empire*. 6 vols. (New York: Knopf, 1993), 3:235–36.

12. Williams and Friell, *Theodosius*, 157.

13. Williams and Friell, *Theodosius*, 157; Michael Grant, *The Fall of the Roman Empire* (New York: Collier Books, 1990), 12.

14. Gibbon, *Decline and Fall of the Roman Empire*, 3:241.

15. Gibbon, *Decline and Fall of the Roman Empire*, 3:241.

16. Grant, *Fall of the Roman Empire*, 12.

17. Grant, *Roman Emperors*, 278, 284.

18. Gibbon, *Decline and Fall of the Roman Empire*, 3:373.

19. Grant, *Fall of the Roman Empire*, 15.

20. Gibbon, *Decline and Fall of the Roman Empire*, 3:428.

21. Gibbon, *Decline and Fall of the Roman Empire*, 3:452.

22. Grant, *Roman Emperors*, 278, 300.

23. Gibbon, *Decline and Fall of the Roman Empire*, 3:461.

24. Gibbon, *Decline and Fall of the Roman Empire*, 3:464; Grant, *Roman Emperors*, 278, 302.

25. Grant, *Roman Emperors*, 278, 300.

26. Gibbon, *Decline and Fall of the Roman Empire*, 3:462.

27. Michael Grant, *From Rome to Byzantium* (London: Routledge, 1998), 19–20.

28. Grant, *Fall of the Roman Empire*, 139.

EPILOGUE

1. Edward Gibbon, *The Decline and Fall of the Roman Empire*. 6 vols. (New York: Knopf, 1993), 4:562.

2. Gibbon, *Decline and Fall of the Roman Empire*, 4:562.

3. Gibbon, *Decline and Fall of the Roman Empire*, 4:562.

4. Gibbon, *Decline and Fall of the Roman Empire*, 4:565.

5. Gibbon, *Decline and Fall of the Roman Empire*, 4:566.

6. Gibbon, *Decline and Fall of the Roman Empire*, 4:567.

7. Gibbon, *Decline and Fall of the Roman Empire*, 4:569.

BIBLIOGRAPHY

Alston, Richard. *Rome's Revolution*. Oxford: Oxford University Press, 2015.

Appian and John M. Carter. *The Civil Wars*. London: Penguin, 1996.

Barlag, Phillip. *The History of Rome in 12 Buildings*. Newburyport, MA: New Page Books, 2018.

Barrett, Anthony. *Livia*. New Haven, CT: Yale University Press, 2002.

Beard, Mary. *SPQR*. New York: Liveright, 2015.

Cary, M. *A History of Rome*. London: Macmillan, 1954.

Cassius, Dio, Earnest Cary, and Herbert Baldwin Foster. *Roman History*. 9 vols. Cambridge, MA: Harvard University Press, 1927.

Champlin, Edward. *Nero*. Cambridge, MA: Belknap Press of Harvard University Press, 2005.

Dando-Collins, Stephen. *Blood of the Caesars*. Hoboken, NJ: Wiley, 2008.

———. *Caligula*. Nashville, TN: Turner, 2019.

———. *The Great Fire of Rome*. Cambridge, MA: Da Capo, 2010.

Dennison, Matthew. *The Twelve Caesars*. New York: St. Martin's, 2012.

Durant, Will. *Caesar and Christ: The Story of Civilization III*. New York: Simon & Schuster, 1944.

Everitt, Anthony. *Augustus*. New York: Random House, 2006.

———. *Cicero*. New York: Random House, 2001.

———. *The Rise of Rome*. New York: Random House, 2012.

Gibbon, Edward. *The Decline and Fall of the Roman Empire*. 6 vols. New York: Knopf, 1993.

Goldsworthy, Adrian. *Augustus*. New Haven, CT: Yale University Press, 2014.

———. *Caesar*. New Haven, CT: Yale University Press, 2006.

———. *How Rome Fell*. New Haven, CT: Yale University Press, 2009.

———. *Pax Romana*. New Haven, CT: Yale University Press, 2016.

Grant, Michael. *The Collapse and Recovery of the Roman Empire*. London: Routledge, 1999.

———. *The Fall of the Roman Empire*. New York: Collier Books, 1990.

———. *The Founders of the Western World*. New York: Scribner, 1991.

———. *From Rome to Byzantium*. London: Routledge, 1998.

———. *The Roman Emperors*. New York: Barnes & Noble, 1997.

Herodian and C. R. Whittaker. *Herodian*. 2 vols. Cambridge, MA: Harvard University Press, 1969–1970.

Holland, Tom. *Dynasty*. New York: Doubleday, 2015.

———. *Rubicon*. New York: Doubleday, 2003.

Hughes, Ian. *Imperial Brothers*. Barnsley: Pen & Sword Military, 2013.

Icks, Martijn. *Crimes of Elagabalus*. London: I. B. Tauris, 2013.

Jones, Brian W. *The Emperor Domitian*. London: Routledge, 1992.

Keaveney, Arthur. *Sulla*. London: Routledge, 2005.

Livius, Titus, and T. J. Luce. *The Rise of Rome: Books One to Five*. Oxford: Oxford University Press, 1998.

Lomas, Kathryn. *The Rise of Rome*. Cambridge, MA: Belknap Press of Harvard University Press, 2018.

Magie, David. *Historia Augusta*. 3 vols. Cambridge, MA: Harvard University Press, 1921–1932.

Marcellinus, Ammianus, and John Carew Rolfe. *Ammianus Marcellinus*. 3 vols. Cambridge, MA: Harvard University Press, 1939–1950.

McLynn, Frank. *Marcus Aurelius*. Cambridge, MA: Da Capo, 2009.

Mellor, Ronald. *The Historians of Ancient Rome*. London: Routledge, 2013.

Murdoch, Adrian. *The Last Pagan*. Rochester, VT: Inner Traditions, 2008.

Pearson, Paul N. *Maximinus Thrax*. New York: Skyhorse, 2017.

Perowne, Steward. *The End of the Roman World*. London: Hodder and Stoughton, 1966.

Plutarch, John Dryden, and Arthur Hugh Clough. *Greek and Roman Lives*. Mineola, NY: Dover, 2005.

Potter, David. *Constantine the Emperor*. Oxford: Oxford University Press, 2013.

———. *The Emperors of Rome*. New York: Metro Books, 2011.

Powell, Lindsay. *Marcus Agrippa*. Barnsley: Pen & Sword Military, 2015.

Romm, James. *Dying Every Day*. New York: Knopf, 2014.

Seager, Robin. *Tiberius*. Victoria, Australia: Blackwell, 2005.

Southern, Patricia. *Mark Antony*. Gloucestershire: Amberley, 2012.

Stambaugh, John E. *The Ancient Roman City*. Baltimore, MD: Johns Hopkins University Press, 1988.

Strauss, Barry. *Ten Caesars*. New York: Simon & Schuster, 2019.

Suetonius, Robert Graves, and J. B. Rives. *The Twelve Caesars*. London: Penguin, 2007.

Tacitus. *The Complete Works of Tacitus*. New York: Modern Library, 1942.

Walker, Charles. *Wonders of the Ancient World*. London: Popular Press, 1988.

Williams, Stephen, and Gerard Friell. *Theodosius*. New Haven, CT: Yale University Press, 1998.

Winterling, Aloys. *Caligula*. Berkeley: University of California Press, 2011.

Woolf, Greg. *Rome*. Oxford: Oxford University Press, 2012.

Zosimus and Ronald T. Ridley. *New History*. Leiden: Brill, 2017.

INDEX

ABOUT THE AUTHOR

Phillip Barlag is a normal suburban guy who is just fascinated by Roman history. He has written about Roman leadership in *The Leadership Genius of Julius Caesar: Modern Lessons from the Man Who Built an Empire* (2016) and Roman travel in *The History of Rome in 12 Buildings: A Travel Companion to the Hidden Secrets of The Eternal City* (2018). He lives in the Atlanta, Georgia, area with his wife and three children.

CPSIA information can be obtained
at www.ICGtesting.com
Printed in the USA
BVHW071521151121
621612BV00002B/2

9 781633 886902